A Rhetorical Reader for ESL Writers

A Rhetorical Reader for ESL Writers

CAROLYN B. RAPHAEL

Queensborough Community College
The City University of New York

ELAINE GORAN NEWMAN

Queens College
The City University of New York

MACMILLAN PUBLISHING CO., INC.
New York

Macmillan Publishing Co., Inc.
866 Third Avenue, New York, New York 10022

Collier Macmillan Canada, Inc.

Library of Congress Cataloging in Publication Data

Main entry under title:

A Rhetorical reader for ESL writers.

 Includes index.
 1. English language—Text-books for foreigners.
2. College readers. 3. English language—Rhetoric.
I. Raphael, Carolyn B. II. Newman, Elaine Goran.
III. Title: Rhetorical reader for E.S.L. writers.
PE1128.R447   1983   808'.0427   82-15161
ISBN 0-02-398300-0   AACR2

Printing: 1 2 3 4 5 6 7 8   Year: 3 4 5 6 7 8 9 0

ISBN   0-02-398300-0

ACKNOWLEDGMENTS

Acknowledgment is gratefully made for permission to reprint the following:

"Bittersweet Farewell of a Grown-up Child" by Randi Kreiss, *The New York
    Times*, March 22, 1979. © 1979 by The New York Times Company. Re-
    printed by permission.

"Samoan Children at Work and Play" by Margaret Mead. With permission from
    Natural History, April 1980. Copyright The American Museum of Natural
    History, 1980.

"Going Wild in San Francisco," from *Stalking the Far Away Places* by Euell
    Gibbons (New York: David McKay, 1973). Reprinted by permission of
    Mrs. Euell Gibbons.

"Norman Rockwell: An Artistic Link to Our Past," from *Close to Home*, by
    Ellen Goodman. Copyright © 1979 by The Washington Post Company.
    Reprinted by permission of Simon & Schuster, a Division of Gulf & Western
    Corporation.

"The Rainbow City" by Pete Hamill, *New York Magazine,* August 18, 1980. Reprinted by permission of International Creative Management. Copyright © 1980 by Pete Hamill. First appeared in *New York Magazine,* August 18, 1980.

"Where James Bond Shops" by Suzie Gharib Nazem, FORTUNE Magazine, July 28, 1980. © 1980 Time, Inc. All rights reserved.

"Cultural Influences on Filipino Patients" by Rosario T. DeGracia, *American Journal of Nursing,* August 1979. Copyright © 1979 by the American Journal of Nursing Company. Reproduced with permission, from *American Journal of Nursing,* August, Vol. 79, No. 8.

"Tests for Conductors" from *More Essays from the World of Music* by Ernest Newman (London: John Calder, 1958). Reprinted by permission of John Calder (Publishers) Ltd., London.

"On Natural Death" from *The Medusa and the Snail* by Lewis Thomas. Copyright © 1974–1979 by Lewis Thomas. Reprinted by permission of Viking Penguin, Inc.

"Ethnic Businesses" from "Businesses that Ride a Rebirth of Ethnic Pride" by Irene Pave. Reprinted from the October 22, 1979 issue of *Business Week* by special permission. © 1979 by McGraw-Hill, Inc., New York, N.Y. 10020. All rights reserved.

"Lofting a Kite Against the Wind" by Francis X. Clines, *Science Digest,* March 1979. Reprinted by permission from *Science Digest.* Copyright © 1979 The Hearst Corporation. All rights reserved.

Bruce Catton, "Grant and Lee: A Study in Contrasts" from *The American Story,* Earl Schenck Miers, editor. © 1956 by Broadcast Music, Inc. Reprinted by permission.

Forbes Magazine, "Japan's Multitier Wage System," August 18, 1980, by Robert C. Wood. Copyright 1980, Forbes, Inc.

"Natural—A Word of Many Meanings" by Patricia Wells, *The New York Times,* March 15, 1978. © 1978/79 by The New York Times Company. Reprinted by permission.

"Reinventing Childhood" by Jonathan Kozol, *Saturday Review,* July 21, 1979. Copyright © 1979 by *Saturday Review.* All rights reserved. Reprinted with permission.

"How to Get Ready for Studying Abroad" by Roger Cox. Reprinted by permission from the 1980 issue of *Nutshell.* © 1980, by Roger Cox.

"Of Writing and Writers" by John Ciardi, *Saturday Review,* April 18, 1964. Copyright © 1964 by *Saturday Review.* All rights reserved. Reprinted by permission.

"What Can We Do about Jet Lag?" by Vicki Goldberg, *Psychology Today,* August, 1977. Reprinted by permission of Liz Darhansoff.

"The System Worked" by Anthony Lewis, *The New York Times,* May 17, 1979. © 1978/79 by the New York Times Company. Reprinted by permission.

"Found! A Cure for Math Anxiety" by Edward B. Fisk, *Parents,* February 1980. Copyright © 1980 Parents Magazine Enterprises. Reprinted from *Parents* by permission.

"Designing the Superman" by Isaac Asimov originally appeared as "From Org to Cyborg to Cyb" in the June 29, 1974 issue of *TV Guide.* Copyright © 1974 by Triangle Publications, Inc. It appears in the book *Science Past—Science Future* by Isaac Asimov. Reprinted by permission of Doubleday & Company, Inc.

"Your Money *and* Your Life" by David A. Cook, *Columbia Journalism Review*, July/August 1979. Reprinted by permission of the author.

"Career Education at the College Level" by Clifton R. Wharton, Jr., *Today's Education*, April/May, 1979. Reprinted by permission of the author.

"Privacy and the Press: Is Nothing Sacred?" by Nat Hentoff, *Saturday Review*, July 21, 1979. Copyright © 1979 by *Saturday Review*. All rights reserved. Reprinted with permission.

Preface

This text is designed for advanced ESL students. We believe that students at this level should read language that is neither simplified nor abridged. Therefore, the essays we have chosen are unedited and unexcerpted, ranging from short to medium length. The reading of good models as an aid to writing has long been established as sound teaching practice.

We further believe in teaching students how to analyze rhetorical forms in the essays that they read. Our hope is that the knowledge of these forms will help them to organize their own ideas as they write themes, term papers, and essay examinations. Thus, the principal table of contents is arranged rhetorically.

An alternate table of contents arranges the essays according to the various subject areas commonly studied in college. Since the interests of most students differ as do their major fields of study, we have offered a wide selection of essays relating to different disciplines, including history, language, business, and technology.

The text begins with a chapter entitled "How to Read an Essay." This is a step-by-step approach to the analysis of an essay. Taking the student through three successive reading stages, this chapter suggests that the student pay increasingly more attention to details at each stage. Then the observations are synthesized into a total appraisal.

The essays are grouped under eight rhetorical headings. Each section begins with a preface explaining the form and often giving sample paragraphs as illustrations. (The careful reader will notice that we have alternated the use of the personal pronoun—assigning "he" to one preface and "she" to the next. In this way we avoid the dual charges of being sexist or stylistically insensitive.)

The essays themselves cover a variety of subjects including travel, the media, industry, and leisure activities. Many of the essays deal with cultural diversity and should provide strong starting points for discussion as well as writing.

The exercises accompanying the essays serve several purposes. They are principally designed to provide vocabulary growth, since vocabulary acquisition is vital for continued development in all language skills. The Study Questions focus on reading comprehension: first on content (Finding the Matter) and then on style (Exploring the Manner). Such exercises as Synonyms, Paraphrase, and Word-Form Study, among others, strengthen and reinforce both reading and writing skills. The Questions for Discussion allow the students to explore issues raised in the essays, some of which may develop into topics for themes. Finally, the Topics for Writing are designed to stimulate individual thought and to give the students practice writing in a particular rhetorical mode. These exercises are accompanied by a minimum of instructions, since it is assumed that advanced ESL students can follow directions on their own, as will be required in most college courses.

The essays are followed by a chapter explaining the uses of the dictionary. Although it is placed at the back of the book as an appendix, the instructor may wish to encourage students to read it early in the term and to refer to it often.

The glossary at the end of the text defines terms such as *transition, thesis,* and *audience.* An asterisk following a word indicates that the word is defined in the glossary. Most of these asterisks are to be found in "Exploring the Manner." This reference guide is intended to help students examine the structure of the model essays and to assist them as they create their own.

It should be stated that the chapters do not have to be studied in order. The instructor always has the option of selecting those chapters that might be pertinent to the needs of a particular class. Moreover, the units may be matched to a grammar review or to the special interests of the students. Whatever approach is followed, it is our conviction that the combination of essay analysis and exercise drill must increase the ESL student's control over written English.

We wish to express our appreciation to our colleagues who offered advice and assistance: Ruth Ames, Sheena Gillespie, and Sandra Seltzer of Queensborough Community College, and Peter Chetta of Iona College. We are indebted to Rachel Erlanger, Claire Kaplan, and Jane Albert of Queens College for testing our chapters in their classes.

We also wish to acknowledge the valuable suggestions that came from our reviewers.

Special thanks are due Claire Kaplan for her diligent work on the *Instructor's Manual*, Lita K. Hofberg for her recommendations, and Victoria Zussin for her invaluable illustrations.

We are grateful to Patricia Finn and Marcia Resnick for typing the manuscript and to Ellen Youngelman for her skillful management of administrative details.

No book can reach publication without the guidance of experts, and we have been fortunate to be able to work with D. Anthony English and Ron Harris of Macmillan.

Finally, we wish to thank our families for their encouragement, support, and understanding: first, of course, our husbands, Lawrence J. Raphael and John B. Newman, and then Melissa and David Raphael, John A. Newman, Jane, Robert, David, and Michael Albert.

* * *

The writing of this book was a labor of love shared by two authors who were both colleagues and friends. The death of Elaine Newman shortly before publication dissolved the partnership but not the love. Here, then, is the fruit of that labor. May it serve as a tribute and a memorial.

C. B. R.

Contents

Contents by Academic Discipline

SCIENCE AND MATHEMATICS

BUSINESS AND TECHNOLOGY

EDUCATION

A Rhetorical
Reader for
ESL Writers

How to Read an Essay

There are many different kinds of reading. There is reading for amusement and relaxation, such as the kind you do at airports, in bed, or while sunning on a beach. Whether you are reading magazines or books, gossip columns or great literature, you certainly do not expect to be tested on content or quizzed on facts and details. You are reading only for pleasure and the excitement of turning the next page. There is also informal reading for information, such as reading baseball scores or editorials in a newspaper. Here you are looking for facts, but you only want to find them and go on. Few people linger over sports pages or reread them the following day. Then there is the kind of reading required in college courses. Here you are required to analyze and understand the material, to remember it, and to produce it upon request from a teacher—in the form of compositions, tests, oral reports, or research projects. No matter what is required, you must begin by being able to read and understand the material.

Special college reading courses concentrate on methods of improving your familiarity with English sentence structure, your speed, your comprehension, and your ability to remember important points. But what about the application of these skills to specific courses? What follows are guidelines to help you approach college reading in an orderly manner. These hints are specifically designed for reading the essay, but you should be able to adapt them to your reading assignments in other courses, whether science, economics, technology, or business.

1

I. Getting Started

A. Removing Distractions

Some students insist that they can read while eating, listening to music, or talking on the phone. Even if this is true, these are not ideal conditions for serious reading. Reading an essay designed for a college-level audience demands your fullest concentration. Whether or not you believe that you can "tune out" any noise, chances are that you will work better if you remove yourself from all possible distractions. This means that while you are reading, you should not watch television, listen to the radio or stereo, or sit in the middle of the living room where other people are talking. Being sociable cannot be combined with serious reading.

B. Finding a Good Place to Study

If you are lucky enough to have a room of your own, close the door and barricade yourself inside. If you have a noisy, bustling family, try the basement, the kitchen, or the school or public library. Once you have decided upon a private place, make certain that the light is sufficient. You will be able to read for longer periods with good light. Finally, choose a comfortable chair—but not too comfortable. Too much comfort encourages sleep instead of study.

C. Focusing Attention

Some researchers claim that television watching has reduced the attention span of today's students to the time between commercials: approximately ten minutes. Whether or not this is your problem, you should be able to read an essay all the way through without stopping. Therefore, if you need to increase your concentration time, you may have to go into training, much as a jogger trains to increase speed or distance. Try to read for 15 minutes without stopping—then 20. Of course, you may want to look up occasionally in order to avoid eyestrain, but you will find that reading for longer periods is more efficient than stopping and starting six times in an hour.

D. Becoming Acquainted

You should become acquainted with an essay before you begin reading it. Look at the title and author's name (and biographical information, if any). Notice the length of the essay so that you can estimate the time needed to read it. Examine the illustration, if there is one, and try to see how it relates to the essay. Next, look at the organization of the essay and observe whether it is divided into sections or written without divisions. Finally, take your English dictionary and look through the article for unfamiliar words—then look them up. If there is a vocabulary list accompanying the chapter, look up the definitions and keep a list in your notebook so that you can refer to it when necessary. Once you have completed these preliminary steps, you are ready to begin.

II. Digging In

A. Vocabulary

As you read the essay for the first time, keep your notebook open to the vocabulary page. When you find a word that is unfamiliar, first see if you can guess its meaning from the context of the sentence. Then check your guesswork against the dictionary definition and go on. (Make certain that you select the definition that applies to the word as it is used in the particular sentence.) Since each sentence adds meaning to what came before, you will do well to understand the new words as you read.

B. Introduction

The beginning of an essay presents the subject and the author's attitude toward it. As you read, notice the way in which the author opens the essay. Does he ask a question, tell an anecdote, or give background information on the subject? How quickly can you tell what the essay is going to discuss?

Find the *thesis* (central idea) of the essay. This is the author's main point, and it is often expressed in a sentence or two. Determine whether the author states his thesis or simply suggests it for you to figure out.

C. Body

Read the middle section of the essay and observe the way or ways in which the author supports the thesis. Ask yourself which point each new idea contributes to the essay and whether or not these ideas support the thesis. Also, follow the movement of the supporting ideas from one to the next. Does there seem to be a smooth progression? Can you follow the author's thinking?

D. Conclusion

Finally, look at the way in which the author brings the essay to a close. Does he restate the thesis or add new information in the closing paragraphs? Does the final paragraph give you a feeling that he has concluded? Is there a feeling of finality in the last few sentences?

After you finish reading the selection, pause for a few minutes and write down your reactions to the subject, the content, and the style of the essay. It may be only a few words or phrases, but first impressions are interesting and important.

III. Rereading

A. Tone

As you read the essay this time, respond to the tone of the writing as you would react to the tone of someone's voice. In speech, tone indicates the relationship between the speaker and listener. The same is true in writing, but here the relationship is between writer and reader. Look closely at a paragraph to discover whether the writer is speaking directly to you in the second person (*you*) or to a general, unnamed audience. Perhaps he is speaking in the first person (*I*) or using the third person (*he, she, it, they*). Decide whether the vocabulary is the kind you would find in a textbook or in a letter from a friend. These answers will enable you to establish the tone as formal or informal and to determine whether the author has assumed a distant or close relationship with you, the reader.

B. Thesis

During this reading you should look more closely at the thesis to make certain that you understand the author's central point. Notice how the thesis helps to focus the subject and how it expresses the author's attitude. If the thesis is implied rather than stated, write it down as you understand it and check to see that the supporting ideas all contribute to it.

C. Structure

Now that you know what and where the thesis is, you can examine the type of essay that you are reading. Depending on the writer's purpose, the essay will be an example of *narration, description, exposition,* or *argumentation.* If the writer wants to relate an incident, he will use narration, as illustrated by this thesis: "I grew up the day that my father left our family." If the intention is to describe a scene, person, or object, the writer will use description, as in this thesis: "My attic bedroom offers me privacy, beauty, and security." If the author's purpose is to explain something, the essay will be exposition, and the thesis might look like this: "The best way to slice a roast turkey is to let it cool first and then use a sharpened carving knife." Finally, the writer who wishes to persuade the reader will use argumentation with a thesis such as this one: "All college students should be guaranteed parking privileges."

The most common kind of essay read or written in college is exposition, and there are many patterns of organizing ideas in an expository essay. These include *illustration* (using examples), *comparison and contrast* (showing similarities and differences), *definition* (telling what something is), *analysis* (breaking something down for study), and *cause and effect* (finding reasons and results). Of course, few full-length essays use a single organizing pattern. Most combine whatever forms seem best suited to the author's purpose, such as including exposition within an argument or illustrating a narration with description.

As you read the essay the second time, determine its category (*narrative, descriptive,* etc.) and its pattern of organization (*examples, definition,* etc.). This knowledge will help you to understand the author's purpose and evaluate how well the essay fulfills that purpose.

D. Supporting Ideas

Try to determine what kinds of information the author has used to support the thesis. Ask yourself these questions: Are there facts, statistics, examples, personal observations? Does the author distinguish between fact and opinion? Is there enough supporting material to convince you that the thesis has been proved? Your answers will help you to understand the author's method of proof.

E. Topic Sentence

Each paragraph should develop a single idea, which is called the *topic sentence.* It may appear anywhere in the paragraph, although the most popular position is at the beginning. The topic sentence serves to unify the paragraph, that is, to help it remain on the topic and not wander off to a new idea. As you read, look at the paragraphs, especially the longer ones, and determine how well the author has developed the topic sentences. When added together, the topic sentences should outline the ideas that support the thesis.

IV. Putting It All Together

A. The Total Essay

As you read the essay for the third time, you should experience the dual pleasures of recognition and discovery. Of course you have read it before and know the subject matter, but now you can explore the fine points. No longer hampered by your search for word definitions and topic sentences, you are free to enjoy the essay as a whole. Moreover, you can now begin to see what kinds of words and types of sentences the author has chosen to create his individual style.

B. The Thesis

Look once more at the author's thesis. Does it reveal the purpose of the essay? Was the author simply narrating an incident for the pleasure of telling a story? Or was he describing a favorite childhood hiding place to share a treasured memory? Perhaps he was trying to persuade you that his opinion of the military draft is the correct one. Once you are certain of the author's purpose, you can evaluate how well he has succeeded in achieving it.

Notice, too, the attitude that the author demonstrates toward his subject in the thesis. Examine this sample thesis: "All high school students should study a foreign language for at least two years." Revealed in this thesis is the author's attitude toward second-language acquisition—perhaps as a qualification for membership in an expanding world community. You may not agree with the author's point of view, but it is essential that you know what it is.

C. The Paragraph

Now that you know what a topic sentence is, be aware of where it appears in the paragraph: beginning, middle, or end. When it appears at the beginning, the topic sentence *introduces* the supporting ideas; in the middle it *connects* them; and at the end it *summarizes* them. No matter where the topic sentence appears, it binds the ideas of the paragraph to give it unity.

Pay particular attention to the ways in which the sentences are connected within the paragraph. A smoothly connected paragraph is said to have *coherence*, and the connectors are called *transitions*. These may be pronouns, repeated words or phrases, synonyms, or various connecting words. If your eyes move comfortably through the paragraph and you can easily follow the development of the topic sentence, the transitions are doing their job.

Notice, too, the way in which the writer uses transitions to connect a new paragraph to the previous one. As the reader progresses from one paragraph to the next, the transitions act as signposts or reminders of what has just been read and as signals of what is to be read next.

D. The Sentence

Choose a paragraph and look at the length of the sentences. Count the words in the first four sentences and see if they are all the same length. Usually, writers try to alternate sentence length for variety.

Another way to achieve variety is by beginning the sentences with different parts of speech. Notice the part of speech that begins each of the following sentences:

Noun	*Love* is a need that is greater than thirst or hunger for most people.
Adjective	*Hot* buttered pancakes can tempt the most serious dieter.
Preposition	*In* an instant, the cat seized the bird and dragged it under the bush.

Look also at word order and sentence types as you observe the various colors of the writer's palette.

E. The Word

When you examined the writer's tone during the second reading, you received an overall impression. Now you can look more closely at the words that help to determine the tone. Whether you are writing or speaking, you adjust your vocabulary to suit the occasion and the audience. If you are writing a letter applying for a job, for example, you will be more formal in your choice of words than you will be when writing an entry in a diary or journal. A job application for a position as editorial assistant in a publishing firm might include a sentence such as this one: "In addition to receiving high grades in my composition and literature courses in college, I have had practical experience writing for my local newspaper, the *Daily Record*, where I wrote a weekly column entitled 'College Life.'" This formal sentence is long and includes no informal or colloquial terms. It is appropriate both for the situation and the reader. On the other hand, an entry describing the application in your private journal might read as follows: "Wrote letter of application to Howell Publishers today. The next step is to blow their minds when they call me for an interview." Here you are writing to and for yourself. Your style may include fragments and colloquialisms because the situation is informal and because you will be the only reader.

In addition to observing the level of formality when you read, you should also be aware of the difference between the strict dictionary definition of a word (*denotation*) and the other meanings that people associate with words (*connotations*). Of course, the associations will depend on the cultural background of the reader, but some connotations are nearly universal.

Often a word is chosen because of the power of its connotations. The word *supervisor*, for example, means "one who oversees" and has basically the same denotation as the word *boss*. But if we want to describe a person who pushes other people around, we will choose the adjective *bossy*, not *supervisory*, because of the often negative connotations associated with the noun *boss*.

Most words have connotations as well as denotations. Therefore, it is important to be aware of the associations linked to a word. The word *mother* has a dictionary meaning of "a female parent," but it is rich in associations. If a person's relationship to his or her mother is warm and loving, the connotations of the word will be positive and pleasant. But if this relationship includes tension and conflict, the word may present a mixture of positive and negative associations for that individual. When you read an essay, see if the author is using connotations as well as denotations. Your sensitivity to connotations will enhance your understanding and appreciation of the essay.

F. A Final Word

Now that you have read the essay at least three times, you probably have had several reactions to it. You may have been interested in the topic, but you may not have enjoyed the author's style. You may have found the vocabulary difficult but the organization easy to follow. Some of your reactions are probably positive and others negative. Nonetheless, like the person who has just completed a 500-piece jigsaw puzzle, you can stand back and enjoy the finished product. As you admire the puzzle (or essay) in its completed state, you will probably feel a certain degree of pride in having worked to bring it to completion.

In college courses, each new reading assignment is like a puzzle. It must be studied, taken apart, and reassembled. Often the procedure is long and painstaking, requiring repeated efforts and perseverance. But it is only by means of successive readings that you can hope to uncover the several layers of meaning in an essay or textbook chapter. If you are willing to spend the time and effort required, you will be rewarded not only with knowledge but also with pleasure.

The pleasure gained from reading need only be enjoyed, but the knowledge must be applied so that it can grow. Repeated readings of the essays in this book will, of course, enable you to analyze and understand the content and style of the essays themselves. In addition, as you read and reread the essays, you will discover how to apply your knowledge to the exercises that follow, including synonyms, paraphrase, and sentence completion. Finally, a thorough familiarity with each essay will help you to participate in classroom discussions and to write a composition on a related subject.

The final word in this chapter should really be *success*. The successful student is one who knows how to read well, and learning to read and analyze an essay is good preparation for studying any text in any course. With modifications for the different kinds of subject matter, the procedure of analysis through repeated readings is a valid study method. And any student will tell you that learning how to study in college is the key to success.

1

Narration

The Form

"Once upon a time . . ." signals the beginning of a story to many young American children. When they hear or read these words, they prepare to share an adventure about princes and dragons, princesses and evil witches. The familiar beginning of the fairy tale allows them to find a comfortable position as they ready themselves for excitement. Then the events become increasingly thrilling as the plot continues until the inevitable and, of course, happy ending. This is one example of fiction, where the primary purpose of the story is the story itself and the sheer enjoyment that the tale delivers.

There are also narratives that have other purposes: to reveal personal history (biography or autobiography), to report events (journalism), or to convince the reader (argument). These are works of nonfiction, and they are supposed to tell the truth. Using real events instead of fictional ones, these narratives appeal to the reader's interest in following a story.

The narrative essay is also a work of nonfiction. Here the writer uses narration to relate a sequence of events and to emphasize the thesis, or central idea. As in the fairy tale, the narrative essay must have a beginning, middle, and end; and the events must progress in a logical time sequence.

The Student Reader

You use narrative whenever you write a letter retelling an exciting incident, such as a surprise birthday party. You use narrative when you relate the events of the day to your family, sitting around the dinner table. The difference between these informal narratives and those in essays is a matter of selection and organization. When you speak or write informally, you do not worry about the careful choosing of details. You simply tell the story as it happened. The writer of a narrative essay, however, wants to choose only the most interesting events to include in her narrative. And she wants to arrange them in chronological (time) order so that the reader can follow the progression of events. Finally, she must choose a narrative point of view, that is, the person who will be telling the narrative. The first person (*I*) lends a personal tone to the essay, whereas the third person (*he, she, it, they*) creates more distance between the author and the reader.

Here is an excerpt from an essay narrating the events that occurred on a camping trip. The author's choice of third-person narrator focuses your attention on the raft-building, not on the narrator. Notice the use of details ("large felling axe," "stout rope") and the chronological arrangement of the events.

> After two hours of walking they arrived at a river and rested while deciding how to cross. Carson said that it looked too deep to wade across, and Smith agreed. Hammond judged it to be too wide by far for a guide rope to be stretched from bank to bank and, after some discussion, the others came around to his point of view. Finally, they decided to build a raft, as there was a plentiful supply of wood next to shore. Smith used the large felling axe to cut down three tall birches, angling them so that they fell parallel to the bank. As soon as the trees were down, Carson and Hammond stripped off the smaller branches and cut the trunks into equal lengths to form the square frame of the raft. Then they laid the shorter branches over the frame to create the platform while Smith used a stout rope to lash all the parts firmly together. By the time the sun had begun to set, they were ready to launch their hastily built craft.

The Professional Writer

Some essays consist entirely of narrative, but more often a narrative incident is used to illustrate the thesis. For example, Randi Kreiss, in her essay "Bittersweet Farewell of a Grown-up Child," recounts her sheltered childhood in a brief narrative to show how difficult it is to see one's parents move away.

The selection of a narrative point of view is also important. In

Margaret Mead's essay "Samoan Children at Work and Play," she presents the first half of her essay in the first person (*I*). After she has related her personal experiences on the tropical island of Samoa, she shifts to the third person so that the reader can concentrate completely on the subject of the essay: the life-style of the Samoan children.

In addition to selecting a point of view, the writer must include carefully chosen details to make the narrative interesting. In his essay "Going Wild in San Francisco," the naturalist Euell Gibbons tells the reader exactly how wild plants can be prepared for eating. Speaking of wild mustard plants, he says, "The buds of the two members of the mustard family could be cooked and served like broccoli." Throughout his essay, Gibbons conveys the sensations of tasting wild plants as he takes the reader with him on his adventure, providing the involvement that is essential to narrative writing.

BITTERSWEET FAREWELL OF A GROWN-UP CHILD

Randi Kreiss

[1] My parents have retired to Florida, and I am suffering an empty nest syndrome. They taught me the value of family, urged me to settle in town, nurtured the love of my children and then they left. I may be 31 years old and a liberated woman, but it still hurts. There are thousands of people like me, experiencing a kind of delayed separation anxiety. Our parents are leaving the old hometown and shaking our roots loose as they go.

[2] In a parody of their ancestors who endured an arduous sea voyage in hopes of a better life, my well-heeled, lively parents tooled down I-95 in search of sunny days and four for bridge. They traded their snow shovels for golf clubs and left us behind to cope with real life.

[3] Part of me is happy for them. Both in their 50's, fit and independent, they have made a gutsy move. Methodically, they lightened their load, sold their house and my father's dental practice, and bought an apartment in Florida.

[4] But somewhere inside, I'm uneasy. Certainly my own life, my husband's life and my children's lives are diminished by their absence.

The daily calls or visits or just sightings of my mother's car parked in town were like touching down for a moment, a warm spot in each day. There were always noncritical ears to hear my side of an argument, a sensible voice to advise compromise. Mainly, the balance they provided on a daily basis is missing, the balance between past and present and the balance between my identity as a child and as a mother. That is all gone, because phone communication is brief and all the news is edited. The daily aches, fears and squabbles are deleted. Good news only, kids, it's Grandma calling.

[5] I wonder about two active people retiring. What will they do for the next 30 or 40 years? Can they really withdraw from the tumult of Northern life and embrace Southern ways? Or are they just exchanging one set of anxieties for another? Perhaps this is self-centered—I may be unwilling to see my parents retire because it is another confirmation that I, too, am getting older.

[6] There is anger in me as well. The child inside is holding her breath and turning blue; an unreasonable reaction, but let me explain.

[7] We live in a lovely community where people don't grow up longing to find a better life for themselves. They long to be able to afford this one, right here.

[8] My parents, sister and I lived in our house in Cedarhurst, L.I., for most of our lives. Not that we were overprotected, but I wouldn't sleep at a friend's house until I was 14. When it came time to go "away" to college, I only made it as far as New York University.

[9] Of course, I married the boy I knew in high school, and we settled just down the road in Woodmere. Only my sister threatened our geographic unity. Always the independent one (she made it to Boston for college), she married and settled in Philadelphia.

[10] I began making phone calls to her. "What if you both get a virus in the middle of the night?" I whispered. "What happens when you have a baby and Mom isn't there to help out?"

[11] After three years, they moved just down the road to Hewlett. So there we were, all settled in, reveling in our togetherness, except Mom and Dad, apparently. They smiled lovingly at us all and announced their impending retirement.

[12] I'm the first one to admit it was childlike, but I was angry. My father was always quoting Margaret Mead on the value of an extended family. Now he wanted to deprive his grandchildren of that experience.

[13] Once the decision was made, my parents began shedding possessions as a dog shakes out fleas. For my husband and me, that house was part of our youth and our romance. Memories mixed with the dust and plaster as pictures came down and relics were hauled up from the basement.

[14] We all thought it would be fun to have a garage sale on the last

weekend before they moved. Bits and pieces of ourselves, our old life together, were strewn about the garage waiting for buyers. But the day was cold and traffic was slow. By afternoon, my father stood outside alone, handing our things to strangers.

[15] Maybe part of the sadness was the air of finality. There were unmentioned but strongly felt parallels to the cleaning out and closing up that accompanies a death. My parents vacuumed up every trace of themselves, and they left town.

[16] The woman in me shouts "bravo" for their daring and the new days before them. They didn't wait for widowhood or illness to force their retirement. They made a free choice.

[17] But there is still the child in me, too, perhaps more petulant in this time of adjustment.

[18] Several months ago, the night before my husband and I left for a vacation alone, I heard my 4-year-old daughter crying in bed. She didn't want us to go, she said. Patiently, logically, I explained that mothers and fathers need time away to themselves. She nodded her head, endured my explanation and asked, "But who will be my mother when you're gone?"

[19] When we said goodbye to my parents, the child in me was asking the same question.

VOCABULARY

Look up the following words in your dictionary. Use the system developed in the dictionary section in the back of the text. Be sure to write the part of speech, the pronunciation, and the meaning(s) of each word.

bit·ter·sweet (bĭt′ər-swēt′) *n.* **1.** A North American woody vine, *Celastrus scandens,* having orange or yellowish fruits that split open to expose seeds enclosed in fleshy scarlet arils. **2.** A sprawling vine, *Solanum dulcamara,* native to Eurasia, having purple flowers and poisonous scarlet berries. Also called "nightshade." **3.** Dark to deep reddish orange. See color. —*adj.* **1.** Bitter and sweet at the same time. **2.** Producing a mixture of pain and pleasure. **3.** Having the color bittersweet.

Definition ©1981 Houghton Mifflin Company. Reprinted by permission from *The American Heritage Dictionary of the English Language, New College Edition.*

syndrome

nurtured

tooled

parody

arduous

diminished

squabbles

deleted

tumult

reveling

strewn

petulant

STUDY QUESTIONS

Finding the Matter

1. What is the meaning of the word *bittersweet* as it is used in the title of the essay?

2. What is the similarity between the journey of Kreiss's parents to Florida and the journey of their ancestors who first came to America? Why does she call her parents' trip a "parody" of the earlier one?

3. What are the differences between daily communication with a parent and long-distance phone calls?

4. In what ways does the author admit that she might have been overprotected as she grew up?

5. Why was the garage sale a sad experience?

Exploring the Manner

1. Kreiss begins her essay using the first person* singular (*I*). Why does she change to first person* plural (*we*) to state the thesis*?

2. Who is the intended audience* for this essay?

3. Why does the author devote only four paragraphs to a chronological narrative of her growing-up years?

SYNONYMS

From the column at the right, select the best synonym for the italicized word in each sentence. Rewrite each sentence using the appropriate synonym.

1. My parents did not have to make a *difficult* voyage to find a better life.

2. Our lives seemed *lessened* since my parents' absence.

3. We don't report all our *fights* when my parents call.

4. We also *omit* reporting on our daily problems.

5. Parts of our lives were *scattered* around the garage floor.

6. I still feel like an *ill-tempered* child when I think of my parents.

A. diminished

B. strewn

C. delete

D. arduous

E. squabbles

F. petulant

PARAPHRASE

Read this paragraph twice, then close your book. Using your own words, rewrite the paragraph as clearly and as completely as you can.

But somewhere inside, I'm uneasy. Certainly my own life, my husband's life and my children's lives are diminished by their absence. The daily calls or visits or just sightings of my mother's car parked in town were like touching down for a moment, a warm spot in each day. There were always non-critical ears to hear my side of an argument, a sensible voice to advise compromise. Mainly, the balance they provided on a daily basis is missing, the balance between past and present and the balance between my identity as a child and as a mother. That is all gone, because phone communication is brief and all the news is edited. The daily aches, fears and squabbles are deleted. Good news only, kids, it's Grandma calling.

VERB FILL-IN

Fill in each blank with the verb form that is appropriate for each sentence.

My parents, sister and I _____ in our house in Cedar-
live

hurst, L.I., for most of our lives. Not that we _____, but I
overprotect

wouldn't _____ at a friend's house until I _____
sleep   be

14. When it came time to go "away" to college, I only _____
make

it as far as New York University.

Of course, I _____ the boy I _____ in high
marry   know

school, and we _____ just down the road in Woodmere.
settle

Only my sister _____ our geographic unity. Always the
threaten

independent one (she _____ it to Boston for college), she
make

_____ and _____ in Philadelphia.
marry   settle

SENTENCE COMPLETION

From the column at the right, select the correct line to complete each of the numbered lines at the left. Write each sentence in its correct form.

1. In a parody of their ances-   A. the balance between past
   tors who endured an ardu-   and present and the bal-

ous sea voyage in hopes of a better life,

2. Our parents are leaving the old hometown

3. Methodically, they lightened their load, sold their house

4. Mainly, the balance they provided on a daily basis is missing,

5. We live in a community where people don't grow up

6. After three years, my sister moved just down the road

7. My father was always quoting Margaret Mead

8. My parents vacuumed up every trace of themselves

9. There is still the child in me, too, perhaps more petulant

ance between my identity as a child and as a mother

B. to Hewlett.

C. and bought an apartment in Florida.

D. on the value of an extended family.

E. and shaking our roots loose as they go.

F. my well-heeled, lively parents tooled down I-95 in search of sunny days and four for bridge.

G. longing to find a better life for themselves.

H. in this time of adjustment.

I. and they left town.

CLOZE EXERCISE

Fill in each blank with the best word to complete the meaning of the sentence.

I wonder about two active people _____. What will they do for the _____ 30 or 40 years? Can they _____ withdraw from the tumult of Northern _____ and embrace Southern ways? Or are _____ just exchanging one set of anxieties _____ another? Perhaps this is self-centered—I _____ be unwilling to see my parents _____ because it is another confirmation that _____, too, am getting older.

SENTENCE COMBINING

Combine each pair of sentences into a single grammatical sentence.

1. There are thousands of people like me.
   There are thousands of people who miss their parents.

2. There were always noncritical ears to hear my side of an argument.
   There were always suggestions for compromise.

3. I wondered if my parents could withdraw from the tumult of Northern life.
   I wondered if they could embrace Southern ways.

4. My father stood outside the garage alone.
   He was handing our things to strangers.

5. My husband and I planned to take a vacation.
   We explained that mothers and fathers need time away to themselves.

PUNCTUATION

Read the following paragraph. Write in the capital letters and place commas, periods, colons, semicolons, dashes, and quotation marks where needed.

the woman in me shouts bravo for their daring and the new days before them they didnt wait for widowhood or illness to force their retirement they made a free choice but there is still the child in me too perhaps more petulant in this time of adjustment several months ago the night before my husband and i left for a vacation alone i heard my 4 year old daughter crying in bed she didnt want us to go she said patiently logically i explained that mothers and fathers need time away to themselves she nodded her head endured my explanation and asked but who will be my mother when youre gone when we said goodbye to my parents the child in me was asking the same

question.

WORD-FORM CHART

Use your dictionary to complete the following table. Follow the example shown with item 1, *nurture*. If there is no commonly used form for a particular part of speech, write the symbol XXX.

Noun	Verb	Adjective	Adverb
1. nurturer	nurture	nurturing	XXX
2. anxiety			
3. independence			
4.	confirm		
5. deprivation			
6.	vacuum		
7.	neglect		

WORD-FORM EXERCISE

Using your completed Word-Form Chart, select the correct form to fit into each sentence. Use the appropriate tense of the verb, the singular or plural form of the noun, and the passive voice where necessary.
Follow the sequence of numbers from the Word-Form Chart to select the correct form.

1. My parents taught me the value of family and _____

   the love of my children.

2. Those of us whose parents leave suffer a kind of delayed separa-

   tion _____.

3. My parents are both healthy, fit, and ⎯⎯⎯⎯⎯⎯.

4. My parents' retirement ⎯⎯⎯⎯⎯⎯ that not only they, but I

   too, am getting older.

5. Their decision to move ⎯⎯⎯⎯⎯⎯ their grandchildren of the

   experience of growing up in an extended family.

6. After the garage sale, my parents ⎯⎯⎯⎯⎯⎯ up every trace of

   themselves.

7. Despite my age, I still feel like a ⎯⎯⎯⎯⎯⎯ child.

QUESTIONS FOR DISCUSSION

1. We have seen how the retirement of her parents affected the author. Has this happened in your family? If so, how did you feel about it? If not, how would you feel if your parents (or grown children) moved far away?

2. What differences are there between parents of grown children moving away and children who are grown moving away from home and parents?

3. To what extent do extended families exist in your native country? What are the advantages and disadvantages?

TOPICS FOR WRITING

1. Write a theme using a narrative incident to illustrate a "childish" quality in your personality.

2. Write an essay about your experience with separation anxiety, either as a child or as an adult.

3. Imagine yourself explaining to your grown children and grandchildren that you are moving far from them. Compose a letter stating your reasons for the decision in a tactful and loving manner.

4. Write a letter to your parents telling them how you feel about their moving away from family and friends.

SAMOAN CHILDREN AT WORK AND PLAY

Margaret Mead

[1] When anthropologists make trips to the far corners of the earth and search out the primitive peoples who live there, they add to our knowledge of the different ways of life under which human existence is possible, of the different kinds of demands which human beings can meet bravely and well.

[2] It was to add to our store of this kind of information that I went to Taū, a little island in American Samoa, and spent nine months living among the few hundred South Sea Islanders who inhabit it. I went there to make a study of Samoan children and Samoan girlhood, to find out if the pains and pangs of growing up were as difficult in Samoa as in America.

[3] This was no problem which could be solved in a flying trip. I could not just walk into the round, unwalled houses, with their high thatched roofs and pebbly floors, sit down on the mat which is always spread for strangers, and say to the guest-house mother who sat nursing one baby while a little older child tangled her half-finished mat, "Well, now, tell me, what are your children's names?

(Courtesy of the American Museum of Natural History.)

How old are they? And Flower is the oldest? Does she take her responsibility seriously? Is she good and obedient? Is she bossy with the other children? Was she jealous when the new baby came?"—and then pass on to the next mother and ask her the same kind of questions, putting the answers all down on cards, to be counted and written up after I got back. If that mother, in her soft Polynesian language in which her children and I made the same mistakes, had answered my questions directly, I should not have understood her answers. For they would have run something like this:

[4] "Names—well, the baby's name is Pandanus Nut, that's what we call it, or just Nut for short. But its name from its father's father's family is 'The One that Does Not Move,' and only yesterday my younger brother gave it his name of 'Lighted House,' so perhaps we will call it that now. And how old is he? Well, he was born after the second Palolo Fish Feast, and before my young cousin, Hibiscus, had her baby girl. He can't walk yet. The next one to the baby is called Bonito Fish. He is a boy. I don't know how old he is. And Flower, she is a girl, is the oldest of my children who are at home. There is that one, a boy, his name is White Stone, who lives with my mother, and the girl, her name is Jelly-fish, who lives with my first husband's sister in the next village. No, my first husband isn't dead! He's married to the sister of that woman with the banana leaf over her head, who is going down to the sea for water. I don't know what you mean by responsibility. Do you mean she has got common sense in her head enough to know that she mustn't play with her brother nor touch any of his things? She listens easily, not like my brother's children, who listen with difficulty to my brother's commands. Is she bossy? Of course she is bossy to all those in the family who are younger than she is, and listens to the wishes of all those who are older. And which new baby do you mean? My sister's baby, or my younger sister's baby, or my brother's wife's baby? But of course she was glad when all the babies were born."

[5] Only after I had learned to speak the language well, and had spent long mornings sitting gossiping over a coconut or a plate of bananas, after I had learned to plait mats and blinds and helped the harassed homeless people rebuild the village after a devastating hurricane, and had spent even more hours with the little girls themselves, searching for shells, weaving flower necklaces, coaxing land crabs with a low, sweet chant, or swimming in a hole in the reef, did I come to know enough about the Samoan way of life so that I could have understood those answers.

[6] Samoan children's names change often, at the whim of any relative. As soon as they are old enough, they are allowed to choose new ones for themselves upon any occasion. And similarly they choose their own homes, living now with a grandmother, now with an uncle. Families are not made up of father and mother and children, but of some fifteen or twenty relatives among whom there is

no oldest child, because a young aunt or cousin will be nearly of an age, among whom the same child is never "youngest" for long. And in these great households the mothers take little care of their children after the babies learn to crawl. The nurses are not young girls but toddling five-year-olds, who trundle about upon their hips babies that are too heavy to be lifted into their arms. Samoan children are not carefully disciplined and supervised until they are five or six, and then, properly trained, given some freedom. They are spoiled and pampered by their baby nurses until they are five, and then, if they are girls, they are turned into nurses themselves; if they are boys, they are turned over to the rough but thorough discipline of older boys. At ten years of age they are sturdy, well-behaved youngsters, although their bringing-up seems so strange to us.

[7] Samoan parents do not hide anything from their children; they tell them no fairy tales about the birth of babies nor do they pack them off to a relative until after a funeral. They believe quite literally that children should be seen but not heard, should be present but make no comments, should learn the important facts of life from careful observation, not from random, groping experimentation. And the children grow up, acquainted with the rhythm of life and death, accepting life as simply and unrebelliously as do their parents.

[8] Nor do Samoan parents think children should not work. The tiniest little staggerer has tasks to perform — to carry water, to borrow fire brands, to fetch leaves to stuff the pig. And these slighter tasks are laid aside for harder ones as soon as the child becomes strong enough or skilled enough. At the preparation for a feast to celebrate a visiting chief, a marriage, or a new canoe, the little children feel very serious and important, and go scurrying about the village, muttering, "There are very great complications in my household." Learning to run errands tactfully is one of the first lessons of childhood, and a child of nine will be trusted to take a valuable piece of bark cloth to barter for a pig.

[9] This attitude toward children as little adults although lacking in experience and sometimes sadly devoid of common sense, makes for a different kind of play also. Samoan children have no dolls, no play houses, no tea sets, no toy boats. For dolls they have real babies; at six they are expected to sweep up the real house and pick all the scraps off the floor. Little boys anxious to become boatmen paddle about in real canoes within the safety of the lagoon. Embryonic eel fishermen hold the bait for their big brothers, but never play-act fishing in a pail, or catch a leaf and pretend it is an eel. Yet they have their games, playing at ball with square light balls made of pandanus, stringing necklaces of flowers, playing round games to merry songs of their own improvising in the dusk. And in all these they but imitate their elders, who follow a morning of work and an afternoon of sleep with an evening of dance and song.

[10] Strangest of all to us is the Samoan opinion of precocious chil-

dren. To be brighter than your age, to stand out conspicuously above other children, this is the sin for which a child is roundly scolded and sometimes whipped. So it is that the happiest children are those who like to be children, who put off responsibility, who do what is asked of them without aspiring to more grown-up tasks, those who answer in lazy content, "I am but young."

VOCABULARY

Look up the following words in your dictionary. Use the system developed in the dictionary section in the back of the text. Be sure to write the part of speech, the pronunciation, and the meaning(s) of each word.

> an·thro·pol·o·gist (an'thrə päl'ə jist) *n.* a student of or specialist in anthropology
> an·thro·pol·o·gy (-jē) *n.* the study of man, esp. of the variety, physical and cultural characteristics, distribution, customs, social relationships, etc. of mankind: often restricted to the study of the institutions, myths, etc. of nonliterate peoples —an'thro·po·log'i·cal (-pə läj'i k'l), an'thro·po·log'ic *adj.* —an'thro·po·log'i·cal·ly *adv.*

Definitions with permission. From *Webster's New World Dictionary*, Second College Edition. Copyright ©1980 by Simon & Schuster, Inc.

primitive

pangs

thatched

pebbly

obedient

common sense

bossy

plait

harassed

devastating

chant

whim

trundle

random

groping

literally

fairy tales

staggerer

scurrying

devoid

embryonic

dusk

precocious

STUDY QUESTIONS

Finding the Matter

1. What did Margaret Mead hope to study when she went to Taū?

2. What was the first skill Mead had to develop before she could learn about the Samoan way of life?

3. Describe the way in which children's names change in Samoa.

4. What are the living arrangements for these children?

5. Who takes care of the babies after they learn how to crawl?

6. Name some of the responsibilities of Samoan children.

7. How does the Samoan concept of play differ from yours?

Exploring the Manner

1. In the opening two paragraphs, does Mead move from a specific idea to a more general one or the reverse?

2. Identify the thesis* of Mead's article.

3. What is the purpose of the long imaginary dialogue* that Mead describes between herself and a Samoan woman? What sentence explains why this conversation never took place?

4. Look at the following two topic sentences.* Besides indicating the main idea of each paragraph, show how they function as transitions*: "Nor do Samoan parents think children should not work." "This attitude toward children as little adults although lacking in experience . . . makes for a different kind of play also."

5. How much of the essay is narration? How would the essay have been different if Mead had left out her personal experience in Samoa?

SYNONYMS

From the column at the right, select the best synonym for the italicized word in each sentence. Rewrite each sentence using the appropriate synonym.

1. While she was learning the language, Margaret Mead spent long mornings gossiping over a plate of bananas and learning to *braid* mats.

2. The little girls stood at the water's edge, coaxing the crabs with a low, sweet *song*.

3. The children played and improvised games at *twilight*.

4. Mead helped the people rebuild the village after a *ravaging* hurricane.

5. Samoan children's names change often, at the *fancy* of any relative.

6. Strangest of all to us is the Samoan opinion of *bright* children.

7. Little children help in the preparation of special events

A. chant

B. devastating

C. precocious

D. plait

E. scurrying

F. whim

G. dusk

and go *scampering* around
the village feeling very
important.

PARAPHRASE

Read this paragraph twice, then close your book. Using your
own words, rewrite the paragraph as clearly and as completely
as you can.

Samoan parents do not hide anything from their children;
they tell them no fairy tales about the birth of babies nor do
they pack them off to a relative until after a funeral. They
believe quite literally that children should be seen but not
heard, should be present but make no comments, should
learn the important facts of life from careful observation, not
from random, groping experimentation. And the children
grow up, acquainted with the rhythm of life and death,
accepting life as simply and as unrebelliously as do their
parents.

VERB FILL-IN

Fill in each blank with the verb form that is appropriate for
each sentence.

When anthropologists _____ trips to the far corners of
make

the earth and _____ out the primitive peoples who live there,
search

they _____ to our knowledge of the different ways of life
add

under which human existence is possible, of the different kinds of

demands which human beings can _____ bravely and well.
meet

It _____ to add to our store of this kind of information
be

that I _____ to Taū, a little island in American Samoa, and
      go

_____ nine months _____ among the South Sea
   spend   live

Islanders who inhabit it. I _____ there to make a study of
      go

Samoan children and Samoan girlhood, _____ if the pains
      find out

and pangs of growing up _____ as difficult in Samoa as in
      be

America.

SENTENCE COMPLETION

From the column at the right, select the correct line to complete each of the numbered lines at the left. Write each sentence in its correct form.

1. Mead went to the South Sea Islands to study Samoan children,

2. Only after Mead had learned to speak the language well

3. Samoan children's names change often,

4. As soon as Samoan children are old enough,

5. Families are not made up of father, mother and children,

6. Children are spoiled and pampered by their baby nurses until they are five,

7. Samoans believe that children should be

A. at the whim of any relative.

B. is a sin for which a child is scolded and sometimes whipped.

C. to find out if the pains of growing up were as difficult in Samoa as in America.

D. they are allowed to choose new names for themselves.

E. and then, if they are girls, they are turned into nurses themselves.

F. but of some fifteen or twenty relatives.

G. did she come to know enough about the Samoan

8. Little boys anxious to become boatmen paddle about

9. In Samoa to be brighter than your age and to stand out above other children

way of life so she could understand the woman's answers.

H. present and make no comments.

I. in real canoes within the safety of the lagoon.

CLOZE EXERCISE

Fill in each blank with the best word to complete the meaning of the sentence.

This was no problem which _____ be solved in a flying

_____. I could not just walk _____ the round,

unwalled houses, with _____ high thatched roofs and pebbly

_____, sit down on the mat _____ is always spread

for strangers, _____ say to the guest-house mother

_____ sat nursing one baby while _____ little older

child tangled her _____ mat. "Well, now, tell me,

_____ are your children's names? How _____

are they? And Flower is _____ oldest? Does she take her

_____ seriously? Is she good and _____? Is she

bossy with the _____ children? Was she jealous when

_____ new baby came?"—and then _____ on to

the next mother _____ ask her the same kind _____

questions, putting the answers all _____ on cards, to be

counted _____ written up after I got _____.

SENTENCE COMBINING

Combine each pair of sentences into a single grammatical
sentence.

1. He is married to the woman with the banana leaf over her head.
   She is going down to the sea for water.

2. She listens easily, not like the other children.
   The other children listen with difficulty to the commands.

3. She is bossy to others.
   She is bossy to those younger than she is.

4. The nurses are not young girls, they're toddling five-year-olds.
   The five-year-olds carry the heavy babies on their hips.

5. Children imitate their elders.
   Their elders follow a pattern of work in the morning and sleep in
   the afternoon.

6. Samoans do not approve of precocious children.
   Samoans scold or whip children who stand out.

PUNCTUATION

Read the following paragraph. Write in the capital letters,
and place commas, periods, colons, semicolons, dashes and
quotation marks where needed.

samoan childrens names change often at the whim of any relative

as soon as they are old enough they are allowed to choose new ones

for themselves upon any occasion and similarly they choose their

own homes living now with a grandmother now with an uncle

families are not made up of father and mother and children but of

some fifteen or twenty relatives among whom there is no oldest child

because a young aunt or cousin will be nearly of an age among whom

the same child is never youngest for long and in these great households the mothers take little care of their children after the babies

learn to crawl

WORD-FORM CHART

Use your dictionary to complete the following table. Follow the example shown with item 1, *pebble*. If there is no commonly used form for a particular part of speech, write the symbol XXX.

Noun	Verb	Adjective	Adverb
1. pebble	pebble	pebbly	XXX
2.	thatch		
3.		bossy	
4.	devastate		
5. trundler			
6.	stagger		
7.	observe		
8. acceptance			
9.		devoid	
10. precocity precociousness			

WORD-FORM EXERCISE

Using your completed Word-Form Chart, select the correct form to fit into each sentence. Use the appropriate tense of the verb, the singular or plural form of the noun, and the passive voice where necessary.
Follow the sequence of numbers from the Word-Form Chart to select the correct form.

1. The thatched-roof houses have _____ on the floor.

2. The Samoans lived in unwalled houses and were experienced in

   _____ their roofs.

3. The mother informed Margaret Mead that the woman

   _____ all those in the family younger than she.

4. The homeless people had been harassed by a _____

   hurricane.

5. The five-year-olds _____ about with babies on their

   hips.

6. The tiniest child _____ around performing tasks like

   carrying water and borrowing fire brands.

7. Children learn about life from careful _____ of their

   elders.

8. The children grow up _____ life as do their parents.

9. The children acted like adults but sometimes showed that they

   were _____ of common sense.

10. The children in the village quickly learned not to display any

    _____ .

QUESTIONS FOR DISCUSSION

1. If you were going on a field trip with an anthropologist to study a particular society, what would you have to know in advance besides the language?

2. How do you feel about the Samoan parents allowing their children to witness birth and death? Explain your reaction.

3. Why is it considered a "sin" for a Samoan child to appear superior in any way to the other children? How might this attitude relate to the welfare of the entire society?

TOPICS FOR WRITING

1. Compare child-raising techniques in your native country with those you have observed in America.

2. Write a theme describing your theory of raising a well-adjusted child in America in the 1980s. Consider such concerns as responsibility, independence, discipline, education, love, play, and family relationships.

3. Try to remember what aspects of being a child made you happy (or unhappy). Write a narrative composition discussing one of these memories in detail.

4. Discuss your reaction to the Samoan philosophy that "children should be seen but not heard, should be present but make no comments, should learn the important facts of life from careful observation, not from random, groping experimentation."

GOING WILD IN SAN FRANCISCO

Euell Gibbons

[1] It was October. The host on an early morning TV show was interviewing me. I had landed at the San Francisco International Airport at 10 P.M. the evening before. This interviewer was interested in the availability of wild foods in the Bay Area. I told him that I had already found three edible wild plants growing as weeds in the flower beds that surrounded the TV studios as I came in, but had to confess that I didn't know a nearby place where I could gather wild foods in quantity. I have probably spent a total of five days in that beautiful city, always as a one-day visitor, and my favorite survival spot was the restaurants on Fisherman's Wharf. However, from the brief glimpse of the flora I had on my way to the station, I was willing to bet that I could find enough wild food for a good vegetarian lunch, and do it before lunchtime.

[2] He called my bluff and offered to send a camera crew along with me to record the gathering. I wanted neither a well-groomed

park nor a dense forest. The camera crew thought we could find a neglected area in a park they knew and we set off. We never got there. As we passed through an urban-renewal area where slum buildings were coming down and jackhammers machinegunned their way through concrete, I spotted a block-long median strip in the wide street that had been allowed to grow completely wild.

[3] This was in the well-watered fog belt and the growth was lush. The strip had been planted in young olive trees several years before, and these were about eight feet tall and beginning to bear. But olive foliage is so thin that it scarcely interfered with the sunlight that filtered through, and wild food plants grew bountiful right up to the bases of the little trees. Before I had even stepped into this natural greengrocery I had spotted eight different wild food plants, and all of them in great abundance.

[4] There were tall lamb's-quarters (*Chenopodium*) and wild beets (*Amaranthus*), both relatives of common garden spinach and furnishing the same kind of vegetable. Wild mustard (*Brassica*), charlock (*Raphanus*), and, as a complete surprise to me, orach (*Atriplex*), which I had seen only by the seaside or growing in saline desert soils. These three could furnish more green vegetables or salads, and the buds of the two members of the mustard family could be cooked and served like broccoli. There was a fat-rooted, biennial thistle (*Cirsium*), and the tender, crisp root had the flavor of a globe artichoke. Between the taller plants, purslane (*Portulaca*) sprawled over the ground, offering crisp, purple stems and leafy tips. Both are very good, raw or cooked. Then there were, of course, dandelions, in every stage of development, offering dandelion greens, crowns, and roots, all good cooked vegetables, and the tender hearts are delicious in salads.

[5] By this time the camera crew was ready to concede that I could not only prepare a lunch from the available wild food here, but could easily vegetable-feed a large family indefinitely from this natural wild food supermarket. We started filming the gathering and immediately attracted a crowd. Although it was during school hours, two little black boys about ten years old attached themselves to us. One was a shy lad wearing a sombrero almost as wide as he was tall. The other was bold, beautiful, and intelligent. He amazed me by joining in the eating of raw purslane and orach, saying that he often came out here and finished up his dinner when the food was scanty at home. He led me through the rank growth to his favorite patch of what he called "wild lemon grass" (*Oxalis*) and we added this acid, lemon-flavored plant with cloverlike leaves to our snack. Then he spotted a tall plant with lacy, dark-green foliage with umbels of yellowish flowers and maturing seed-heads at its top. He grew excited and pointed, "Hey, I know what that plant is, that's lickwish." It was a wild anise plant, but many think anise and licorice taste almost identical. He started

pulling the blooms and immature seeds of the umbels and cramming them into his mouth, saying around a mouthful of anise, "Man, just taste that sweetness. Sometimes I call this lickwish and sometimes I just call it sugar." A thrill shot through me to find a modern boy who knew how to get his sweets from the wild. He had thought it all through about sanitation also, for he later said, "This lickwish out here is clean, cause no dogs ever come out here. When it grows close to the sidewalk you ought not to eat it because it might have dog wee-wee on it."

[6]   Then I found a clump of wild lettuce (*Lactuca*) with plants in all stages of development, from just peeping through the ground to seeding. The California climate is wonderful, but it is apparently confusing to plants trying to figure out when spring has come. It is just about spring all year. There had recently been an abundance of rain and everything was growing enthusiastically, with a whole crop of new plants coming up. I was able to gather very young wild lettuce, which is good for cooking like spinach, one of the most palatable of all wild greens, and also to gather tender stems from older plants that, when peeled, make a very good cooked vegetable.

[7]   We also located a nice patch of sheep sorrel. This would make a good addition to a purslane salad, can form the main ingredient in a gourmet soup and can even be cooked with sugar to make a fruitlike dessert. The olive trees, while not exactly wild, would come within my rules of fair foraging, which is "reaping where you did not sow, but only if the food would go unused unless you take it." They were just beginning to bear, but in the block-long median strip with its two rows of young olive trees, there were many bushels of olives just turning from green to bluish-black. An olive is inedible straight from the tree. To prepare them for eating is a long, complicated pickling process, but the nearly ripe olives would be just right for making olive oil. Strangely enough, making olive oil is a simpler process than making the olives edible. Slightly underripe olives merely need the seeds removed, then the meat is pressed. It is better to put them in a cloth bag, place the bag between two boards and load the top board with heavy stones. This gently squeezes out the "virgin" oil, the very finest of olive oils.

[8]   I was beginning to wish that I had brought along my camping gear and back-pack tent. I would have loved to set up my tent right there in the midst of the noisy city, gathered and cooked my food from the wild for a day or so, and proved that nature can do her thing wherever man will let a small plot of fertile soil alone.

[9]   I would still like to return and try that stunt with my two oldest grandchildren, Mike and Colleen, who like wild food as well as I do. But I doubt that it will be possible in exactly the same place. The film the crew made was shown on television the next day, and within two hours the median strip was covered with curious people who

came to see what had been there all the time. They had been unable to see it until their eyes had been opened.

VOCABULARY

Look up the following words in your dictionary. Use the system developed in the dictionary section in the back of the text. Be sure to write the part of speech, the pronunciation, and the meaning(s) of each word.

ed·i·ble (ĕd′ə-bəl) *adj.* **1. a.** Capable of being eaten. **b.** Fit to eat; nonpoisonous. **2.** Ready to be eaten. —*n.* Something fit to be eaten; food. Usually used in the plural. [Late Latin *edibilis,* from Latin *edere,* to eat. See **ed-** in Appendix.*] —**ed′·i·bil′i·ty, ed′i·ble·ness** *n.*

Definition ©1981 Houghton Mifflin Company. Reprinted by permission from *The American Heritage Dictionary of the English Language, New College Edition.*

survival

flora

well-groomed

dense

jackhammers

median

lush

foliage

bountiful

abundance

saline

biennial

scanty

rank

palatable

forage

reap

sow

STUDY QUESTIONS

Finding the Matter

1. What point does Gibbons make by including the incident involving the two little black boys?

2. Why is it more interesting to think of Gibbons trying to make a meal out of wild ingredients in the middle of San Francisco rather than in the countryside?

3. Do you think Gibbons's morning adventure made a good television program? Why?

4. Why couldn't Gibbons return to the same strip the next day for another wild vegetable lunch?

Exploring the Manner

1. Usually, students are taught to connect related sentences by using transitions.* Could Gibbons's first four sentences have been improved by connecting them? If so, how would you do it? Would you rearrange the order of the ideas?

2. Although he is known for his unusual eating habits, Gibbons says in his first paragraph that on previous visits to San Francisco, Fisherman's Wharf, with its many restuarants, was his "favorite survival spot." How does this admission bring the author closer to his reader?

3. In this narrative essay, the author speaks in the first person* (*I*). How would the essay have been different if it had been told by one of the camera crew (with regard to details, tone,* attitude)?

4. Would Gibbons's narrative have been as interesting if it had not been told in chronological order*? Explain your answer.

SYNONYMS

From the column at the right, select the best synonym for the italicized word in each sentence. Rewrite each sentence using the appropriate synonym.

1. I had only a brief glimpse of the *flora* on my way to the station.	A. eatable
	B. insufficient
2. I wanted neither a well-groomed park nor a *dense* forest.	C. crowded
	D. wealth
3. In the past, I had seen certain plants growing by the seaside or in *salty* soil.	E. gathering
	F. tasty
4. There was an *abundance* of wild food plants.	G. planted
	H. saline
5. The boy claimed that food at home was *scanty*.	I. biennial
	J. plants

6. Some plants had a *two-year* growth period.

7. We were *reaping* the food that otherwise would not be used.

8. The seeds were *sown* by the winds.

9. We found many *edible* plants.

10. Spinach is one of the most *palatable* plants of all wild greens.

PARAPHRASE

Read this paragraph twice, then close your book. Using your
own words, rewrite the paragraph as clearly and as completely
as you can.

He called my bluff and offered to send a camera crew along
with me to record the gathering. I wanted neither a well-
groomed park nor a dense forest. The camera crew thought
we could find a neglected area in a park they knew and we set
off. We never got there. As we passed through an urban-
renewal area where slum buildings were coming down and
jackhammers machinegunned their way through concrete. I
spotted a block-long median strip in the wide street that had
been allowed to grow completely wild.

VERB FILL-IN

Fill in each blank with the verb form that is appropriate for
each sentence.

It _____ October. The host on an early morning TV
         be

show _____ me. I _____ at the San Francisco
         interview   land

International Airport at 10 P.M. the evening before. This interviewer

_____ in the availability of wild foods in the Bay Area.
to be interested

I _____ him that I _____ three edible plants grow-
      tell   find

ing as weeds in the flower beds that surrounded the TV studios as I

_____ in, but I _____ to confess that I
      come   have

_____ a nearby place where I _____ gather wild
   do not know   can

foods in quantity.

SENTENCE COMPLETION

From the column at the right, select the correct line to complete each of the numbered lines at the left. Write each sentence in its correct form.

1. The interviewer was interested in

2. From the brief glimpse of the flora I had on my way to the station

3. Olive foliage is so thin that it scarcely interfered with the sunlight that filtered through, and wild food

4. Then there were dandelions in every stage of development offering greens, crowns and roots, all good

5. Although it was during school hours,

6. He led me through the rank growth to his favorite patch of what

7. He started pulling the blooms and immature seeds of the umbels and cramming them into his mouth, saying,

8. The California climate is wonderful, but it is apparently confusing to plants trying to

9. "This lickwish here is clean, cause

10. Sheep sorrel can form the main ingredient in a gourmet soup

11. To prepare olives for eating is a long, complicated pickling process,

A. plants grew bountiful right up to the bases of the little trees.

B. "Man, just taste that sweetness."

C. the median strip was covered with curious people who came to see what had been there all the time.

D. I was willing to bet that I could find enough wild food for a good vegetarian lunch.

E. but the nearly ripe olives would be just right for making olive oil.

F. no dogs ever came out here."

G. two little black boys about ten years old attached themselves to us.

H. place the bag between two boards and load the top board with heavy stones.

I. he called "wild lemon grass" and we added this to our snack.

J. the availability of wild foods in the Bay Area.

K. right there in the midst of the noisy city.

L. figure out when spring has come.

12. It is better to put olives in a cloth bag,

13. I would have loved to set up my tent

14. I would still like to return and try that stunt with my two oldest grandchildren,

15. The film the crew made was shown on television the next day, and within two hours

M. and can even be cooked with sugar to make a fruit-like dessert.

N. who like wild food as well as I do.

O. cooked vegetables, and the tender hearts are delicious in salads.

CLOZE EXERCISE

Fill in each blank with the best word to complete the meaning of the sentence.

Then I found a _____ of wild lettuce with

_____ in all stages of _____, from just peeping

through _____ ground to seeding. The _____ cli-

mate is wonderful, but _____ is apparently confusing to

_____ trying to figure out _____ spring has come.

It _____ just about spring all _____. There had

recently been _____ abundance of rain and _____

was growing enthusiastically, with _____ whole crop of new

_____ coming up. I was _____ to gather very young

_____ lettuce, which is good _____ cooking like

spinach, one _____ the most palatable of _____

wild greens, and also _____ gather tender stems from

_____ plants that, when peeled, _____ a very good

cooked _____.

SENTENCE COMBINING

Combine each pair of sentences into a single grammatical sentence.

1. I didn't want a well-groomed park.
    I didn't want a dense forest.

2. I spotted a block-long median strip in the wide street.
    This strip had been allowed to grow completely wild.

3. It was during school hours.
    Two little black boys about ten years old attached themselves to us.

4. The other boy was bold.
    He was also beautiful and intelligent.

5. The olive trees would come within my rules of fair foraging.
    The olive trees were not exactly wild.

6. He started pulling the blooms and immature seeds of the umbels.
    He started cramming them into his mouth.

7. I was able to gather very young wild lettuce.
    Wild lettuce is good for cooking like spinach.

PUNCTUATION

Read the following paragraph. Write in the capital letters and place commas, periods, colons, semicolons, dashes, and quotation marks where needed.

although it was during school hours two little black boys about ten years old attached themselves to us one was a shy lad wearing a sombrero almost as wide as he was tall the other was bold beautiful and intelligent he amazed me by joining in the eating of raw purslane he noticed something and grew excited and pointed hey i know what that plant is thats lickwish it was a wild anise plant but many think anise and licorice taste almost identical he started pulling the blooms and immature seeds of the umbels and cramming them into his

mouth saying around a mouthful of anise man just taste that sweet-

ness sometimes i call this lickwish and sometimes i call this sugar a

thrill shot through me to find a modern boy who knew how to get

his sweets from the wild

WORD-FORM CHART

Use your dictionary to complete the following table. Follow
the example shown with item 1, *availability*. If there is no
commonly used form for a particular part of speech, write
the symbol XXX.

Noun	Verb	Adjective	Adverb
1. availability	avail	available	availably
2.	quantify		
3.	neglect		
4.		allowable	
5.		easy	
6.	join		
7.		apparent	
8. preparation			
9.		showy	

WORD-FORM EXERCISE

Using your completed Word-Form Chart, select the correct form to fit into each sentence. Use the appropriate tense of the verb, the singular or plural form of the noun, and the passive voice where necessary.
Follow the sequence of numbers from the Word-Form Chart to select the correct form.

1. The TV-show host was interested in the _____ of wild foods in the Bay Area of San Francisco.

2. Gibbons was not familiar with the area and therefore was not certain of finding a place where a _____ of wild foods could be gathered.

3. The camera crew knew of a _____ area of a nearby park.

4. Gibbons spotted a block-long median strip that _____ to grow completely wild.

5. The camera crew was ready to concede that I could _____ vegetable-feed a large family from the wild food here.

6. The boy amazed Gibbons by _____ in the eating of some of the natural food.

7. The California climate is wonderful, but it is _____ confusing to plants trying to figure out when spring has come.

8. _____ the olives for eating is a long, complicated pickling process.

9. The film that the TV crew made _____ on television and people crowded the strip within a very short time.

QUESTIONS FOR DISCUSSION

1. What kind of experience or knowledge must one have to survive in the wild?

2. If you could save $25 on your monthly grocery bill, would you consider eating the foods Gibbons ate? How might you prepare them?

3. If Gibbons were a guest in your country, where would you take him to test his foraging skills?

TOPICS FOR WRITING

1. Write a narrative essay telling of an adventure that you had as a result of accepting a bet or a dare.

2. Tell of a meal that you ate in which there was nothing that you enjoyed eating.

3. Relate an incident in which you tried to get closer to nature by camping, hiking, or cooking out.

4. Write a theme telling of an incident that might cause a meat-eating person to become a vegetarian.

2

Description

The Form

Descriptive writing is word painting. Whereas a painter uses oils, pastels, or watercolors to communicate his impressions, the writer uses words. First, the writer observes something; then he transforms the image into words. The readers must then decode the words into their own interpretations of the original image. It sounds complicated, but this is what we do whenever we read.

All writing is word painting, but descriptive writing is the most visual. Here the writer uses carefully selected words in order to convey a particular image. Details are essential. For example, if I say, "I saw a bird this morning," I have allowed the readers to imagine any bird they want. But if I say, "I saw the first robin of spring this morning—a plump male—his red breast glowing in the sun," then the readers receive a clear picture. Details can employ any or all of the five senses. The feel of a fabric, the sound outside a window, the writer's reaction to a particular color, taste, or smell—all these sensations can be conveyed to the readers through the writer's words.

The focus in a descriptive essay is *space*. Whether one is describing a favorite person, a food, or an emotion, there must be a logical arrangement of ideas. When describing a bedroom, for example, the writer might lead the reader on an imaginary tour through the door and around the room in a single direction, pointing out the furniture, carpeting, curtains, and accessories along the way. Of

51

course, random description can be less exciting than a description with a purpose. Simply describing a room may not create much interest, but a thesis such as this one is likely to arouse the reader's curiosity: *Although it horrifies my parents, I find the messiness of my room comforting.*

The way in which an author organizes his ideas depends on the subject. If he is describing a ship, he might proceed from front to back (bow to stern). A beautiful statue might be described from top to bottom (head to foot), although the reverse is also possible. If he is describing a landscape painting, he might discuss the foreground first and then the background.

When a description deals with an abstract idea, the organization is not spatial. Rather, the organizing principle is the author's dominant impression of whatever he is describing. Thus, if he were to describe his fear of heights, he might talk about the different physical sensations that he has (heavy perspiration, rapid heartbeat, dizziness) as well as the emotional reactions (fear of falling, helplessness, dependence).

Sometimes complete essays are written in the descriptive mode. More often, description is used in combination with other modes, such as narrative, argument, or comparison. In fact, it is difficult to think of any essay that does not contain descriptive detail.

The Student Reader

When you read a descriptive essay, take note of sensory details and the author's method of organizing the ideas. Also be aware of the manner in which the author treats his subject. Perhaps the description is *objective*, written as a scientist would describe a tissue sample seen under a microscope. Objective description excludes personal opinion and judgment, concentrating solely on factual observation. Some descriptions are *subjective*, however, allowing the author to include his opinions, attitudes, and biases. In his essay "University Days," James Thurber writes a delightfully subjective description of his experience with a microscope.

> I passed all the other courses that I took at my University, but I could never pass botany. This was because all botany students had to spend several hours a week in a laboratory looking through a microscope at plant cells, and I could never see through a microscope. I never once saw a cell through a microscope. This used to enrage my instructor. He would wander around the laboratory pleased with the progress all the students were making in drawing the involved and, so I am told, interesting structure of flower cells, until he came to me. I would just be standing there. "I can't see anything," I would say. He would begin patiently enough, explaining how anybody can see through a micro-

scope, but he would always end up in a fury, claiming that I could *too* see through a microscope but just pretended that I couldn't. "It takes away from the beauty of flowers anyway," I used to tell him. "We are not concerned with beauty in this course," he would say. "We are concerned solely with what I may call the *mechanics* of flars [flowers]." "Well," I'd say, "I can't see anything." "Try it just once again," he'd say, and I would put my eye to the microscope and see nothing at all, except now and again a nebulous milky substance—a phenomenon of maladjustment. You were supposed to see a vivid, restless clockwork of sharply defined plant cells. "I see what looks like a lot of milk," I would tell him. This, he claimed, was the result of my not having adjusted the microscope properly, so he would readjust it for me, or rather, for himself. And I would look again and see milk.

No one could confuse Thurber's personal reminiscence with a clin-
ically objective description.

The Professional Writer

Another example of subjective description can be found in Pete Hamill's essay "The Rainbow City." Hamill, a lifelong New Yorker, does not describe the city objectively, as a travel brochure would, but subjectively, as a native son: "But in the face of anger, tumult, harsh words, and bitterness from older New Yorkers, the new immigrants have become a permanent part of the city." This is not merely a descriptive sentence; it is a distinctive point of view.

A far more objective description appears in Susie Nazem's article "Where James Bond Shops." Here the factual details of the various surveillance items bought by the famous and powerful are so intriguing that the author's personal opinion becomes unimportant.

Whether the descriptions are objective or subjective, the authors achieve their purpose through the careful selection and arrangement of details.

NORMAN ROCKWELL: AN ARTISTIC LINK TO OUR PAST

Ellen Goodman

[1] Now he's gone, the tall skinny man with a shock of white hair who always looked like a Norman Rockwell portrait as he bicycled across the small-town set of Stockbridge, Massachusetts.

[2] Now, for a few days his fans and detractors alike suddenly feel a kind of nostalgia . . . for his nostalgia.

[3] There were, of course, critics who called him the Lawrence Welk of the art world, insisting that bubbles floated off the ends of his brushes and that his work was sticky with sweetness. There were others who adored him, saying that he was the artist among con artists. But now they can both be heard calling him an artistic link to our past, a visual historian.

[4] Norman Rockwell was a craftsman, an artist who insisted upon being called an illustrator, and a gentle, sophisticated man. But no, not a historian. His folksy vision of this country was no more accurate than the bleak world of Edward Hopper. His magazine work was no more a total reflection of our society than the photographs of Walker Evans.

[5] Rockwell wasn't a man of many words, but these few were significant: "Maybe as I grew up and found the world wasn't the perfectly pleasant place I had thought it to be, I unconsciously decided that if it wasn't an ideal world, it should be and so painted only the ideal aspects of it—pictures in which there were no slatterns or self-centered mothers, in which to the contrary, there were only Foxy Grandpas who played baseball with the kids and boys fishing from logs and got-up circuses in the backyard."

[6] He knew that he didn't portray America. He portrayed Americana.

[7] I suppose that every society carries in its soul some collective longings, some common spiritual values. We invest these back into our history and then hold them aloft as a standard of comparison for the present. For most of his eighty-two years, through 360 magazine covers, that was what Rockwell recorded: our ideals and our common myths.

[8] As a chronicler, he was born at a perfect time in a perfect place: in New York City, a few years before the end of the nineteenth century. He grew up into the world of hustle and boosters and made it in the competitive and high-pressure business of magazine illustrators. Like many of us, he must have looked back with some longing on the century of Simpler Times and Smaller Towns. So, he made a click, a link with others, sharing with them some vast and powerful yearning for a way of life which he defined as American.

(Courtesy of the estate of Norman Rockwell and its agent, Raines & Raines, New York ©1929 by the family of Norman Rockwell.)

[9] Rockwell painted our American religion—The Four Freedoms— and our real heroes—the common people. He then went on to en- grave images of our strongest ideas—not those of equality or even justice—but those of everyday decency.

[10] In the world of Americana, his boys were all Tom Sawyers, his doctors made house calls and his dogs were puppies. But his subjects were usually the old or the young—as if even he had trouble finding a place for the real, midlife American in his scheme.

[11] He spent his work life reaching back to make connections. His illustrations in the 1920s often carried the feeling of the 1900s. His paintings of the 1930s have more of the patina of a Teddy than a Franklin Roosevelt. In wartime he carefully drew our peaceful nature and even in his self-consciously relevant work of the 1960s, Rockwell pushed the buttons of the past.

[12] It was as a hard-working artist, a businessman, a husband of

three wives that he portrayed the imagined ease of everyday life. His subjects had foibles rather than problems. They lived through a comedy of manners rather than human tragedies. So, it wasn't a mirror he held up to society, but the hungering eye of a man of his time. A man who filled his canvases with what many of us felt was missing.

[13] In the 1960s, after President Johnson rejected a portrait of himself by John Hurd, Rockwell went to paint him. "Hurd, of course, had painted him as he was," Rockwell said later, "while I had done him as he would like to think he is."

[14] Well, consciously or not, he painted America as we would like to think it was. As we would like to think it is at root. His legacy is an interior landscape . . . of our very best side.

VOCABULARY

Look up the following words in your dictionary. Use the system developed in the dictionary section in the back of the text. Be sure to write the part of speech, the pronunciation, and the meaning(s) of each word.

shock¹ (shŏk) *n.* **1.** A violent collision or impact; heavy blow. **2.** Something that jars the mind or emotions as if with a violent, unexpected blow. **3.** The disturbance of function, equilibrium, or mental faculties caused by such a blow; violent agitation. **4.** A severe offense to one's sense of propriety or decency; an outrage. **5.** *Pathology.* A generally temporary state of massive physiological reaction to bodily trauma, usually characterized by marked loss of blood pressure and the depression of vital processes. **6.** The sensation and muscular spasm caused by an electric current passing through the body or through a bodily part. **7. Shock therapy** *(see).* —*v.* **shocked, shocking, shocks.** —*tr.* **1.** To strike with great surprise and agitation. **2.** To strike with disgust; offend; scandalize: *"His actions shocked the bartender, who hurriedly asked them to go."* (Nathanael West). **3.** To induce a state of shock in (a person). **4.** To subject (an animal or person) to an electric shock. —*intr. Archaic.* To come into contact violently, as in battle; collide. [Old French *choc,* from *choquer†,* to strike (with fear).]
shock² (shŏk) *n.* A number of sheaves of grain stacked upright in a field for drying: *"A few shocks of corn in a corner of a fallow mead stood up as if alive."* (D.H. Lawrence). —*tr.v.* **shocked, shocking, shocks.** To gather (grain) into shocks. [Middle English *shokke,* probably from Middle Dutch or Middle Low German *schok,* shock, group of sixty, akin to Old Saxon *scok†.*] —**shock′er** *n.*
shock³ (shŏk) *n.* A thick, heavy mass: *"The wind moving gently his great shock of voluminous white hair"* (Melville D. Post). —*adj.* Thick and shaggy. [Perhaps from SHOCK (stack).]

Definitions ©1981 Houghton Mifflin Company. Reprinted by permission from *The American Heritage Dictionary of the English Language, New College Edition.*

portrait

detractors

nostalgia

sophisticated

folksy

bleak

significant

slatterns

chronicler

hustle

boosters

engrave

patina

foibles

STUDY QUESTIONS

Finding the Matter
1. What did Norman Rockwell look like?
2. What subjects did he most enjoy painting?
3. What was Rockwell's philosophy of painting?
4. Although he praised small-town life, where was Rockwell born?
5. What early experiences caused Rockwell to wish for a simpler time and place?

Exploring the Manner
1. What stylistic qualities suggest that this article was originally written for a newspaper or magazine rather than a book?
2. What effects does Goodman achieve by repeating the words *now* and *nostalgia* in the first two paragraphs of the essay?
3. Goodman occasionally places similar words next to each other so that the reader can discover the differences in their meanings. Compare the meanings of *America* and *Americana* in these sentences: "He knew that he didn't portray America. He portrayed Americana."

4. Why does Goodman call Rockwell an "artist" but say that he insisted on being called an "illustrator"? Which word has a more favorable connotation* in the art world?

5. Would you call Goodman's essay objective* or subjective* description? Support your opinion.

SYNONYMS

From the column at the right, select the best synonym for the italicized word in each sentence. Rewrite each sentence using the appropriate synonym.

1. People feel a kind of *homesickness* for Rockwell's Americana.

2. Rockwell's folksy vision of this country was no more accurate than the *barren* world of Edward Hopper.

3. Rockwell expressed *meaningful* ideas about the world as he saw it.

4. As a *recorder* of his era, he was born at a perfect time.

5. Rockwell *carved* images of our strongest ideas, those of everyday decency.

6. The subjects of his paintings had small *faults* rather than serious problems.

A. significant

B. foibles

C. nostalgia

D. engraved

E. chronicler

F. bleak

PARAPHRASE

Read this paragraph twice, then close your book. Using your own words, rewrite the paragraph as clearly and completely as you can.

There were, of course, critics who called him the Lawrence Welk of the art world, insisting that bubbles floated off the ends of his brushes and that his work was sticky with sweetness. There were others who adored him, saying that he was the artist among con artists. But now they can both be heard calling him an artistic link to our past, a visual historian.

VERB FILL-IN

Fill in each blank with the verb form that is appropriate for each sentence.

Now he _____, the tall skinny man with a shock of
            go

white hair who always _____ like a Norman Rockwell
                look

portrait as he _____ across the small-town set of Stock-
            bicycle

bridge, Massachusetts.

Now, for a few days his fans and detractors alike suddenly

_____ a kind of nostalgia . . . for his nostalgia.
      feel

There _____, of course, critics who _____ him
        be   call

the Lawrence Welk of the art world, _____ that bubbles
                    insist

_____ off the ends of his brushes and that his work
     float

_____ sticky with sweetness. There were others who
     be

_____ him, _____ that he was the artist among
     adore   say

con artists. But now they can both be _____ calling him an
                 hear

artistic link to our past, a visual historian.

SENTENCE COMPLETION

From the column at the right, select the correct line to complete each of the numbered lines at the left. Write each sentence in its correct form.

1. There were critics who adored Rockwell,

2. He knew that what he portrayed was not America,

3. He was born at a perfect time,

4. Rockwell made it in the competitive and high-pressure

5. His subjects were either the old or the young, for Rockwell

6. His subjects lived through a comedy of manners rather than

A. but Americana.

B. a few years before the end of the nineteenth century.

C. had difficulty finding a place for midlife America in his scheme.

D. saying that he was the artist among con artists.

E. living through human tragedies.

F. business of magazine illustrators.

CLOZE EXERCISE

Fill in each blank with the best word to complete the meaning of the sentence.

He spent his work life reaching _____ to make connections. His illustrations _____ the 1920s often carried the _____ of the 1900s. His paintings _____ the 1930s have more of _____ patina of a Teddy than _____ Franklin Roosevelt. In wartime he _____ drew our peaceful nature and _____ in his self-consciously relevant work _____ the 1960s, Rockwell pushed the _____ of the past.

It was _____ a hard-working artist, a businessman,

_____ husband of three wives that _____ portrayed

the imagined ease of _____ life. His subjects had foibles

_____ than problems. They lived through _____

comedy of manners rather than _____ tragedies. So, it

wasn't a _____ he held up to society, _____ the

hungering eye of a _____ of his time. A man _____

filled his canvases with what _____ of us felt was missing.

SENTENCE COMBINING

Combine each pair of sentences into a single grammatical
sentence.

1. His critics called him the Lawrence Welk of the art world.
   His critics insisted that his work was sticky with sweetness.

2. Rockwell wasn't a man of many words.
   His few words were significant.

3. Every society carries in its soul some collective longings.
   It also carries some common spiritual values.

4. He grew up in a world of hustlers.
   He made it in the high-pressure business of magazine illustrators.

5. His subjects were the old and the young.
   He had trouble finding a place for the midlife American.

6. Hurd had painted President Johnson as he was.
   Rockwell painted him as he wanted to think he was.

PUNCTUATION

Read the following paragraph. Write in the capital letters and place commas, periods, colons, semicolons, dashes, and quotation marks where needed.

rockwell wasnt a man of many words but these few were significant maybe as i grew up and found the world wasnt the perfectly pleasant place i had thought it to be i unconsciously decided that if it wasnt an ideal world it should be and so painted only the ideal aspects of it pictures in which there were no slatterns or selfcentered mothers in which to the contrary there were only foxy grandpas who played baseball with the kids and boys fishing from logs and gotup circuses in the backyard

WORD-FORM CHART

Use your dictionary to complete the following table. Follow the example shown with item 1, *bicycle*. If there is no commonly used form for a particular part of speech, write the symbol XXX.

Noun	Verb	Adjective	Adverb
1. bicycle	bicycle	XXX	XXX
2.			visually
3.		unconscious	
4. spiritualism			
5.		powerful	
6. canvas			

WORD-FORM EXERCISE

Using your completed Word-Form Chart, select the correct
form to fit into each sentence. Use the appropriate tense of
the verb, the singular or plural form of the noun, and the
passive voice where necessary.
Follow the sequence of numbers from the Word-Form Chart
to select the correct form.

1. Rockwell looked like a portrait of himself as he _____

   across Stockbridge.

2. Rockwell was considered to be a _____ historian.

3. Rockwell _____ decided that if the world was not ideal,

   he would paint only the ideal aspects of it.

4. Every society carries in its soul some common _____

   values.

5. He shared with others a _____ yearning for a life which

   he defined as American.

6. Rockwell was a man who filled his _____ with what

   many of us felt was missing.

QUESTIONS FOR DISCUSSION

1. Lawrence Welk is an orchestra leader who is known for playing
   old-fashioned music for the older generation. In what way can he
   be compared to Norman Rockwell?

2. Walker Evans, an American photographer, took journalistic pictures that often showed the sadness of unemployed men on bread
   lines during the Great Depression of the 1930s. Why does Goodman say that his pictures, like Rockwell's, were not "a total
   reflection of our society"?

3. Goodman suggests that America's strongest ideas are not *equality*
   or *justice* but *decency*. Look up these words and then decide
   whether you agree or disagree with her statement.

TOPICS FOR WRITING

1. Goodman's description of Rockwell's contribution to American life is a eulogy, or a written remembrance in praise of someone who has died. Write a eulogy describing and praising someone who has had a lasting effect on your life.

2. Write a composition in which you describe the personality of a close friend or relative. First describe the person as he or she really is, flaws and all. Then describe this person in ideal terms, as you would like him or her to be.

3. Write a composition in which you describe the personality and lasting accomplishments of a famous poet, artist, writer, military or political leader of your native country.

THE RAINBOW CITY

Pete Hamill

[1] New York is the rainbow city. All the colors and the races of the world are here, all languages, religions, and dreams. Our triumph is plural, and throughout our history, the New York rainbow has drawn the adventurous and the brilliant, the mad, the brave, and the ambitious. For many, of course, there was no pot of gold at the foot of the rainbow; New York is above all a human, imperfect city. But for most the rainbow was enough. Welcome to the rainbow.

[2] I was born and raised here, but if you ask me to explain New York and show you its sights, I'll sometimes mumble about ghosts. More than any large American city, New York is a place where the past keeps shoving its way into the present. I see the great bridge across the Narrows on a summer morning from the Belt Parkway, and I also see Giovanni da Verrazano on that morning in 1524, nosing his tiny caravel into the wide, inviting harbor, to be welcomed with flowers by the original native New Yorkers.

(Courtesy of the Port Authority of N.Y. and N.J.)

[3] I look at the skyline at dusk, rising from the harbor, in Truman Capote's phrase, "like a diamond iceberg." But I also see the Dutch erecting their wooden forts while slaves ripped from Africa worked their way into the rainbow from a camp at 75th Street and the East River. At the Battery, I see the English lowering the Dutch flag at musket-point in 1664, changing the names of the Dutch towns ('t Vlackbos, for example, became Flatbush), building a flourishing slave market on Wall Street, and then giving us, in spite of their almost congenital hypocrisy, double-dealing, and cruelty, a common language and common law.

[4] I walk lower Broadway, above the bones of the old town, and in my mind's eye I see, coming out of Maiden Lane, Aaron Burr, teeming with irony and schemes, devising ways to rescue the revolutionary triumph from Hamilton's aristocrats, and inventing Tammany Hall. Burr is there, among the West Indian messenger boys, the Puerto Rican girls going to work in the banks, and the commuters in from the suburbs; so are Diamond Jim Brady and Boss Tweed, Commodore Vanderbilt and Jay Gould, all those grasping brigands of the nineteenth century, and so are the 1969 Mets, champions of the world, drowning in ticker tape and torn-up phone books on the last day in New York when everyone I knew was happy.

[5] But much of the time, I think about the immigrants, those millions of Irish, Jewish, Italian, German, and Polish men and women who came here in flight from czars, kings, poverty, and injustice. They survived the hazards of the Atlantic crossing and then were jammed into an old quarantine station on Staten Island or the round stone fort called Castle Garden, and, after 1892, into Ellis Island. They were humiliated in those holding pens, or robbed, or scorned; their names were sometimes arbitrarily changed; they stammered in their own languages before the steady, arrogant force of English and shivered in the winter cold or broiled in the stinking summer heat; and when they were finished, when the papers were signed and stamped, when the degrading and patronizing processes of entry were over, they picked up their sad, cheap suitcases tied with rough cord, and walked out the door and built America.

[6] This is their city: impatient, traditional, tough, generous, and plural. It's a port city, an archipelago with only the Bronx of our five boroughs attached to the mainland. And since World War II, it has been the port of entry for still another great migration, this time from the American South and the Caribbean, from South America, and, increasingly, from Asia. The new arrivals have strained our resources to the breaking point, because many jobs available to the earlier immigrants have vanished, or gone to the Sun Belt and other places.

[7] But in the face of anger, tumult, harsh words, and bitterness

from older New Yorkers, the new immigrants have become a permanent part of the city. None of them have starved. None of their children have been denied schooling. And in return they've given us music, art, food, a denser, darker texture, a wider sense of the world. This is their city too. You can't see this multilayered New York from an airplane or a hotel room, because the city is too specific and too local. Here are a few places that will give you the sense of our pluralism: our past, our present, our future. Go out and walk around. You might even trip over a pot of gold.

VOCABULARY

Look up the following words in your dictionary. Use the system developed in the dictionary section in the back of the text. Be sure to write the part of speech, the pronunciation, and the meaning(s) of each word.

rain·bow (rān′bō′) *n.* **1. a.** An arc of spectral colors appearing in the sky opposite the sun as a result of the refractive dispersion of sunlight in drops of rain or mist. **b.** Any similar arc, as in a waterfall mist or graded display of colors. **2.** An illusory hope: *the rainbow of making a quick fortune.* [Middle English *reinbowe*, Old English *rēnboga*. See **reg-²** in Appendix.*]

Definition ©1981 Houghton Mifflin Company. Reprinted by permission from *The American Heritage Dictionary of the English Language, New College Edition.*

triumph

mumble

caravel

congenital

hypocrisy

teeming

irony

schemes

brigands

hazards

humiliated

scorned

arbitrarily

arrogant

degrading

patronizing

impatient

archipelago

tumult

STUDY QUESTIONS

Finding the Matter

1. Who were the "original native New Yorkers who greeted Giovanni da Verrazano in 1524"?

2. Who ruled New York after the Dutch?

3. Which one of the five boroughs is attached to the mainland of the United States?

4. Where were immigrants received in New York after 1892?

Exploring the Manner

1. Why is the rainbow a suitable image* to describe New York City?

2. What descriptive examples does Hamill use to blend the past and the present of the city?

3. Explain Hamill's use of the terms *impatient, traditional, tough, generous,* and *plural,* as they apply to New York City.

4. Since Hamill is not writing a geographic description of New York City, he does not use spatial organization. What descriptive method does he use?

SYNONYMS

From the column at the right, select the best synonym for the italicized word in each sentence. Rewrite each sentence using the appropriate synonym.

1. With all the races and colors in New York, our *victory* is plural, a mixture of languages, religions, and dreams.

2. Giovanni da Verrazano directed his tiny *ship* into the wide, inviting harbor of New York.

3. Diamond Jim Brady and Boss Tweed were typical of the grasping *bandits* of the nineteenth century.

4. The immigrants survived the *risks* of frightening Atlantic crossings.

5. On Ellis Island the immigrants were robbed and *despised.*

6. They were helped very little by the *proud* English-speaking officers on the island.

7. The whole process on Ellis Island was *debasing* for the immigrants.

8. The officers on the island used *condescending* and humiliating practices.

9. New York is a restless city, a busy city, a port city that *teems* with immigrants.

10. In spite of all the *turbulence*, new immigrants have become a permanent part of the city.

A. brigands

B. tumult

C. degrading

D. hazards

E. patronizing

F. triumph

G. scorned

H. caravel

I. abounds

J. arrogant

PARAPHRASE

Read this paragraph twice, then close your book. Using your own words, rewrite the paragraph as clearly and completely as you can.

This is the city of immigrants: impatient, traditional, tough, generous, and plural. It's a port city, an archipelago with only the Bronx of our five boroughs attached to the mainland. And since World War II, it has been the port of entry for still another great migration, this time from the American South and the Caribbean, from South America and, increasingly, from Asia. The new arrivals have strained our resources to the breaking point, because many jobs available to the earlier immigrants have vanished, or gone to the Sun Belt and other places.

VERB FILL-IN

Fill in each blank with the verb form that is appropriate for each sentence.

New York _____ the Rainbow City. All the colors and
                              be

the races of the world _____ here. Our triumph
                                    be

_____ plural, and throughout our history, the New York
         be

rainbow _____ the adventurous, the brilliant, and the ambi-
                     draw

tious. For many there _____ no pot of gold at the foot of
                                 be

the rainbow. But for most the rainbow _____ enough. The
                                                    be

immigrants _____ New York. They _____ their
                      love   appreciate

new freedoms and they ———————— quickly to a new way of life.
                        adjust

New York ———————— part of a new dream.
            become

SENTENCE COMPLETION

From the column at the right, select the correct line to complete each of the numbered lines at the left. Write each sentence in its correct form.

1. More than any large American city,

2. I look at the skyline at dusk, rising from the harbor

3. On lower Broadway, one can dream of Aaron Burr devising ways

4. Much of the time, I think about the millions of Irish, Jewish, Italian, German, and Polish men and women

5. They survived the hazards of the Atlantic crossing

6. They were humiliated in those holding pens and their names

7. New York is a port city, an archipelago with only the Bronx of our five boroughs

8. The new arrivals have strained our resources to the breaking point

9. No immigrants have starved and none of their children

10. If you walk around New York, the city of opportunity,

A. you just might trip over a pot of gold.

B. have been denied schooling.

C. attached to the mainland.

D. and then were jammed into an old quarantine station on Staten Island.

E. New York is a place where the past keeps shoving its way into the present.

F. were changed to something other than what they stammered in their own language.

G. who came here in flight from Czars, kings, poverty, and injustice.

H. because many jobs available to earlier immigrants have vanished.

I. like a diamond iceberg.

J. to rescue the revolutionary triumph from Hamilton's aristocrats.

CLOZE EXERCISE

Fill in each blank with the best word to complete the meaning of the sentence.

I was born and _____ here, but if you _____

me to explain New _____ and show you its _____,

I'll sometimes mumble about _____. More than any large

_____ city, New York is _____ place where the past

_____ shoving its way into _____ present. I see

the _____ bridge across the Narrows _____ a

summer morning from _____ Belt Parkway, and I

_____ see Giovanni da Verrazano _____ that

morning in 1524, _____ his tiny caravel into _____

wide, inviting harbor, to _____ welcomed with flowers by

_____ original native New Yorkers.

SENTENCE COMBINING

Combine each pair of sentences into a single grammatical sentence.

1. New York is above all a human, imperfect city.
   New York contains people of many colors and races.

2. In a dream I can see Aaron Burr.
   Aaron Burr was teeming with schemes to rescue the revolutionary triumph from Hamilton's aristocrats.

3. I think about the immigrants.
   The immigrants were Irish, Jewish, Italian, German, and Polish.

4. The immigrants stammered their names in their own languages.
   The immigrants ended up with new, strange-sounding American names.

5. New York is a port city.
   New York has five boroughs.

6. None of the immigrants has starved.
   None of their children has been denied schooling.

PUNCTUATION

Read the following paragraph. Write in the capital letters and place commas, periods, colons, semicolons, dashes, and quotations marks where needed.

i look at the skyline at dusk rising from the harbor in truman capotes phrase like a diamond iceberg but i also see the dutch erecting their wooden forts while slaves ripped from africa worked their way into the rainbow from a camp at seventy fifth street and the east river at the battery i see the english lowering the dutch flag at musket point in 1664 changing the names of the dutch town building a flourishing slave market on wall street and then giving us in spite of their almost congenital hypocrisy double dealing and cruelty a common language and common law

WORD-FORM CHART

Use your dictionary to complete the following table. Follow the example shown with item 1, *mumbler*. If there is no commonly used form for a particular part of speech, write the symbol XXX.

Noun	Verb	Adjective	Adverb
1. mumbler	mumble	mumbling	mumblingly
2.			ironically
3. survivor			
4.		arbitrary	
5.	degrade		
6.		traditional	
7. migration			
8.	vanish		
9.			tumultuously
10.		plural	

WORD-FORM EXERCISE

Using your completed Word-Form Chart, select the correct form to fit into each sentence. Use the appropriate tense of the verb, the singular or plural form of the noun, and the passive voice where necessary.
Follow the sequence of numbers from the Word-Form Chart to select the correct form.

1. Hamill states that he was born and raised in New York and

   that if someone asks him to explain New York, he finds him-

   self ＿＿＿＿＿＿＿＿ about ghosts.

2. He sees Aaron Burr teeming with ＿＿＿＿＿＿＿＿ and schemes.

3. The immigrants _____ the hazards of crossing the

Atlantic Ocean.

4. Their names were _____ changed.

5. The _____ processes of Ellis Island left a firm imprint

on the immigrants.

6. New York is a city full of ethnic _____.

7. New York is still the port of entry for great _____,

such as those people now coming from South America and the

Caribbean.

8. Many jobs that were formerly available in New York now

_____.

9. In spite of the face of anger, _____ and bitterness, new

immigrants have become a permanent part of the city.

10. There are many places that will give a person a sense of the

_____ aspects of New York.

QUESTIONS FOR DISCUSSION

1. What was the reason for the famous duel between Aaron Burr and
   Alexander Hamilton?

2. Why does Hamill use the term *brigands* to describe Diamond Jim
   Brady, Boss Tweed, Commodore Vanderbilt, and Jay Gould?

3. How are immigrants usually treated today when they first arrive
   in America?

TOPICS FOR WRITING

1. Write a theme describing the main features of your home town or city. Like Hamill, use history, specific places, and people to illustrate your point.

2. Describe three sights in your native country as if you were showing them to foreign visitors.

3. Describe your first impression of America.

4. Write a theme using a central image* to describe the main features of one of the following:
    a. The street on which you are living.
    b. The neighborhood in which you are working.
    c. The particular part of the city or town in which you live.

WHERE JAMES BOND SHOPS

Susie Gharib Nazem

> ## THE PASSENGERS IN THIS CAR CANNOT BE HURT.
> ## NOT BY BULLETS, BOMBS OR TERRORIST ATTACK.
>
> **The VIP Security Sedan.**
>
> *Fully bulletproof construction—clear, curved windows that*
> *up to a 30 caliber carbine.*
>
> *Fully bomb proof—protects against bombs, hand*
> *grenades.*
>
> *Remote ignition and electric*
> *¼ mile away for safety*
>
> *Kidnap recovery sy*
> *or stolen auto*
>
> *Oil slick emis*

[1] This is no joke. Advertisements like the one above have been appearing in a half dozen newspapers including the *New York Times*, the *Wall Street Journal*, and *Le Monde*. What's for sale is a $245,000 1979 Cadillac that the Shah of Iran ordered two years ago. After the Iranian ruler lost the Peacock Throne, he turned down delivery, forfeiting his $50,000 deposit on the car. For one thing, the silver gray Caddy was too wide for the dirt roads in Mexico, where the Shah made his first home in exile.

[2] The price tag now: $155,000. Still sound a bit steep for a set of wheels? Consider the extras. As the ad goes on to say, the car is bulletproof and can withstand the impact of a hand grenade on the roof or a land mine under the body. It comes equipped with everything from machine-gun mounts to a hand-held bomb sniffer to ducts that spray tear gas to distances of 50 feet. A gadget under the rear bumper can spill as much as 30 gallons of diesel fuel on the road to give pursuers the slip. (Diesel fuel is slicker than oil.)

[3] Any unwelcome passenger is in extreme peril. Under the seat next to the driver are three shotgun shells, pointed upward. If someone in that seat were to threaten or otherwise displease the driver, a flick of a switch will literally blow his tail off. (The builders of the car considered installing a device that would instantaneously squash the seat and its occupant against the roof of the car. They decided that would be too messy.) When all else fails, the trunk of the car hides an escape vehicle—a bright red minibike powered with a motorcycle engine. The bike can cruise at speeds up to 65 miles per hour.

[4] The Shah didn't ignore fuel economy. He ordered his electronic palace, which is 1,000 pounds heavier than an ordinary 1979 Cadillac, without any gas-eating emission-control devices. It gets an open-road average of 17 miles per gallon, compared with an unmodified Cadillac's 14. (Presumably an American buyer would have to reinstall the antipollution equipment, cutting gas mileage to 12.) Carmine O. Pellosie, a vice president of CCS Communication Control Inc., the privately held New York company that produced the car, says: "It's ideal for the man who has everything—and wants to keep it."

[5] The Shah's car is one of 400 automobiles for the security-minded that CCS has turned out since it was founded five years ago by Ben Jamil, now 47. Suave, swarthy, and Brooklyn-born, Jamil is fluent in English, French, Arabic, and Russian. (His father is Yemeni and his mother is French. He picked up Russian at Brooklyn College.) Jamil looks and acts very much like a moviegoer's notion of a secret agent—and is a mighty tenacious businessman besides. He got his start in 1955 by rewiring antique French telephones. Soon his com-

pany, Telephones Unlimited, was selling them to stores like Saks Fifth Avenue and Neiman-Marcus, ringing up annual sales of $7 million. That's when AT&T sued. In 1969, after a long court battle, Jamil won.

[6] He then sold the company and turned his attention from designing telephones to protecting them from eavesdroppers. "It's so simple to tap a telephone," he says. "With a piece of wire that costs 60 cents anyone can play James Bond." (In a process called "backstrapping," you hook the wire at a central switching point to the telephone line you want to tap and connect it with a line of your own.) At first CCS turned out just ten products—mostly debugging devices—and the company's first-year sales were $2 million. The Europeans—especially Italians, notes Jamil—were the first to snap up CCS's debugging products: "They were pragmatic about the facts of life." After Watergate, he adds, "there was a very sober attitude about bugging" in the U.S. too, and sales here began to grow.

practical in a positive way

[7] Today, CCS still sells a dozen kinds of "Bug Alerts," which Jamil says are becoming as popular as pocket calculators with customers who can afford them. Priced from $500 to $12,000, and no bigger than a match head, the devices fit into a wristwatch, a pack of cigarettes, or even the binding of a spiral notebook. Walk within ten feet of a bug and a red diode lights up. The company also makes and sells many other protective devices. Plants in New York, London, and Toronto—a fourth is under construction in Kuwait—manufacture more than 75 products that would leave James Bond breathless. So might Jamil's profit margins. In 1979, he says, pretax earnings reached $12 million on revenues of $18 million. A third of those sales come from overseas.

[8] CCS is one of the largest and best-known companies in the fast-growing $600-million-a-year surveillance and monitoring industry, and it is the job of 38-year-old Carmine Pellosie to keep it that way. A former investigator for a law firm and director of security for a small New Jersey bank, Pellosie is as ebullient as Jamil is controlled. Jamil hired him two years ago to supply marketing razzle-dazzle. He is now the only person other than Jamil to own stock in CCS.

enthusiastic

[9] The company's client list is sprinkled with big names: Du Pont, Gulf, Fiat, General Foods, Mobil, Renault, Philip Morris, Texaco. In May CCS sold over $2 million of anti-bugging equipment to movie-company executives attending the Cannes Film Festival (suspicious folks, those moviemakers). In June, an oil company that is drilling in Prudhoe Bay ordered a slew of anti-wiretapping devices to protect its telephone conversations from snoopy competitors.

many / large amount

[10] Nearly 500 police departments in the U.S., as well as kings, college professors, and rock stars, turn to CCS for everything from bulletproof vests to Dick Tracy-esque wristwatch microphones. But Pellosie is mum about specifics: "If I sold cigarette lighters, sure, I'd say King Hussein carries one. But not in this business."

[11] Prudence, rather than paranoia, motivates most of CCS's customers. The world is a dangerous place for the powerful and prosperous these days. Acts of terrorism around the world—including assassinations, kidnappings, bombings, and personal assaults—are running at the rate of 250 a month. Of the 100 Americans kidnapped since 1970, more than half were businessmen. In that period kidnappers collected about $180 million in ransom.

[12] A recent victim of an unprovoked attack was Percy Wood, the 60-year-old president of United Airlines. In mid-June he was seriously injured by the explosion of a letter-bomb delivered to his home. Since the UAL incident, claims Pellosie, requests for CCS's security devices—especially letter-bomb detectors at about $2,000 each—have doubled. Says he: "Protection is not an expense, but a cost-saving item. It costs a lot of money to lose a good man."

[13] The CCS catalogue reads as though it had been written by Ian Fleming. Take the 007 Bionic Briefcase—or try to. It is bulletproof and stealing it is virtually impossible. When the alarm circuits are set, moving the case activates a siren that blares for four hours. A person carrying the case inserts fingers into two rings; if anyone tries to snatch the case away, pulling out the rings, the alarm goes off. (Tip: reinserting both rings stops the noise. It isn't easy.) In the briefcase are compartments for a bomb sniffer, a high-powered lamp so bright that it can blind an attacker for up to 14 hours, and an electronic location signaler. With all that, there's still room in the briefcase for business papers. The price, fully equipped: $15,000.

[14] CCS's best seller is a machine with the wordy name Voice Stress Analyzer System Mark IX-P. It's a lie detector. But unlike a conventional polygraph, it measures stress levels in a person's voice rather than changes in pulse rate. Since it does not have to be physically attached to the subject, a speaker's veracity can be checked without his knowing it. ("Now you can ask a waiter if the clam chowder is really fresh," says Pellosie.) The machine costs $8,000 and is finding buyers among lawyers and businessmen—and even jealous spouses.

[15] A hot item on the concert circuit, because of the pirating of live recordings, is the TRD 009, a tiny contraption that electronically detects working tape recorders. In concert halls, a long wand attached to the device is swept over the heads of the audience to check for recorders. In the next six months Pellosie expects to market a tape-recorder nullifier that will make the 009 obsolete. The new invention will generate a low-frequency tone inaudible to the human ear but capable of obliterating anything recorded on tape.

[16] Pellosie is full of exuberant ideas for other new inventions. The company's six engineers are working on an atomic-powered tracking device with a 15-year battery life that can be surgically implanted in a person's body. "If [Italian Prime Minister] Aldo Moro had had one of these," says Pellosie, "we could have found

him." CCS has already received orders for the yet-to-be-invented device.

[17] Right now, says Pellosie, CCS is having trouble just keeping pace with demand for products it already has. While most companies like to boast about their growth in backlog as a measure of their success, CCS tries to avoid having one. Declares Pellosie: "If you need security, you need it now. You can't wait a week."

[18] It is CCS policy to sell nothing to citizens of countries rated unfriendly to the U.S. These days, Iranians, Russians, Czechs, and Poles get the cold shoulder. The Mafia, of course, is also blacklisted, but Pellosie says it would be hard for CCS to know if it had sold to a mobster on some occasion. "If we did," he says, "it was probably through a Wall Street lawyer in a three-piece suit." The only known investigation of the company by a federal law-enforcement agency — subject unspecified — was dropped without any action being taken.

[19] Once the company accepts a customer, there's no problem about paying. Whatever the amount, just whip out your credit card — American Express, Diners Club, or MasterCard. And why not? If that Voice Stress Analyzer Mark IX-P is all it's said to be, it should be the best credit check in the business.

VOCABULARY

Look up the following words in your dictionary. Use the system developed in the dictionary section in the back of the text. Be sure to write the part of speech, the pronunciation and the meaning(s) of each word.

for·feit (fôr'fĭt) *n.* **1.** Something surrendered as punishment for a crime, offense, error, or breach of contract; a penalty or fine. **2.** Something placed in escrow and then redeemed after payment of a fine. **3.** A forfeiture. **4.** *Plural.* A game in which forfeits are required. —*adj.* Surrendered or alienated for a crime, offense, error, or breach of contract. —*tr.v.* **forfeited, -feiting, -feits. 1.** To surrender or be forced to surrender as a forfeit. **2.** To subject to forfeiture. [Middle English *forfet,* forfeit, transgression, from Old French *forfet,* from *for(s)faire,* to commit a crime : *fors-,* beyond (here, beyond what is permitted), from Latin *foris,* outside (see **dhwer-** in Appendix*) + *faire,* to do, act, from Latin *facere* (see **dhē-¹** in Appendix*).] —**for'feit·a·ble** *adj.* —**for'feit·er** *n.*

Definition ©1981 Houghton Mifflin Company. Reprinted by permission from *The American Heritage Dictionary of the English Language, New College Edition.*

steep

gadget

flick

squash

cruise

tenacious — *stubborn - holding strong - persistant*

eavesdroppers

pragmatic *practical in a positive way*

sober

surveillance

monitoring

ebullient *enthusiastic*

razzle-dazzle

suspicious

slew — *many - large amount*

prudence *Caution*

paranoia *fearful*

ransom

activates

veracity *truthfulness*

nullifier *nutural/ze*

obliterating *wipe out*

exuberant *exciting*

STUDY QUESTIONS

Finding the Matter

1. Name four of the unusual features installed in the $245,000 1979 Cadillac produced by CCS Communication Control, Inc.

2. How did the founder of CCS, Ben Jamil, begin his career? How did his first company lead him to his second?

3. What is a Bug Alert, and how is it commonly concealed?

4. Name the special equipment that is included in the 007 Bionic Briefcase.

5. How does the Voice Stress Analyzer System differ from the conventional lie detector?

Exploring the Manner

1. Is the thesis* of the article specifically stated or suggested? Find or formulate the thesis sentence.

2. Would the VIP Security Sedan have attracted your attention if Nazem had described it merely as a "Fortress on wheels, impregnable to attack"? Why not? Which of the details about the car is the most interesting to you?

3. Nazem is careful to connect a new paragraph to the previous one by using transitions*. For example, after discussing Jamil's first business, rewiring antique French telephones, she begins a new paragraph as follows: "He then sold the company and turned his attention from designing telephones to protecting them from eavesdroppers." Find other examples* of good transitions connecting paragraphs.

SYNONYMS

From the column at the right, select the best synonym for the italicized word in each sentence. Rewrite each sentence using the appropriate synonym.

1. The Shah turned down delivery of his special Cadillac, thereby *losing* his $50,000 deposit.

2. Do you think that $155,000 is *high-priced* for a bullet-proof car?

3. A *device* under the rear bumper can spill as much as 30 gallons of diesel fuel on the road.

4. The builders thought of installing a special device in the seat that would *crush* its occupant against the roof of the car.

A. gadget

B. tenacious

C. ebullient

D. steep

E. forfeiting

F. sober

G. prudence

H. squash

I. activates

J. veracity

5. Jamil is a mighty *persistent* businessman who acts very much like a moviegoer's notion of a secret agent.

6. After Watergate, Jamil's sales increased, because people in the United States took a very *serious* attitude toward bugging.

7. Pellosie is very *enthusiastic* about this fantastic business.

8. By ordering these devices, people exhibit *caution* rather than paranoia.

9. In this special briefcase, alarm circuits are set, and moving the case *starts* a siren that blares for four hours.

10. The *truth* in the person's voice can be checked by a voice stress analyzer.

PARAPHRASE

Read these paragraphs twice, then close your book. Using your own words, rewrite the paragraphs as clearly and completely as you can.

Prudence, rather than paranoia, motivates most of CCS's customers. The world is a dangerous place for the powerful and prosperous these days. Acts of terrorism around the world—including assassinations, kidnappings, bombings, and personal assaults—are running at the rate of 250 a month. Of the 100 Americans kidnapped since 1970, more than half were businessmen. In that period kidnappers collected about $180 million in ransom.

A recent victim of an unprovoked attack was Percy Wood, the 60-year-old president of United Airlines. In mid-June he was seriously injured by the explosion of a letter-bomb delivered to his home. Since the UAL incident, claims Pellosie, requests for CCS's security devices—especially letter-bomb

detectors at about $2,000 each—have doubled. Says he:
"Protection is not an expense, but a cost-saving item. It
costs a lot of money to lose a good man."

VERB FILL-IN

Fill in each blank with the verb form that is appropriate for
each sentence.

1. Advertisements for these new gadgets _____ in a half
                                              appear

   dozen famous newspapers for the last few years.

2. The builders of the car considered _____ a device under
                                            install

   the seat that would immediately squash its occupant.

3. The trunk of the car _____ an escape vehicle.
                             hide

4. Jamil _____ Pellosie two years ago to supply marketing
              hire

   razzle-dazzle.

5. The company's client list _____ with big names like
                                  sprinkle

   DuPont, Gulf, and General Foods.

6. An oil company that _____ in Prudhoe Bay ordered a
                            drill

   slew of anti-wire-tapping devices.

7. Acts of terrorism around the world _____ at a rate of
                                            run

   250 a month.

8. The president of United Air Lines ⎯⎯⎯⎯⎯⎯⎯⎯ very seriously

   injure

   by the explosion of a letter-bomb.

9. A new invention, a tape-recorder nullifer, ⎯⎯⎯⎯⎯⎯⎯⎯ a

   generate

   low-frequency tone inaudible to the human ear.

10. The only known investigation of CCS by a federal law-

    enforcement agency ⎯⎯⎯⎯⎯⎯⎯⎯ without any action being

    drop

    taken.

SENTENCE COMPLETION

From the column at the right, select the correct line to complete each of the numbered lines at the left. Write each sentence in its correct form.

1. In this special car any unwelcome passenger is

2. The escape vehicle can cruise at speeds

3. Jamil got his start in 1955 by rewiring

4. With a piece of wire that costs 60 cents,

5. Bug Alerts are now becoming as popular as

6. CCS is a fast-growing surveillance

7. These days the world is a dangerous place

A. antique French telephones.

B. that can blind an attacker for 14 hours.

C. in extreme peril.

D. and monitoring company.

E. there's no problem about paying for these devices.

F. pocket calculators with customers who can afford them.

G. that can be surgically implanted in a person's body.

H. for the powerful and prosperous.

8. In the briefcase is a high-powered lamp

9. The Voice Stress Analyzer is finding buyers among

10. The company's engineers are working on an atomic-powered tracking device

11. It is the policy of CCS to sell nothing to citizens of countries

12. If a customer has a credit card,

I. up to 65 miles per hour.

J. rated unfriendly to the United States.

K. lawyers, businessmen, and even jealous spouses.

L. anyone can play James Bond.

CLOZE EXERCISE

Fill in each blank with the best word to complete the meaning of the sentence.

Any unwelcome passenger is in _____ peril. Under the seat next _____ the driver are three shotgun _____, pointed upward. If someone in _____ seat were to threaten or _____ displease the driver, a flick _____ a switch will literally blow _____ tail off. (The builders of _____ car considered installing a device _____ would instantaneously squash the seat _____ its occupant against the roof _____ the car. They decided that _____ be too messy.) When all _____ fails, the trunk of the _____ hides an escape vehicle—a _____ red minibike powered with a _____ engine. The bike can cruise _____ speeds up to 65 miles _____ hour.

SENTENCE COMBINING

Combine each pair of sentences into a single grammatical
sentence.

1. The car can withstand the impact of a hand grenade on the roof.
   The car can withstand a land mine under the body.

2. The trunk of the car hides an escape vehicle.
   The escape vehicle is a bright red minibike powered with a motorcycle engine.

3. The special Cadillac is ideal for the man who has everything.
   It is ideal for the man who wants to keep everything.

4. Jamil turned his attention from designing telephones.
   He turned his attention to protecting telephones from eavesdroppers.

5. The company has plants in New York, London, and Toronto.
   The company manufactures products that would leave James
   Bond breathless.

6. Nearly 500 police departments use everything from bulletproof
   vests to Dick Tracy-esque microphones.
   Kings, college professors, and rock stars use everything from
   bulletproof vests to Dick Tracy-esque microphones.

PUNCTUATION

Read the following paragraph. Write in the capital letters
and place commas, periods, colons, semicolons, dashes, and
quotation marks where needed.

the shah didnt ignore fuel economy he ordered his electronic

palace which is 1000 pounds heavier than an ordinary 1979 cadillac

without any gas eating emission control devices it gets an open road

average of 17 miles per gallon compared with an unmodified cadillacs

14 presumably an american buyer would have to reinstall the anti-

pollution equipment cutting gas mileage to 12 carmine o pellosie a

vice president of ccs communication control inc the privately held new york company that produced the car says its ideal for the man

who has everything and wants to keep it

WORD-FORM CHART

Use your dictionary to complete the following table. Follow the example shown with item 1, *delivery*. If there is no commonly used form for a particular part of speech, write the symbol XXX.

Noun	Verb	Adjective	Adverb
1. delivery	deliver	XXX	XXX
2.			electronically
3. ebullience			
4.		simple	
5.	secure		
6. revenue			
7.	terrorize		
8. pirate piracy			
9.	obliterate		
10.		payable	

WORD-FORM EXERCISE

Using your completed Word-Form Chart, select the correct
form to fit into each sentence. Use the appropriate tense of
the verb, the singular or plural form of the noun, and the
passive voice where necessary.
Follow the sequence of numbers from the Word-Form Chart
to select the correct form.

1. After the Iranian ruler lost the throne, he turned down

    _____ of his special car.

2. The Shah had ordered his _____ palace without any

    emission-control devices.

3. Jamil hired Pellosie, a very _____ man.

4. Telephones are easy to work with; they can be tapped

    _____.

5. Pellosie was an investigator for a law firm and a _____

    director for a small bank.

6. Jamil's company reached _____ of $18 million.

7. Acts of _____ around the world are becoming common.

8. Because some people _____ live recordings, it is now

    necessary to detect working tape recorders.

9. The new invention will be able to _____ anything

    recorded on tape.

10. Once CCS accepts a customer, there's no problem about

    _____.

QUESTIONS FOR DISCUSSION

1. What was the Watergate incident, referred to by Nazem, and how did it change American attitudes about "bugging"?

2. What trade secrets might CCS try to protect for clients such as DuPont, Mobil Oil, and General Foods?

3. Why might kings, rock stars, and college professors be customers of CCS? Who else might contact the company and for what purposes?

4. How would you feel about submitting to a Voice Stress Analyzer to determine your truthfulness in a legal case?

TOPICS FOR WRITING

1. Pretend that you are the advertising director for an organization similar to CCS. Write a business letter to a prospective client describing three of your most effective security devices.

2. Choose one of the items mentioned in Nazem's article and write an essay describing how, when, and where you would use it.

3. In 1949, the English writer George Orwell wrote a novel entitled *1984*, in which he envisioned a society where "Big Brother" (the government) would always be watching. Since we have almost arrived at this date, write an essay describing the ways in which people in your native country or America have lost their privacy because of government or other intrusions.

4. Write a theme describing an imaginary day in a futuristic society where your every move is monitored.

CULTURAL INFLUENCES ON FILIPINO PATIENTS

Rosario T. DeGracia

[1] Who in any major city of the United States has not met at least one person with a Chinese-Malayan face, Spanish surname, and American nickname? This person, a Filipino, could easily be mistaken for a Japanese, Chinese, Korean, or Vietnamese national. In the decade ending in 1974, a total of 120,269 Filipinos migrated to the United States, the annual numbers rising from 3,130 in 1965 to 32,857 in 1974; while the annual numbers of temporary workers, trainees, and exchange visitors increased from 2,691 to 32,203.[1]

[2] Before World War II, only a handful of Filipinos came to the United States, mostly laborers brought over for the big plantations in Hawaii and the farms of California and the Pacific Northwest. Recently, more professionals have migrated to America, usually bringing with them their immediate families.[1] Modern U.S. technology, seen as a means of improving professional competence and enhancing socioeconomic status, is one of the reasons for this migration.

[3] Essentially, the Filipino is an Asian with a strong Malayan base,

derived from the highly complex culture of the Indonesian Madjapa-hit Empire.

[4] In the sixteenth century, the West started influencing the Philippines. The 300 years or so of Spanish hegemony began when Ferdinand Magellan first claimed the Philippine Islands for Spain in 1521. Then, as an outcome of the Spanish-American War, the Philippines was ceded to America for $20 million, a sale consummated without the knowledge or consent of the Filipino people.

[5] Another country that has exerted tremendous influence on Filipino thought and behavior is China, which traded with the Filipinos from the Tang dynasty in the seventh century. Thus, Rustia defines a Filipino as "an Asian, basically Malay, with a generous admixture of the Chinese and the Spanish, and with a cultural overlay of the American for good measure."[2]

Filipino Culture

[6] Although the Filipino culture has arisen from such a mixed heritage, there are some basic traits that most Filipinos will manifest. Individualization is necessary, for of course, no one person will demonstrate all the elements of his culture.

[7] The Philippines consists of roughly 7,000 islands, big and small. Filipinos display characteristics that differ, depending on the region they hail from. Due to the Chinese influence on family solidarity, people from the same region tend to socialize only among themselves. This clannishness is evident among the many organizations in Filipino communities, which to some observers might appear to be rivalry. Thus, lack of spontaneous cooperation is not surprising, but it is both a weakness and a strength.

[8] If at all possible, the nurse should identify her Filipino patients' regional idosyncrasies. She can probably obtain help in this from a Filipino worker in the hospital.

[9] The younger generation's values in some ways clash with the traditional. In the Philippines today, youths resemble their western counterparts, particularly in matters of dress, music, and social values. In the U..S., one sees this orientation, whether they were brought up by parents who had migrated or they are third-generation American children. Despite this, one may still observe in them such traditional values as respect for elders, love of family, and preservation of self-esteem.

[10] The strong feeling for family, a quality derived from the Chinese influence, is manifested by old-fashioned patterns imposed by the family patriarch or the equally authoritative matriarch. Respect and deference are always given to one's elders, whose words and decisions one dares not question. The young receive solicitous protection from their elders. In the absence of both parents, the eldest child has the say and must be obeyed.

[11] The implications for health care are important. Filipino patients always have their families hovering over them, perhaps to the irritation of the nursing staff. The sick Filipino child feels lost without his mother constantly at his bedside. When grandparents are ill, sons, daughters, and even grandchildren take turns keeping them company and supporting their husbands or wives.

[12] A daughter newly delivered follows traditional customs related to activity, food, and hygiene, which may be contrary to what the doctor or nurse prescribes.

[13] Single adults with no relatives in the vicinity have swarms of visitors. These are concerned friends, who recognize the loneliness that illness can bring. Nurses would do well to capitalize on this custom for whatever assistance it provides the patient. Certainly, family-centered nursing is indicated.

[14] Filipinos are deeply religious and God-fearing. They have a deep sense of destiny, a heritage from the Asian religions of pre-Spanish times, coupled with their firmly rooted faith in the God whom the Spanish missionaries brought to the islands, Spain's greatest contribution to the collective Fillipino soul.

[15] An expression often used, whose origin Filipinos themselves may not know, is *Bahala na*. It is a corruption of *Bathala*, the name of the ancient god of the pagan Filipinos. In uttering *Bahala na*, Filipinos are saying that they are leaving things in the hands of God.

[16] Another expression they may use is *talaga*, meaning "destined, inevitable." Ill Filipinos tend to attribute their condition to the will of God and to cope with their illness by praying and hoping that whatever God's will is, it is the best for them. Although both patients and families find it hard to accept a poor prognosis, they keep on hoping despite their resignation. This attitude explains why Filipino patients are uncomplaining and frequently suffer in silence.

[17] The nurse can try to penetrate the facade of cheerfulness, silence, or fatalism, including the family in her explorations. Filipino patients and their families appreciate openness on the part of their doctors and nurses, for their reliance on God and fate strengthens them and enables them to cope.

Temperament

[18] Filipinos, being essentially Asian, have gentle, mild, and passive temperaments—the temper of people whose collective unconscious has been anchored in the idea of a harmonious balance between man and nature. They generally are neither assertive nor aggressive. They appear guarded or reticent. This, unfortunately, can be misconstrued as an inferiority complex. Too often, they are labeled as passive-aggressive, as having a personality disorder with anger as its underlying cause. This anger produces anxiety, which is usually handled through covert and passive means. Behavioral mani-

-festations of this disorder and behavior common to Filipinos are procrastination and stubbornness, associated with intense cravings for acceptance, generosity, and verbal demands for attention. Whether this behavior in Filipinos is a personality disorder is difficult to determine. I would venture to say that this attitude stems from centuries of Spanish repression, which inhibited a proud people. As a result of more than three centuries of Spanish hegemony, Filipinos learned the value of silence and prudence. To preserve security, they are submissive to authority and reluctant to express their opinions.

[19] No wonder they regard doctors and nurses as authority figures and do not question whatever regimen is imposed on them. They easily win the labels "good patient," "cooperative," and "uncomplaining." Yet, is this how one should perceive such behavior? Shouldn't the nurse use assessment skills to determine what is behind this behavior?

Interpersonal Relationships

[20] Filipinos generally behave agreeably, even to the extent of personal inconvenience. This is called *pakikisama*, which means going along with others.[3]

[21] Related to *pakikisama* is *hiya* or "shame," which is Asian. The Chinese and the Japanese call it "face," and the Spanish *orgullo*, or "self-pride." *Hiya* is a painful emotion arising from a relationship with an authority or society that inhibits self-assertion in a situation perceived as dangerous to one's ego.[4]

[22] Another trait is *amor propio*, which is Spanish and means "self-esteem." When a Filipino's *amor propio* is wounded, he preserves his dignity through silence or aloofness, believing that to do otherwise would demonstrate a lack of self-pride. Filipinos believe that having accepted the doctors or nurses implies that they have confidence and, by the same token, they trust that it is mutual.

[23] On the other hand, even when they mistrust the doctor or nurse, Filipino patients seldom tell them to their faces. They beat around the bush for fear of hurting the other person's feelings or, perhaps, have a family member or friend make known their feelings.

[24] Commonly, a hesitant yes means no. This is an effort to avoid a direct, blunt no. Still another custom is the use of a euphemism, such as *kuwan*, meaning "thing." It can replace any expression one does not ordinarily use in polite company, and its nonverbal counterpart is a nod, which means yes.

[25] The Filipino language has hierarchical terms for yes and no. The term depends on whether a Filipino is speaking to a person of lower, equal, or superior status. When a Filipino does not know another's status, a silent nod avoids giving possible offense. Filipino patients often address a physician or nurse properly as "Dr. Jones" or "Ms. Smith." If they don't know their names, they nod.

[26] A silent nod may also be a defense in a belittling situation. If an authority figure gives instructions in a belittling way, a Filipino patient may nod. If a nurse rattles off instructions and the patient nods, it could mean he understands, or it could mean that her instructions are inadequate but he wants to spare her feeling and preserve his *amor propio.*

Food Preferences

[27] Eating habits vary with Filipinos' region of origin.

Drawing origin from various cultures but displaying regional characteristics, Filipino food was prepared by the series of Malay migrations . . . spiced by commercial relations with Chinese traders, stewed in 300 years of Spanish rule and hamburgered by American influence on the Philippine way of life. [5]

[28] The main influence in this potpourri is Spanish cookery. Certainly, to Europeans and South Americans, nothing can be very strange about Filipino dishes.

[29] The French will recognize a lighter bouillabaisse in our *sinigang,* which is fish in a tart broth with tomatoes and tamarind (a fruit noted for its tartness, native to the Philippines). The Germans will find *arroz con caldo* like their *Suppenham.* Both are rice in chicken broth. Our *arroz con goto* is similar to Italian minestrone.

[30] Despite regional differences, there are national dishes known all over the Philippines. Among these are *adobo* (pork, chicken, beef, or a combination simmered in vinegar and garlic sauce) and *dinuguan* (pork flesh and innards spiced with whole peppers and stewed). Another is *pancit* (long, uncut rice noodles sautéed with meat and vegetables). Still another is *lumpia* (a roll of vegetables and meat in a paper-thin rice wrapper). Filipinos like *lechon* (whole pig roasted outdoors for long hours over charcoal). Some Americans, no doubt, have been treated to some of these foods by their Filipino friends.

[31] The Filipino staple is rice, ordinarily boiled to fluffiness. It is eaten at every meal. For breakfast, rice usually is fried with a touch of garlic and eaten with an egg, sausage, or fried fish. Rice is the main bulk of Filipino meals, a must on the dinner table.

[32] Attractively served western dishes may not suit Filipino patients, even when they are familiar with American food which lacks spices. Perhaps the hospitalized Filipinos may eat the first few meals, then start craving rice and home-cooked dishes. A Filipino child might ignore other foods but pick at ice cream and desserts. Food from home can help, but the nurse needs to tell the family that they can bring food.

[33] Filipinos use salt generously. On top of the already salted and

spiced dishes, Filipinos pour a salty, brownish clear liquid called *patis*, a preparation of fish or shrimp extract. Some use soy sauce. Another sauce used on shrimp and other dishes, while cooking or at the table, is *bagoong*, which is highly salted. In fact, a humble meal can be made with a cup of rice doused with *bagoong*, plus tomatoes or any leafy vegetable. For Filipino patients who must limit their salt intake, a careful examination of food habits is essential.

References

1. U.S. Immigration and Naturalization Service. *Annual Reports 1965–74. Charts Nos. 8A and 16.*
2. Rustia, Erlinda. Keynote speech for conference on the Filipino culture, in Seattle, Wash. November 8, 1974. Sponsored by the Washington Cluster Group, WCHEN project on Faculty Development to Meet Minority Needs.
3. Lynch, Frank. Social acceptance reconsidered. In *Four Readings on Philippine Values*, ed. by Frank Lynch, 3d ed. Quezon City, Ateneo de Manila University Press, 1970.
4. Bulatao, Jaime. Hiya. *Philippine Studies* 12:424–438, July 1964.
5. Getting to know Philippine food. *ARCHIPELAGO* (The International Magazine of the Philippines) 1:47, Feb. 1974.

VOCABULARY

Look up the following words in your dictionary. Use the system developed in the dictionary section in the back of the text. Be sure to write the part of speech, the pronunciation, and the meaning(s) of each word.

mi·grate (mī′grāt′) *intr.v.* **-grated, -grating, -grates.** **1.** To move from one country or region and settle in another. **2.** To change location periodically; move seasonally from one region to another: *"The birds that fish the cold sea for a living must either migrate or starve."* (Rachel Carson). [Latin *migrāre.* See **mei-**[1] in Appendix.*]
   Usage: *Migrate* is used with reference both to the place of departure and the destination, and can be followed by *from* or *to.* It is said of persons, animals, and birds, and sometimes implies lack of permanent settlement (notably seasonal movement). *Emigrate* pertains to a single move by persons, and implies permanence. It has specific reference to the place of departure, emphasizes movement from that place, and is usually followed by *from*. *Immigrate* specifies a single move by persons, and implies permanence. But it refers to the destination, emphasizes movement there, and is followed by *to*.

Definition ©1981 Houghton Mifflin Company. Reprinted by permission from *The American Heritage Dictionary of the English Language, New College Edition.*

competence

enhancing

hegemony

ceded

consummated

admixture

heritage

manifest

spontaneous

idiosyncrasies

patriarch

matriarch

deference

solicitous

hovering — movement of the wings.

destined

inevitable

prognosis

penetrate

facade

cope

harmonious

guarded

reticent — reserved

anxiety — worry

covert

procrastination — delay to put

cravings

prudence

inhibits

euphemism

hierarchical

belittling – underestimate – depreciate

potpourri

STUDY QUESTIONS

Finding the Matter

1. Which countries have influenced Filipino culture?

2. What is the connection between the Filipinos' feeling for family and health care?

3. How do the Filipinos' religious beliefs affect their attitudes toward illness?

4. If a Filipino patient nods his or her head, what different meanings can this gesture have?

5. What food appears on the Filipino's table at every meal?

Exploring the Manner

1. Who is the intended audience* for this article? How do you know?

2. Why does the author write seven paragraphs of introduction* before mentioning the role of the nurse in dealing with Filipino patients?

3. Examine the descriptions of the Filipino patient with regard to temperament, self-esteem, and food preferences. What details help you to understand the special qualities of this culture?

4. Why does the author give three words to describe one emotion: *shame, face,* and *self-pride*?

5. Would you call this description objective* or subjective*? Does the fact that the author is a Filipino affect your answer? Explain.

SYNONYMS

From the column at the right, select the best synonym for the italicized word in each sentence. Rewrite each sentence using the appropriate synonym.

1. Filipinos see U.S. technology as a means of improving their professional *ability*.

2. There are certain basic traits that most Filipinos will *show* even though they come from a mixed heritage.

3. Among Filipinos the lack of *self-generated* cooperation is not surprising.

4. The young people always receive *concerned* protection from their elders.

5. When Filipinos use the expression "talaga," they use it to mean "*fated*."

6. These people have intense *longings* for acceptance.

7. Filipinos have learned the values of silence and *caution*.

8. Sometimes the Filipino has to deal with a society that *restrains* him or her from exhibiting self-assertion.

9. Eating habits vary among Filipinos, but the main influence of their cultural *mixture* is Spanish.

10. The Filipinos exhibit a great deal of *worry* even though they appear to be unassertive.

A. solicitious

B. inhibits

C. manifest

D. anxiety

E. destined

F. potpourri

G. spontaneous

H. cravings

I. competence

J. prudence

PARAPHRASE

Read this paragraph twice, then close your book. Using your
own words, rewrite the paragraph as clearly and completely
as you can.

The Philippines consists of roughly 7,000 islands, big and
small. Filipinos display characteristics that differ, depending
on the region they hail from. Due to the Chinese influence on
family solidarity, people from the same region tend to
socialize only among themselves. This clannishness is evident
among the many organizations in Filipino communities,
which to some observers might appear to be rivalry. Thus,
lack of spontaneous cooperation is not surprising, but it is
both a weakness and a strength.

VERB FILL-IN

Fill in each blank with the verb form that is appropriate for
each sentence.

In the sixteenth century, the West _____ influencing the
                                                start

Philippines. The 300 years or so of Spanish hegemony _____
                                                                          begin

when Ferdinand Magellan first _____ the Philippine Islands
                                              claim

for Spain in 1521. Then, as an outcome of the Spanish–American

War, the Philippines _____ to America for $20 million, a
                                  cede

sale _____ without the knowledge or consent of the Fili-
        consummate

pino people.

Another country that _____ tremendous influence on
                                  exert

Filipino thought and behavior _____ China, which
                             be

_____ with the Filipinos from the Tang dynasty in the
    trade

seventh century. Thus, Rustia _____ a Filipino as "an Asian,
                          define

basically Malay, with a generous admixture of the Chinese and the

Spanish, and with a cultural overlay of the American for good

measure."

SENTENCE COMPLETION

From the column at the right, select the correct line to complete each of the numbered lines at the left. Write each sentence in its correct form.

1. Essentially, the Filipino is an Asian with a strong Malayan base,

2. Because of the Chinese influence on family solidarity,

3. The strong feeling for family, a quality derived from the Chinese influence

4. Filipino patients always have their families hovering over them,

5. Single adults with no relative in the vicinity

6. Filipinos have a deep sense of destiny,

7. Filipino patients and their families appreciate openness on the part of their doctors and nurses,

A. derived from the highly complex culture of the Indonesian Madjapahit Empire.

B. perhaps to the irritation of the nursing staff.

C. a heritage from the Asian religions of pre-Spanish times.

D. have swarms of visitors.

E. then start craving rice and home-cooked dishes.

F. it could mean he understands.

G. people from the same region tend to socialize only among themselves.

8. Filipinos generally behave agreeably,

9. If a nurse rattles off instructions and the patient nods,

10. Perhaps the hospitalized Filipinos may eat the first few meals, and

H. for their reliance on God and fate strengthens them and enables them to cope.

I. is manifested by old-fashioned patterns imposed by the family patriarch.

J. even to the extent of personal inconvenience.

CLOZE EXERCISE

Fill in each blank with the best word to complete the meaning of the sentence.

The strong feeling for family, _____ quality derived

from the Chinese _____, is manifested by old-fashioned

patterns _____ by the family patriarch or _____

equally authoritative matriarch. Respect and _____ are

always given to one's _____, whose words and decisions one

_____ not question. The young receive _____

protection from their elders. In _____ absence of both

parents, the _____ child has the say and _____

be obeyed.

SENTENCE COMBINING

Combine each pair of sentences into a single grammatical sentence.

1. Respect is always given to one's elders.
   Deference, derived from the Chinese influence, is always given to one's elders.

2. Families are always hovering over the Filipino patients.
   The nursing staff is irritated by the families.

3. Filipino patients are uncomplaining.
   They frequently suffer in silence.

4. The Filipino food staple is rice.
   Rice is eaten at every meal.

5. The Filipino will eat the first few meals in the hospital.
   The Filipino will crave rice and home-cooked dishes.

6. Before World War II, only a handful of Filipinos came to the
   United States.
   Mostly laborers were brought over to work the big plantations.

PUNCTUATION

Read the following paragraph. Write in the capital letters
and place commas, periods, colons, semicolons, dashes, and
quotation marks where needed.

commonly a hesitant yes means no this is an effort to avoid a

direct blunt no still another custom is the use of a euphemism such

as *kuwan* meaning thing it can replace any expression one does not

ordinarily use in polite company and its nonverbal counterpart is a

nod which means yes the filipino language has hierarchical terms for

yes and no the term depends on whether a filipino is speaking to a

person of lower equal or superior status when a filipino does not

know anothers status a silent nod avoids giving possible offense

filipino patients often address a physician or nurse properly as dr

jones or ms smith if they dont know their names they nod.

WORD-FORM CHART

Use your dictionary to complete the following table. Follow the example shown with item 1, *migration*. If there is no commonly used form for a particular part of speech, write the symbol XXX.

Noun	Verb	Adjective	Adverb
1. migration	migrate	migratory migrational	XXX
2. behavior			
3.			basically
4.	resemble		
5. patriarch			
6.		constant	
7.			passively
8. authority			
9.		mistrustful	
10. situation			

WORD-FORM EXERCISE

Using your completed Word-Form Chart, select the correct form to fit into each sentence. Use the appropriate tense of the verb, the singular or plural form of the noun, and the passive voice where necessary.

Follow the sequence of numbers from the Word-Form Chart to select the correct form.

1. One of the reasons the Filipinos have _____ to America

   is for the benefits that they can derive from modern U.S.

   technology.

2. A country that has exerted tremendous influence on Filipino thought and _____ is China.

3. Although the Filipino culture has arisen from such a mixed heritage, there are some _____ traits that most Filipinos will manifest.

4. In the Philippines today, youths _____ their western counterparts, particularly in matters of dress, music, and social values.

5. The Filipinos do not have a _____ society.

6. The sick Filipino child feels lost without his or her mother _____ at the bedside.

7. Filipinos have gentle, mild, and _____ temperaments.

8. Filipinos regard doctors and nurses as _____ figures.

9. Even when they _____ the doctors or the nurses, the Filipino patients will seldom tell them to their faces.

10. A Filipino may nod as a defense in a belittling _____.

QUESTIONS FOR DISCUSSION

1. What might a nurse do for a Filipino patient on a low-salt diet who will return home to meals that are heavily salted?

2. What advice would you give a doctor and nurse about a member of your family to help them provide proper hospital care?

3. Imagine that a visitor from your native country becomes seriously ill and is confined to a hospital. How might his or her religious beliefs affect the visitor's response to medical treatment?

TOPICS FOR WRITING

1. Write a theme describing the particular problems that a member of your family might have in a hospital (language, diet, cultural differences).

2. Write a composition describing a gesture (such as nodding the head) that has one meaning in your native culture and a different meaning in American culture.

3. List the main subjects of a training course that you are designing to make hospital personnel sensitive to the cultural differences among their patients. Then write a composition describing the importance of these subjects.

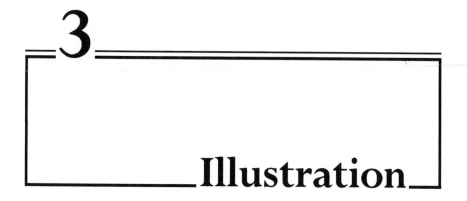

3

Illustration

The Form

A Roman poet once wrote: *Verba movent, exempla trahunt.* ("Words move people, but examples compel them.") His words are still true today. If someone tells us that she had an exhausting day, we may nod in sympathy. But if she explains that the dog ran away, the bathtub overflowed, the car broke down, and she was late to work, then we can really understand her misery.

Examples give flavor to writing as spices do to sauces. Without either, the result is bland. Of course, the examples used must be appropriate, sufficient in number, and detailed. When carefully chosen and developed, examples can arouse and hold the reader's interest.

The Student Reader

When you read an essay using illustration, notice how the specific examples bring the author's thesis (or topic sentence) from the general down to the specific. In this paragraph, the several illustrations help the writer to explain the process of blending because they are interesting and easy to remember.

Another way in which new words come into the English language is through the process of blending. Blends are words formed by com-

111

bining the beginning of one word with the end of another. One example of this process is the word *smog*, which combines the beginning of *smoke* with the end of *fog*. The word *motel* is a blend of *motor* and *hotel*. Other commonly heard blends are *squash* (*squeeze* plus *crash*), *splatter* (*splash* plus *spatter*), *smash* (*smack* plus *mash*), and *brunch*. Most blends pass out of the language quickly; only a small percentage, such as those noted above, survive for any considerable length of time.

The Professional Writer

No matter what the subject or style, details enliven all writing. In his essay on kites, Francis X. Clines presents numerous examples from many places and different times. Instead of simply telling the reader that the Chinese first used kites 2,500 years ago, Clines says: "A Chinese warlord wrote of hoisting a soldier high into the sky on a giant kite to spy down on an embattled castle." At this point and in other parts of the essay, the example attracts our attention and encourages us to read on.

Lewis Thomas, in his essay "On Natural Death," explores a mouse's apparent lack of pain when a cat carries its dying victim in its mouth. He explains that when it is wounded by the cat, the mouse's body releases pain-killing hormones: "Thus it is that the mouse seems always to dangle languidly from the jaws, lies there so quietly when dropped, dies of his injuries without a struggle. If a mouse could shrug, he'd shrug." In this example Lewis is trying to illustrate the mouse's seeming indifference to pain. The graphic quality of the illustration emphasizes Lewis's point and remains in the mind long after the end of the essay. This is the power of illustration.

Illustration 113

TESTS FOR CONDUCTORS

Ernest Newman

[1] The public in general, and the sob brothers of the non-musical Press, who always come out in force when a child does some simple thing that older people have been doing for years without finding the mental strain unbearable, evidently have the quaintest notions about conducting. The conductor, as they see him, is a combination of the hypnotist and the lion-tamer. The orchestral players, however, do not see him in that light; apart from some half-dozen really great conductors, for whom, like the rest of us, they have a profound respect, they size him up as a man doing the easiest of musical jobs and not always doing it dazzlingly well.

[2] Witness the old story of the player who couldn't tell an inquirer who had conducted that evening's concert because he had "forgotten to look." Only the other day a friend of mine told me that he had asked an eminent concert soloist who had recently been amusing himself with the baton how he enjoyed conducting. "Not at all," he replied, "it's too easy after playing the _____." (I omit the name of the instrument, as that might serve to identify him.) Or witness, again, the answer of a player in the London Symphony

Orchestra who was asked what he thought of the talented boy from Italy. "He's certainly the best conductor we've had this season," a judgment which all concerned, including the public, can take in whatever sense they choose.

[3] What is the *raison d'être* of the conductor? A string quartet manages without one, although the right performance of, say, the Beethoven C sharp minor quartet is a far more exciting business than that of the C-minor symphony, and the second quartet of Ernest Bloch much more difficult, technically and intellectually, than the "Oberon" overture or "L'apprenti sorcier." The string quartet manages without a human semaphore in front of it because it is made up of first-rate artists who know every nook and cranny of the work in hand, and by long association have learned to function as an organic unity. It is only when a great increase in the number of the players weakens the inner binding principle that some sort of external clamp becomes necessary.

[4] This part of conducting is a routine that anyone can learn who will apply himself to it, though some, of course, will be better at it than others. But conducting in the greater sense means much more than this: it means fineness of spirit, a wide musical culture that enables the possessor of it to distinguish between the mind of one composer and that of another, and between different orders of musical imagination, and an experience of life that makes him imaginatively one, with all that a great composer has felt and suffered and said in his music. It stands to reason that no child, however gifted, can possibly be a conductor in this greater sense of the term.

[5] Conducting a few standard works which the orchestra knows by heart is a feat well within the powers of any naturally musical boy. What anyone can do by going through the business of practising it is not surely a matter for blank amazement, and the age at which we can expect a child to be able to do this or that in music is progressively falling as educational methods improve. Has the reader heard the story of old Moriz Rosenthal and the fond mother who was convinced that her boy was a pianistic wonder such as the world had never yet seen? At last Rosenthal consented to hear the prodigy, and something like the following dialogue ensued. "So you are going to play to me?" "Please sir, yes sir." "And what are you going to play?" "Please sir, the 'Tchaikovsky Concerto in B flat minor.'" "Oh that? And how old are you?" "Please sir, four-and-a-half sir." "Four-and-a-half? Too old!"

[6] I myself will begin to be amazed at a conductor of tender age when he shows his quality not in a few standard works well known to the orchestra but in the rehearsal and first performance of a new symphony by a living composer. If he comes brilliantly through that test he can be sure of counting on me among his warmest admirers.

Illustration 115

And while we are on the subject of tests, why not arrange for one for conductors in general, that might decide whether those people are right or wrong who say that, ruling out some half-dozen really great conductors, an audience would be hard put to it to distinguish between ninety per cent of the others if it did not see them? Will one of our orchestras be a sport and give us a concert something after this fashion? Let the orchestra (invisible to us) play three times without a conductor some standard work or other, and, in between, play it under three conductors—no age or sex barred—without our seeing them or being told their names. After that, let the audience try to decide which performance was which. It ought to be good fun—if the conductors chosen will consent.

VOCABULARY

Look up the following words in your dictionary. Use the system developed in the dictionary section in the back of the text. Be sure to write the part of speech, the pronunciation, and the meaning(s) of each word.

quaint (kwānt) *adj.* **quainter, quaintest. 1.** Agreeably curious, especially in an old-fashioned way: *"Smoke drifted lazily from a multitude of quaint chimneys."* (Stephen Crane). **2.** Unfamiliar or unusual in character; strange. **3.** Highly inappropriate or illogical. Used ironically: *They fought the war out of a quaint sense of honor.* —See Synonyms at **strange.** [Middle English *queinte, cointe,* clever, skillfully made, from Old French *cointe,* expert, elegant, from Latin *cognitus,* past participle of *cognōscere,* to be acquainted with : *com-,* with + *gnōscere,* to know (see **gnō-** in Appendix*).] —**quaint′ly** *adv.* —**quaint′ness** *n.*

Definition ©1981 Houghton Mifflin Company. Reprinted by permission from *The American Heritage Dictionary of the English Language, New College Edition.*

hypnotist

dazzlingly

witness

eminent

semaphore

nook

cranny

binding

clamp

feat

standard

prodigy

tender

invisible

consent

STUDY QUESTIONS

Finding the Matter

1. Why does Newman include the anecdote about the musician who didn't know who was conducting the orchestra because he hadn't looked?

2. How can string quartets perform without a conductor?

3. Why did the famous musician Moriz Rosenthal tell a 4½-year-old pianist that he was "too old" to play the Tchaikovsky Piano Concerto? Was he serious? How do you know?

Exploring the Manner

1. The term *sob sisters* usually refers to female journalists who write sentimental newspaper columns designed to bring tears to the eyes of the reader. How do you interpret Newman's use of the phrase "sob brothers of the non-musical Press"? What is his attitude* toward these journalists?

2. What is Newman's thesis* in this essay? Is it stated or only suggested? How do the examples support the thesis*?

3. Sometimes Newman uses a word in a figurative* manner. One example occurs when he describes the musicians in a string quartet, "who know every nook and cranny of the work in hand." How do you know that he doesn't mean *nook* and *cranny* in their literal* sense?

Illustration   *117*

SYNONYMS

From the column at the right, select the best synonym for the italicized word in each sentence. Rewrite each sentence using the appropriate synonym.

1. People have *strange* notions about the talents and capabilities of child prodigies.

2. Musicians do not always think the conductor is doing his job *brilliantly*.

3. Some *prominent* musicians do not enjoy conducting; they think it's too easy.

4. Guessing the hidden conductor would be fun if the conductors chosen would *agree*.

5. Any talented boy can conduct a few *familiar* works of music.

6. String quartet musicians can perform without a conductor because of an inner *uniting* principle.

A. eminent

B. consent

C. quaint

D. binding

E. standard

F. dazzlingly

PARAPHRASE

Read this paragraph twice; then close your book. Using your own words, rewrite the paragraph as clearly and completely as you can.

This part of conducting is a routine that anyone can learn who will apply himself to it, though some, of course, will be better at it than others. But conducting in the greater sense means much more than this: it means fineness of spirit, a wide musical culture that enables the possessor of it to distinguish between the mind of one composer and that of another, and between different orders of musical imagination, and an experience of life that makes him imaginatively one, with all that a great composer has felt and suffered and said in his music. It stands to reason that no child, however gifted, can possibly be a conductor in this greater sense of the term.

VERB FILL-IN

Fill in each blank with the verb form that is appropriate for each sentence.

I myself _____ to be amazed at a conductor of tender
                begin

age when he _____ his quality not in a few standard works
                  show

well known to the orchestra but in the rehearsal and first perfor-

mance of a new symphony by a living composer. If he _____
                                                                    come

brilliantly through that test he _____ be sure of counting on
                                          can

me among his warmest admirers. And while we _____ on
                                                          be

the subject of tests, why not _____ for one for conductors
                                    arrange

in general, that might _____ whether those people
                              decide

_____ right or wrong who say that, _____ out
       be   rule

some half-dozen really great conductors, an audience would be hard

put to it to distinguish between ninety per cent of the others if it did

not _____ them?
         see

Illustration 119

SENTENCE COMPLETION

From the column at the right, select the correct line to complete each of the numbered lines at the left. Write each sentence in its correct form.

1. The public sees the conductor as a combination

2. A string quartet always manages to play well

3. When there is a large number of musicians playing together,

4. Conducting in the greater sense

5. No child, however gifted,

6. Let an orchestra play three times without a conductor and three times with a conductor

A. without a conductor.

B. means a fineness of spirit, a wide musical culture, and an experience of life that makes the conductor one with his music.

C. so that the audience can try to see which performance was which.

D. can possibly be a conductor.

E. of the hypnotist and the lion tamer.

F. it then becomes necessary to have a conductor.

CLOZE EXERCISE

Fill in each blank with the best word to complete the meaning of the sentence.

Conducting a few _____ works which the _____ knows by heart _____ a feat well _____ the powers of _____ naturally musical boy. _____ anyone can do _____ going through the _____ of practising it _____ not surely a _____ for blank amazement, _____ the age at _____ we can expect _____ child to be _____ to do this _____ that in music _____ progressively falling as _____ methods improve.

SENTENCE COMBINING

Combine each pair of sentences into a single grammatical sentence.

1. A child who performs like an adult is considered to be a prodigy.
   A prodigy is an unusually gifted child.

2. An eminent concert soloist didn't enjoy conducting.
   This concert soloist had been amusing himself with the baton.

3. A great number of experienced musicians can play well together.
   Experienced musicians need a conductor.

4. An orchestra usually knows a few standard works well.
   A naturally musical boy can conduct an orchestra that plays standard works.

5. A mother brought her young son to Moriz Rosenthal.
   He consented to hear the prodigy.

PUNCTUATION

Read the following paragraph. Write in the capital letters and place commas, periods, colons, semicolons, dashes, and quotations marks where needed.

has the reader heard the story of old moriz rosenthal and the fond mother who was convinced that her boy was a pianistic wonder such as the world had never yet seen at last rosenthal consented to hear the prodigy and something like the following dialogue ensued so you are going to play to me please sir yes sir and what are you going to play please sir the tchaikovsky concerto in b flat minor oh that and how old are you please sir four and a half sir four and a half too old

Illustration 121

WORD-FORM CHART

Use your dictionary to complete the following table. Follow
the example shown with item 1, *combination*. If there is no
commonly used form for a particular part of speech, write
the symbol XXX.

Noun	Verb	Adjective	Adverb
1. combination	combine	combinational	XXX
2.		functional	
3. music			
4.	rehearse		
5.	admire		
6.		distinguishable	

WORD-FORM EXERCISE

Using your completed Word-Form Chart, select the correct
form to fit into each sentence. Use the appropriate tense of
the verb, the singular or plural form of the noun, and the
passive voice where necessary.
Follow the sequence of numbers from the Word-Form Chart
to select the correct form.

1. Most people see the conductor as a _____ of the hyp-

   notist and the lion tamer.

2. A string quartet, by long association, has learned to _____

   as an organic unity.

3. A conductor must possess a wide knowledge of musical culture

   and also have a _____ imagination.

4. A young conductor should be able to show his quality in the

   _____ and first performance of a new symphony by a

   living composer.

5. If he comes through this test, he will have many _____.

6. Audiences cannot generally _____ the work of conduc-

   tors unless they see them.

QUESTIONS FOR DISCUSSION

1. What qualities of the conductor are similar to those of a hypnotist
   and a lion tamer?
2. Are musicians in orchestras the best judges of conductors, or
   should conductors be judged by other conductors, by composers,
   by audiences, or by music critics?
3. Why does Newman say that a superior conductor has to be able to
   "distinguish between the mind of one composer and that of
   another"?
4. Is the composer always the best interpreter of his own music,
   either as performer or conductor? Consider either classical composers or popular ones, such as Barry Manilow.

TOPICS FOR WRITING

1. Think of the qualities that a great leader must have. Specify the
   kind of leader (conductor, politician, teacher, religious leader,
   executive) and choose the three most important qualities to write
   about. Illustrate each quality with details.
2. Some popular music groups have lead singers. Write a composition
   illustrating the functions of one such performer. Give at least one
   example of each function.
3. Newman suggests that orchestras may be able to perform well
   without conductors. Write a theme in which you give examples
   of other groups that might be able to function satisfactorily
   without a leader (athletic teams, theatrical groups, student
   organizations).

Illustration   *123*

ON NATURAL DEATH

Lewis Thomas

[1] There are so many new books about dying that there are now special shelves set aside for them in bookshops, along with the health-diet and home-repair paperbacks and the sex manuals. Some of them are so packed with detailed information and step-by-step instructions for performing the function that you'd think this was a new sort of skill which all of us are now required to learn. The strongest impression the casual reader gets, leafing through, is that proper dying has become an extraordinary, even an exotic experience, something only the specially trained get to do.

[2] Also, you could be led to believe that we are the only creatures capable of the awareness of death, that when all the rest of nature is being cycled through dying, one generation after another, it is a different kind of process, done automatically and trivially, more "natural," as we say.

[3] An elm in our backyard caught the blight this summer and dropped stone dead, leafless, almost overnight. One weekend it was a normal-looking elm, maybe a little bare in spots but nothing alarming, and the next weekend it was gone, passed over, departed, taken. Taken is right, for the tree surgeon came by yesterday with his crew of young helpers and their cherry picker, and took it down branch by branch and carted it off in the back of a red truck, everyone singing.

[4] The dying of a field mouse, at the jaws of an amiable household cat, is a spectacle I have beheld many times. It used to make me wince. Early in life I gave up throwing sticks at the cat to make him drop the mouse, because the dropped mouse regularly went ahead and died anyway, but I always shouted unaffections at the cat to let him know the sort of animal he had become. Nature, I thought, was an abomination.

[5] Recently I've done some thinking about that mouse, and I wonder if his dying is necessarily all that different from the passing of our elm. The main difference, if there is one, would be in the matter of pain. I do not believe that an elm tree has pain receptors, and even so, the blight seems to me a relatively painless way to go even if there were nerve endings in a tree, which there are not. But the mouse dangling tail-down from the teeth of a gray cat is something else again, with pain beyond bearing, you'd think, all over his small body.

[6] There are now some plausible reasons for thinking it is not like that at all, and you can make up an entirely different story about the mouse and his dying if you like. At the instant of being trapped and

penetrated by teeth, peptide hormones are released by cells in the
hypothalamus and the pituitary gland; instantly these substances,
called endorphins, are attached to the surfaces of other cells responsible for pain perception; the hormones have the pharmacologic
properties of opium; there is no pain. Thus it is that the mouse seems
always to dangle so languidly from the jaws, lies there so quietly
when dropped, dies of his injuries without a struggle. If a mouse
could shrug, he'd shrug.

[7] I do not know if this is true or not, nor do I know how to prove
it if it is true. Maybe if you could get in there quickly enough and administer naloxone, a specific morphine antagonist, you could turn
off the endorphins and observe the restoration of pain, but this is
not something I would care to do or see. I think I will leave it there,
as a good guess about the dying of a cat-chewed mouse, perhaps
about dying in general.

Illustration   125

[8] Montaigne had a hunch about dying, based on his own close call in a riding accident. He was so badly injured as to be believed dead by his companions, and was carried home with lamentations, "all bloody, stained all over with the blood I had thrown up." He remembers the entire episode, despite having been "dead, for two full hours," with wonderment:

> *It seemed to me that my life was hanging only by the tip of my lips. I closed my eyes in order, it seemed to me, to help push it out, and took pleasure in growing languid and letting myself go. It was an idea that was only floating on the surface of my soul, as delicate and feeble as all the rest, but in truth not only free from distress but mingled with that sweet feeling that people have who have let themselves slide into sleep. I believe that this is the same state in which people find themselves whom we see fainting in the agony of death, and I maintain that we pity them without cause. . . . In order to get used to the idea of death, I find there is nothing like coming close to it.*

[9] Later, in another essay, Montaigne returns to it:

> *If you know not how to die, never trouble yourself; Nature will in a moment fully and sufficiently instruct you; she will exactly do that business for you; take you no care for it.*

[10] The worst accident I've ever seen was on Okinawa, in the early days of the invasion, when a jeep ran into a troop carrier and was crushed nearly flat. Inside were two young MPs, trapped in bent steel, both mortally hurt, with only their heads and shoulders visible. We had a conversation while people with the right tools were prying them free. Sorry about the accident, they said. No, they said, they felt fine. Is everyone else okay, one of them said. Well, the other one said, no hurry now. And then they died.

[11] Pain is useful for avoidance, for getting away when there's time to get away, but when it is end game, and no way back, pain is likely to be turned off, and the mechanisms for this are wonderfully precise and quick. If I had to design an ecosystem in which creatures had to live off each other and in which dying was an indispensable part of living, I could not think of a better way to manage.

VOCABULARY

Look up the following words in your dictionary. Use the system developed in the dictionary section in the back of the text. Be sure to write the part of speech, the pronunciation, and the meaning(s) of each word.

ex·ot·ic (ĕg-zŏt'ĭk, ĭg-) *adj.* **1.** From another part of the world; not indigenous; foreign. **2.** Having the charm of the unfamiliar; strikingly and intriguingly unusual or beautiful. —See Synonyms at **fantastic.** —*n.* One that is exotic. [Latin *exōticus,* from Greek *exōtikos,* from *exō,* outside, from *ex,* out (see **eghs** in Appendix*).] —**ex·ot'i·cal·ly** *adv.* —**ex·ot'ic·ness** *n.*

Definition ©1981 Houghton Mifflin Company. Reprinted by permission from *The American Heritage Dictionary of the English Language, New College Edition.*

cycled

trivially

blight

cherry picker

amiable

spectacle

wince

abomination

receptors

plausible

penetrated

pituitary

endorphins

pharmacologic

languidly

shrug

hunch

lamentations

ecosystem

Illustration 127

STUDY QUESTIONS

Finding the Matter

1. Why does Thomas believe that a mouse in the jaws of a cat might feel no pain?

2. What did Montaigne, the French essayist (1533–1592), have to say about his close encounter with death?

3. What surprised Thomas about the two young MPs who were wounded in a Jeep on Okinawa?

4. Dr. Thomas is a highly respected physician and research scientist. Where does the article suggest his background?

Exploring the Manner

1. Explain how the elm tree incident illustrates Thomas's concept of "natural death."

2. As Thomas accumulates examples of painless deaths, he moves toward his thesis* that death is both natural and well designed. Why does he wait until the end of the essay to present his thesis? Is this an effective technique? Explain your opinion.

3. Is Thomas's thesis* based on fact, opinion, or a combination of both?

4. Which words indicate that the author is giving his opinion?

5. For what kind of audience* is Thomas writing? Support your answer with specific examples from the text.

6. What different shade of meaning is suggested by each of the words Thomas uses to describe the dead elm tree (*gone, passed over, departed, taken*)?

SYNONYMS

From the column at the right, select the best synonym for the italicized word in each sentence. Rewrite each sentence using the appropriate synonym.

1. One gets the impression that proper dying is an *unusual* experience, something only the trained get to do.

   A. amiable
   B. blight
   C. abomination

2. The elm tree caught a *disease*
   and, almost overnight,
   dropped stone dead.

3. The fieldmouse died in the
   jaws of a *friendly* household
   cat.

4. I looked at this cat and
   mouse realizing it was a
   show I had seen many times.

5. Because of the relation of
   the cat and mouse, I felt
   nature was an *abhorrence*.

6. One can make up many
   believable stories concerning
   the process of dying.

7. The mouse dangled *listlessly*
   from the cat's jaws.

D. languidly

E. exotic

F. spectacle

G. plausible

PARAPHRASE

Read this paragraph twice; then close your book. Using
your own words, rewrite the paragraph as clearly and completely as you can.

   It seemed to me that my life was hanging only by the tip of
my lips. I closed my eyes in order, it seemed to me, to help
push it out, and took pleasure in growing languid and letting
myself go. It was an idea that was only floating on the
surface of my soul, as delicate and feeble as all the rest, but
in truth not only free from distress but mingled with that
sweet feeling that people have who let themselves slide into
sleep. I believe that this is the same state in which people
find themselves whom we see fainting in the agony of death,
and I maintain that we pity them without cause. . . . In order
to get used to the idea of death, I find there is nothing like
coming close to it.

VERB FILL-IN

Fill in each blank with the verb form that is appropriate for
each sentence.

1. Some of the books about dying ―――――――― with detailed
                                         pack

Illustration 129

information and step-by-step instructions for performing the

function.

2. One gets the impression that proper dying _____ an
become

extraordinary experience.

3. The elm in the backyard _____ the blight in the summer
catch

and dropped stone dead.

4. The dying of a field mouse, at the jaws of an amiable cat, is a

spectacle I _____ many times.
behold

5. Nature, I _____, was an abomination.
think

6. Montaigne _____ a hunch about dying, based on his
have

own close call in a riding accident.

7. He _____ dead by his companions.
believe

8. He _____ home with lamentations.
carry

9. Montaigne said, "In order to get used to the idea of death, I

_____ there is nothing like coming close to it."
find

10. The worst accident I _____ was in Okinawa.
see

SENTENCE COMPLETION

From the column at the right, select the correct line to complete each of the numbered lines at the left. Write each sentence in its correct form.

1. There are so many books about dying

2. The strongest impression the casual reader gets

3. One weekend it was a normal looking elm,

4. The tree surgeon came by with his crew and their cherry picker

5. Early in life I gave up throwing sticks at the cat

6. The blight seems a relatively painless way to go

7. Some substances called endorphins

8. If a mouse could shrug,

9. Montaigne had a hunch about dying

10. The worst accident I've ever seen was on Okinawa

A. and the next weekend it was gone.

B. to make him drop the mouse.

C. even if there are nerve endings in a tree.

D. that there are now special shelves set aside for them in bookstores.

E. he'd shrug.

F. and took the elm down branch by branch.

G. is that proper dying has become an extraordinary experience.

H. when a jeep ran into a troop carrier.

I. based on his own close call in an accident.

J. are peptide hormones.

CLOZE EXERCISE

Fill in each blank with the best word to complete the meaning of the sentence.

Pain is useful for avoidance, for _____ away when

there's time to get _____, but when it is end game,

_____ no way back, pain is likely _____ be turned

off, and the mechanisms _____ this are wonderfully precise

and quick. _____ I had to design an ecosystem

Illustration 131

———————— which creatures had to live off ———————— other

and in which dying was ———————— indispensable part of living,

I could ———————— think of a better way to ————————.

SENTENCE COMBINING

Combine each pair of sentences into a single grammatical
sentence.

1. The elm was normal-looking one weekend.
   The elm was dead the next weekend.

2. The tree surgeon took down the elm branch by branch.
   The tree surgeon carted it off in the back of his red truck.

3. I gave up throwing sticks at the cat to make him drop the mouse.
   The mouse died anyway.

4. I don't know if this fact is true.
   I don't know how to prove it if it is true.

5. They said they were sorry about the accident.
   They said they felt fine.

6. Pain is useful for avoidance.
   When there's no way back, pain is likely to be turned off.

PUNCTUATION

Read the following paragraphs. Write in the capital letters
and place commas, periods, colons, semicolons, dashes, and
quotation marks where needed.

i do not know if this is true or not nor do i know how to prove

it if it is true maybe if you could get in there quickly enough and

administer naloxone a specific morphine antagonist you could turn

off the endorphins and observe the restoration of pain but this is

not something i would care to do or see i think i will leave it there as a good guess about the dying of a cat chewed mouse perhaps about

dying in general

montaigne had a hunch about dying based on his own close call

in a riding accident he was so badly injured as to be believed dead

by his companions and was carried home with lamentations all

bloody stained all over with the blood he had thrown up he remem-

bered the entire episode despite having been dead for two full hours

with wonderment

WORD-FORM CHART

Use your dictionary to complete the following table. Follow the example shown with item 1, *detail.* If there is no commonly used form for a particular part of speech, write the symbol XXX.

Noun	Verb	Adjective	Adverb
1. detail	detail	detailed	XXX
2.			strongly
3.		aware	
4.	take		
5.	dangle		
6.		entire	
7. float			
8.		bad	
9. mortal			
10.	avoid		

Illustration   133

WORD-FORM EXERCISE

Using your completed Word-Form Chart, select the correct
form to fit into each sentence. Use the appropriate tense of
the verb, the singular or plural form of the noun, and the
passive voice where necessary.
Follow the sequence of numbers from the Word-Form Chart
to select the correct form.

1. Many of these special books are packed with ＿＿＿＿＿＿＿＿

   information.

2. The ＿＿＿＿＿＿＿＿ impression the casual reader gets is that

   dying has become an exotic experience.

3. We can be led to believe that we are the only creatures capable

   of the ＿＿＿＿＿＿＿＿ of death.

4. One weekend it was a normal-looking elm, the next weekend it

   was gone, passed over, departed, ＿＿＿＿＿＿＿＿.

5. The mouse ＿＿＿＿＿＿＿＿ tail-down from the teeth of the cat is

   something else again.

6. You can make up an ＿＿＿＿＿＿＿＿ different story about the

   mouse.

7. Montaigne said, "It was an idea that ＿＿＿＿＿＿＿＿ on the sur-

   face of my soul."

8. The ＿＿＿＿＿＿＿＿ accident I have ever seen was on Okinawa.

9. Men were trapped in bent steel, ＿＿＿＿＿＿＿＿ hurt.

10. Pain is useful for ＿＿＿＿＿＿＿＿, for getting away when there's

    time to get away.

QUESTIONS FOR DISCUSSION

1. Does the possible absence of pain make the idea of death more acceptable to you, as it does to Thomas? Explain your answer.

2. Thomas pokes gentle fun at the numerous books and articles on death and dying because they attempt to teach something as "natural" as ceasing to live. One of the most famous of these books is *On Death and Dying* (1970), by Elisabeth Kübler-Ross. She tries to show people how to come to terms with their own deaths or with the deaths of those they love, especially in the case of long illness. Do you believe that a person can learn how to accept death, or do you believe that death is "natural" and does not need to be taught or learned? Examine the reasons for your answer.

TOPICS FOR WRITING

1. Write a theme listing (and discussing) the characteristics that a good doctor should possess other than being well trained in medicine.

2. Study the following topics and choose the one that appeals to you:
   a. Give three qualities that you believe a "good death" should have.
   b. Give three qualities that a soldier might believe a "good death" should have.
   c. Give three qualities that a member of the clergy might believe a "good death" should have.
   Once you have selected your topic, list the qualities in order of increasing importance and incorporate them into an essay.

3. Should a patient who is terminally ill be permitted to die a "natural death" or be helped to die? Write a theme discussing the reasons for your viewpoint.

4. Discuss an experience you had during which you almost died. Give specific examples of your thoughts and sensations during this experience.

5. Examine the attitudes toward death in your native country.

Illustration   135

ETHNIC BUSINESSES

Irene Pave

[1] Ethnic businesses, those traditionally unsophisticated counter-parts of mainstream U.S. enterprise, are moving into the big time. Their growing prosperity stems from the national discovery—and affirmation—that the U.S. is a pluralistic society, not a melting pot. The process began in the 1960s, when Americans with foreign roots (many inspired by the black awareness movement) concluded that if black was beautiful, so was Polish, German, Italian, or Greek. Today these people express their rediscovered ethnicity by eating ethnic foods, listening to ethnic music, and participating in ethnic festivals. Exposed to such exotica for the first time, their nonethnic neighbors are following suit.

[2] The result is new business for the ethnic merchant—a person who formerly catered to an urban neighborhood of first- or second-generation fellow-countrymen by selling them the products that mainstream retailers failed to provide. He survived, often barely, only because his community supported him. Now he is doing business in the mainstream society that formerly all but ignored his presence.

[3] Moreover, ethnic festivals, offering ethnic foods, music, dancing, and handicrafts, have proved so appealing to Americans of all back-grounds that city officials have begun using them to promote interest

in declining urban centers. The festivals "have a binding effect on the morale of a city," explains Irving M. Levine, director of the Institute on Pluralism & Group Identity in New York City.

[4] The new ethnicity that produced this situation is more than a fad, says Monsignor Geno Baroni, the Roman Catholic priest who founded the National Center for Urban Ethnic Affairs in Washington in 1971. "Deep down, there is a need for traditions and values," says Baroni, who is currently an Assistant Secretary of the Housing & Urban Development Dept. Baroni believes that the ethnic revival represents a reaction by people who for generations felt pressure to discard their pasts and "be American." America, he says, "never wanted to deal with ethnicity before." Now, he adds, it must— although it lacks real information for the task.

[5] The Census Bureau records a person's spoken language and the birthplace of his parents but does not inquire into his self-identification. The Commerce Dept., which since 1969 has identified nearly 400,000 businesses owned by blacks, Hispanics, Asian-Americans, and American Indians, lumps businesses owned by entre-preneurs of European origin into a vague "other" category. "This area is extremely under-researched," says John A. Kromkowski, director of the national ethnic center. The center is just beginning to gather ethnic business data, as is Levine's institute. Up to now, both have concentrated on revitalizing ethnic neighborhoods and easing strains between ethnic groups.

[6] As a result, no one can offer dollars-and-cents figures on ethnic businesses, most of them family-run establishments dealing in food. But traffic in ethnic stores and restaurants is visibly up, and food and handicraft booths at the ethnic festivals that have sprung up in nearly every major city do a land-office business. The grocers, restaurateurs, and other ethnic businessmen, often third- or fourth-generation Americans who have narrowly survived the past two decades, clearly welcome the new clamor for homemade kielbasa or baklava. And they are starting to take steps to widen their traditional markets permanently.

[7] Typical is Victor Ostrowski & Son Inc., an East Baltimore manufacturer and retailer of Polish sausage. The company was founded in 1919, and John K. Ostrowski, its third-generation owner, has seen its annual output double from 50,000 lb. to 100,000 lb. in the past 12 years and his clientele change from 80% Polish 20 years ago to less than 50% Polish today. Originally, the store sold to Polish-Americans in the neighborhood and to retailers in outlying districts. When supermarkets wiped out these outlets, the customers began coming directly to the store—some twice a month, others twice a year. Recently, they have begun to bring their non-Polish friends, and Ostrowski has begun to advertise at holiday time in newspapers in Washington and Silver Spring, Md.

[8] His experience points up a common problem for ethnic busi-

Illustration   137

ness: an eroding base of local support. As immigrants' incomes rose and their old neighborhoods crumbled, many joined the middle-class exodus to the suburbs. They continued to support the ethnic merchants who satisfied their specific consumer demands, but beyond that they kept few ties to the community. Many of their children drifted even farther away. Consequently, the influx of non-ethnic buyers comes in the nick of time.

[9] "We almost died here in the 1950s and 1960s," recalls Anthony Leo Ellison, head of Detroit's 30-member "Greektown" business-men's association. Ths city responded to its cries for help with a $230,000 beautification project in 1976, planting trees and replacing concrete sidewalks with brick to bring back the area's warm, old-time atmosphere. Today, Monroe Street, the areas's main stem, is one of Detroit's liveliest streets, with lines forming nightly in front of the numerous Greek restaurants and coffee shops. Ellison's 67-year-old market, boutique, and gift shop, founded by his grandfather, has tripled in value since 1969 to $1.5 million.

[10] A $4.8 million expansion project for Greektown promises even better things to come. New craft shops, artists' studios, restaurants, and entertainment facilities will be housed in a stroll-through complex of renovated buildings that were formerly part of a tannery. "I fear commercialization," says Ellison. "But it'll work as long as they keep it ethnic."

[11] Retaining the ethnic flavor that makes their goods different has been a real struggle for many merchants. The most successful, such as Gus Sarno of South Philadelphia, have refused to compromise the quality of their products to keep pace with expenses. In Sarno's 75-year-old Isgro Pastries (where the customers were once 80% Italian and are now 70% non-Italian), the use of a specially prepared cream is a house rule despite the trouble and expense of cooking natural ingredients in a double boiler. Sarno stopped advertising when the Italian-language newspaper that carried his ads went out of business, but the bakery has become well enough known to draw frequent business offers. "A lot of people want to go wholesale with us, but it would be impossible to maintain the quality," Sarno says. "We're proud of what we do."

[12] This insistence on the genuine has captured nonethnic allegiance for many ethnic businesses. Says one longtime observer of the Italian business scene in Chicago: "They've seen a renaissance because they toughed it out."

[13] Typically, they toughed it out with little outside help. Funds for starting ethnic businesses or expanding them traditionally come from friends and relatives or from the ethnic group's credit unions or savings and loan associations. Edward S. Dulcan of the national ethnic center, who directs commercial projects in multi-ethnic cities, says, "It is gratifying to see the private resources that are available."

[14] Some of the credit unions and savings and loan associations

have begun accepting members outside their ethnic groups, but others, including a strong national network of Ukrainian credit unions, remain fiercely ethnic. Even today the manager of Chicago's National Bank of Greece, George F. Kostis, spends 60% of each day speaking Greek with customers.

[15] Unlike black and Spanish-speaking groups, European ethnics for the most part still shun mainstream bankers and government agency funding. While the Small Business Administration's minority program has been boosted to $3 billion this year—blacks alone received 2,262 contracts worth $554 million in 1978—talk of promoting participation by other ethnics has died unheeded. "There isn't any organization of ethnics fighting for minority status" or lobbying for special consideration from the government, says Michael Novak, a writer who specializes in ethnic affairs.

[16] Many ethnics are not even aware that the SBA exists, says Aloysius Mazewski, president of the 300,000-member Polish National Alliance in Chicago. Requests for help, such as the Greektown plea to the city of Detroit, are a new phenomenon, usually tied to a citywide push for urban renewal.

[17] Prosperity is clearly the immediate prospect for ethnic businesses, but whether they will be able to continue functioning in traditional family style is in doubt. Some studies note that fourth-generation ethnics often opt for college degrees and white-collar jobs. On the other hand, newly arrived cousins and nephews tend to follow the old ethnic patterns. They are often more than willing to wait on tables until the time comes to take over the restaurant.

VOCABULARY

Look up the following words in your dictionary. Use the system developed in the dictionary section in the back of the text. Be sure to write the part of speech, the pronunciation, and the meaning(s) of each word.

eth•nic (ĕth'nĭk) *adj.* Also eth•ni•cal (-nĭ-kəl). 1. Of or pertaining to a social group within a cultural and social system that claims or is accorded special status on the basis of complex, often variable traits including religious, linguistic, ancestral, or physical characteristics. 2. Broadly, characteristic of a religious, racial, national, or cultural group. 3. Pertaining to a people not Christian or Jewish; heathen; pagan: *"These are ancient ethnic revels, / Of a faith long since forsaken"* (Longfellow). —*n. Informal.* A member of a particular ethnic group. [Late Latin *ethnicus,* heathen, foreign, from Greek *ethnikos,* of a national group, foreign, from *ethnos,* people, nation. See seu-² in Appendix.*] —eth'ni•cal•ly *adv.*

Definition ©1981 Houghton Mifflin Company. Reprinted by permission from *The American Heritage Dictionary of the English Language, New College Edition.*

Illustration   139

unsophisticated

affirmation

pluralistic

exotica

mainstream

morale

binding

revival

lumps

data

eroding

crumbled

influx

stroll

renovated

tannery

genuine

allegiance

renaissance

gratifying

fiercely

shun

boosted

phenomenon

STUDY QUESTIONS

Finding the Matter

1. What did the "black awareness" movement have to do with the buildup of ethnic businesses in the 1960s?

2. How have ethnic festivals created interest in "declining urban centers"?

3. Why are ethnic businessmen continuing to survive after the immigrants who buy from them move away?

4. How did the city of Detroit help its Greek businessmen to survive?

Exploring the Manner

1. How do the examples of the Polish, Greek, and Italian businesses add interest to the article?

2. What is the special effect of the slang* expression describing the Italian businesses in Chicago, "They've seen a renaissance because they *toughed it out*"? How does the choice of words help to describe the speaker?

3. What is the reason for including such factual details as this one: In Gus Sarno's 75-year-old pastry shop, the customers "were once 80% Italian and are now 70% non-Italian"? What other factual details can you find?

SYNONYMS

From the column at the right, select the best synonym for the italicized word in each sentence. Rewrite each sentence using the appropriate synonym.

1. The Commerce Department *groups* black, Hispanic, and Asian business into one category.

2. Ethnic businessmen were more *naive* than their counterparts in the mainstream of U.S. enterprise.

3. Old neighborhoods *disintegrated* as their successful

A. gratified

B. shun

C. lumps

D. unsophisticated

E. stroll

F. renovated

G. genuine

H. crumbled

Illustration 141

inhabitants moved to the suburbs.

4. In the new expansion projects, people will be able to *walk* through areas with various entertainment facilities.

5. These projects will have many buildings that have been *redone* to hold craft shops, artists' studios, and restaurants.

6. People want ethnic foods to be *real*—the true products of the countries from which they had come.

7. Private resources helped in the renovation and people were *pleased* by their cooperation.

8. European ethnics usually *avoid* mainstream bankers and government agency funding.

PARAPHRASE

Read this paragraph twice; then close your book. Using your own words, rewrite the paragraph as clearly and completely as you can.

Prosperity is clearly the immediate prospect for ethnic businesses, but whether they will be able to continue functioning in traditional family style is in doubt. Some studies note that fourth-generation ethnics often opt for college degrees and white-collar jobs. On the other hand, newly arrived cousins and nephews tend to follow the old ethnic patterns. They are often more than willing to wait on tables until the time comes to take over the restaurant.

VERB FILL-IN

Fill in each blank with the verb form that is appropriate for each sentence.

Ethnic festivals, _____ ethnic foods, music, dancing,
                        offer

and handicrafts, _____ so appealing to Americans of all
                      prove

backgrounds that city officials _____ using them to promote
                                      begin

interest in declining urban centers. The festivals _____ to
                                                          prove

have a binding effect on the city, and this effect _____ to
                                                          work

the benefit of all residents.

SENTENCE COMPLETION

From the column at the right, select the correct line to complete each of the numbered lines at the left. Write each sentence in its correct form.

1. Ethnic businesses, those counterparts of the mainstream,

2. People express their rediscovered ethnicity

3. Ethnic merchants provide products that

4. Most ethnic businesses are

5. As immigrants' incomes rose and their old neighborhoods crumbled,

6. In Detroit, the city itself responded to cries of help

7. Renovated buildings will house

A. mainstream retailers fail to provide.

B. by providing a beautification project in the shopping area's main street.

C. has been a real struggle for many merchants.

D. are moving into the big time.

E. for ethnic businesses.

F. to accept members outside their ethnic groups.

G. many joined the middle-class exodus to the suburbs.

H. by eating ethnic foods.

Illustration　143

8. Retaining the ethnic flavor that makes their goods different

9. Some of the credit unions and savings and loan associations have begun

10. Prosperity is clearly the immediate prospect

I. craft shops, artists' studios, restaurants, and entertainment facilities.

J. family-run establishments dealing in food.

CLOZE EXERCISE

Fill in each blank with the best word to complete the meaning of the sentence.

Mr. Ostrowski points up _____ common problem for

ethnic _____: an eroding base of _____ support.

As immigrants' incomes _____ and their old neighborhoods

_____, many joined the middle-class _____ to the

suburbs. They _____ to support the ethnic _____

who satisfied their specific _____ demands, but beyond that

_____ kept few ties to _____ community. Many of

their _____ drifted even further away. _____, the

influx of nonethnic _____ comes in the nick _____

time.

SENTENCE COMBINING

Combine each pair of sentences into a single grammatical sentence.

1. Ethnic merchants usually catered to their own ethnic groups. Ethnic merchants now cater to the general public.

2. The Census Bureau records a person's spoken language and the birthplace of his or her parents.
   The Bureau does not inquire into a person's self-identification.

3. Immigrants went to live in ethnic neighborhoods.
   When their incomes rose they moved to the suburbs.

4. Gus Sarno stopped advertising in the Italian-language newspaper.
   The Italian newspaper went out of business.

5. The ethnic credit unions traditionally granted funds only to their own community.
   They now do business with others from outside their own groups.

6. European ethnics shun mainstream bankers.
   Black and Spanish-speaking groups use mainstream bankers.

PUNCTUATION

Read the following paragraph. Write in the capital letters and place commas, periods, colons, semicolons, dashes, and quotation marks where needed.

the new ethnicity that produced this situation is more than a fad

says monsignor geno baroni the roman catholic priest who founded

the national center for urban ethnic affairs in washington in 1971

deep down there is a need for traditions and values says baroni who

is currently assistant secretary of the housing and urban development

dept baroni believes that the ethnic revival represents a reaction by

people who for generations felt pressure to discard their pasts and be

american america he says never wanted to deal with ethnicity before

now he adds it must although it lacks real information for the task

Illustration 145

WORD-FORM CHART

Use your dictionary to complete the following table. Follow the example shown with item 1, *affirmation*. If there is no commonly used form for a particular part of speech, write the symbol XXX.

Noun	Verb	Adjective	Adverb
1. affirmation	affirm	affirmable	affirmably
2. caterer			
3. presence			
4.	revive		
5. datum			
6.	erode		
7. renaissance			
8.		phenomenal	
9.	boost		
10.		fierce	

WORD-FORM EXERCISE

Using your completed Word-Form Chart, select the correct form to fit into each sentence. Use the appropriate tense of the verb, the singular or plural form of the noun, and the passive voice where necessary.

Follow the sequence of numbers from the Word-Form Chart to select the correct form.

1. What has come about is an _____ that the United States

   is a pluralistic society.

2. The ethnic merchant usually _____ to an urban neigh-

   borhood of first- or second-generation fellow countrymen.

3. This businessman now acts in the mainstream of the society, that formerly ignored his _____.

4. The ethnic _____ represents a reaction by people who felt pressure to discard their pasts.

5. The national ethnic center is just beginning to gather ethnic business _____ in order to help these merchants.

6. Because many immigrants moved from their old neighborhoods, there was an _____ base of local support.

7. These businesses have become successful and have seen a _____ because they stayed in the neighborhoods and made every effort to succeed.

8. Urban businesses that request help from the city are a new _____ which is usually tied to urban renewal.

9. The Small Business Administration's minority program has been _____ this year in order to provide blacks with greater opportunities.

10. Most ethnic credit unions remain _____ ethnic.

QUESTIONS FOR DISCUSSION

1. Compare the idea of America as a melting pot with the newer concept of America as a pluralistic society. Discuss the good and bad points of each.

2. Would you prefer to work in a family-owned ethnic business or to attend college and choose your own career? Give reasons for your answer.

Illustration 147

TOPICS FOR WRITING

1. Monsignor Geno Barone, founder of the National Center for Urban Ethnic Affairs, believes that there is an ethnic revival because "there is a need for traditions and values." Write a theme including three examples of the traditions or values that you brought from your native country and wish to maintain in America.

2. Choose an ethnic store in your neighborhood and write a composition giving examples of the particular products that are sold there that are not sold in nonethnic stores.

3. If you work for an ethnic business or have a relative or close friend who owns one, write a theme discussing how he got started, how and with whom he runs it, and who his customers are. Give examples of reasons for his success.

Illustration   149

LOFTING A KITE AGAINST THE WIND

Francis X. Clines

[1] Quickly, before the commercial resurgence of kite-flying reaches ancient levels of popularity where emperors had to ban kites at crop harvesting time, let us celebrate this simple means by which you and I can take a joyous hand in aerodynamics.

[2] The Americanization of the kite is fast arriving with sales of 150 million kites a year in a price range rising from 50 cents for the reliable old two-stick diamond kite to thousands of dollars for customized kits. All are available through new kite specialty stores that have opened in recent years across the country.

[3] Fortunately, even though sales charts are booming, there seems little danger of this industry's burgeoning into sidelines of kite warmup suits and shoes, or of doctors writing books on how to avoid heart attack and impotence through kite-flying.

[4] For history reveals no way to cheapen the naive charm of flying a kite—an inventive act of mankind that goes back at least 2,500 years to a time when a Chinese warlord wrote of hoisting a soldier high into the sky on a giant kite to spy down on an embattled castle. This was a time when Chinese farmers tethered night kites equipped with "hummer" strings whose sound warnings would increase with crop-threatening winds. Equally clever Pacific islanders used kites made of fronds to drop their fishing lines far offshore for the richer catches.

[5] Fascination with the kite in the western world had peaked at the beginning of this century, just as the kite helped give birth to the airplane that then overtook it in the public mind. The Wright brothers led up to their historic flight by first testing kite gliders of the sort developed 50 years earlier by Sir George Cayley, aeronautics pioneer. The kite was, in effect, the prototype of the first airplane wing.

[6] At that time, no less a revered scientist than Alexander Graham Bell was experimenting feverishly and grandiosely with kites as the key to manned flight. Even by today's standards, his Cygnet kite would be a wonder in the skies again if its body of 3,393 tetrahedral cells could be reconstructed. This kite, which resembled a huge honeycomb or a free floating football stadium light stanchion, was launched in 1907. Towed by a steamship for initial lift, it could carry a man 17 stories up into the air. It was the Hughes Spruce Goose of its day.

[7] The "man-lifting" capabilities of kites had long since been tried in the Orient. (Marco Polo did not bring back kites but told of Oriental sea captains having men hoisted up on kites in a rough-and-tumble test of sailing omens.)

[8] In the West, the first record of such a phenomenon is attributed to George Pocock, a marvelously eccentric British schoolteacher of about 150 years ago who lived for kite-flying. He designed a horse-less carriage pulled by kites, then went on to adapt an armchair to be carried up by a kite. Finally, in 1825, he sent his daughter, Martha, up in the chair, claiming a height of 300 feet. "On descending, she expressed herself much pleased at the easy motion of the kite," Pocock wrote, "and the delightful prospect she had enjoyed."

[9] Modern loners who go up on hang-gliders now experience this "delightful prospect," and while some purists insist that without a ground tether there can be no true kite, other kite experts say this is a mere technicality, that these single-frame craft obviously owe everything to kite evolution.

[10] The science of kite design is hardly stuck in the past, inci-dentally. The modern science of meteorology got a big lift from the invention of the box kite at the turn of this century by Lawrence Hargrave, a meticulous Australian who worked on the problems of

Illustration 151

manned flight. (150 years before that, two Scotsmen, Alexander Wilson and Thomas Melvill, sent a train of six kites up with thermometers to take the first high-altitude temperature readings.)

[11] And the ingenious design departure of a flexible kite was patented in 1951 by Francis Rogallo, an aeronautical engineer with NASA, whose ideas are employed now by hang-glider enthusiasts and by aircraft engineers searching for new, simpler craft. With the help of his wife, Gertrude, he experimented with this non-rigid kite at home, improvising a wind tunnel from a doorway and an electric fan.

[12] Rogallo, of course, is in that tradition of curiosity and fun exemplified best by Ben Franklin. As a boy, years before he teased lightning from the sky in his historic experiment, Franklin experienced the pulling power of a kite across a pond and theorized a trip from Dover to Calais. (An adventurous American, S. F. Cody, did exactly that in 1903, using a box kite for sailing power.)

[13] For Franklin, curiosity about the nature of lightning grew out of his fascination with the scientific device then making the rounds, known as the Leyden jar. It reacted with a spark and crackle when presented with static electricity. He sent a kite up as a storm arrived, a kite with a foot-long wire extending from it, trying to get some lightning down the silk kite string to see whether it would set off the Leyden jar. He succeeded, and thus demonstrated the similarity of lightning and electricity, and went on to invent the lightning rod. Imitators soon popped up everywhere, some of them electrocuting dogs and cats in demonstrations, other electrocuting themselves when they neglected to ground the lines.

[14] That's about as sadistic as the history of the kite ever became, although you'll hear some claims that medieval kites were rigged to dump fireballs on siege targets. Right before World War I a military kite was perfected that could haul an observer up to 3,500 feet into the air, along with the firearm, telephone, and spyglass, but the airplane made that obsolete before it was used widely.

[15] So the kite is one of the few marvelous inventions to be spared infamy, a fact which should only add to its simple pleasure as it rises in popularity once again in forms that currently range from large tetrahedral wedges to postage-stamp-size models bobbing like sylphs on silken thread. You can find at least two excellent books on the subject: *Kites, An Historical Survey,* by Clive Hart, an Australian scholar with an interesting theory on how kites may have evolved from pennants and windsocks; and *The Complete Book of Kites and Kite Flying,* by Will Yolen, a journalist who is a pioneer in the resurgence of the kite.

[16] It is possible to get didactic about kites: Where would radio be if Marconi had not hoisted his antenna on a kite? Where would tourism be if the first bridge across Niagara gorge had not begun with a string (then a rope and cable) carried across by a kite?

[17] But it seems just as important to observe that the kite's ultimate value for humans is blessedly ambivalent, skittering upward along a fine line between pure science and pure fun and letting you relax and wonder about life, feeling the wind in your hand.

VOCABULARY

Look up the following words in your dictionary. Use the system developed in the dictionary section in the back of the text. Be sure to write the part of speech, the pronunciation, and the meaning(s) of each word.

aer·o·dy·nam·ics (âr'ō-dī-năm'ĭks) *n.* Plural in form, used with a singular verb. The dynamics of gases, especially of atmospheric interactions with moving objects. **—aer'o·dy·nam'ic** *adj.*

Definition ©1981 Houghton Mifflin Company. Reprinted by permission from *The American Heritage Dictionary of the English Language, New College Edition.*

resurgence

ban

booming

burgeoning

impotence

naive

hoisting

embattled

tethered

fronds

peaked

prototype

grandiosely

tetrahedral

Illustration   153

stanchion

phenomenon

meteorology

meticulous

ingenious

sadistic

obsolete

infamy

sylphs

pennants

windsocks

didactic

ambivalent

skittering

STUDY QUESTIONS

Finding the Matter

1. Clines mentions the several uses of kites through the centuries. These include helping men to spy as well as dropping fishing lines far off shore. What other examples can you find in the essay?

2. Why was the kite so important to the Wright brothers?

3. Benjamin Franklin is the most famous American kite flyer. What was the practical application of his experiment?

Exploring the Manner

1. The author says that his purpose in this essay is to "celebrate the simple means by which you and I can take a joyous hand in aerodynamics." What does his use of the words *celebrate* and *joyous hand* tell about his attitude* toward kites?

2. Would the essay have been improved if the author had arranged the examples in chronological order*? Explain your answer.

3. Clines describes in detail the incident in which George Pocock's daughter rose 300 feet in an armchair lifted by a kite. How is this used as a transition* to the following paragraph on hang gliders?

SYNONYMS

From the column at the right, select the best synonym for the italicized word in each sentence. Rewrite each sentence using the appropriate synonym.

1. Among young people today, there is a new *resurgence* in kite flying.

2. There is no law that *bans* kite flying in any park or field.

3. Kite sales are *booming* all over the country.

4. A Chinese warlord wrote of *hoisting* a soldier high into the sky.

5. The kite was a *prototype* of the first airplane wing.

6. Pacific islanders used kites made of *fronds* to drop their fishing lines far offshore.

7. There is a certain *naive* charm in flying a kite.

8. Some would-be investors were unwittingly *sadistic* in using animals for their experiments.

9. Some people think that kites originally evolved from *pennants* used in ancient times.

A. flourishing
B. darting
C. example
D. leaves
E. prohibits
F. innocent
G. raising
H. rise
I. cruel
J. flags

Illustration   155

10. It is great fun to watch a
    kite *skittering* upward in
    the wind.

PARAPHRASE

Read this paragraph twice; then close your book. Using
your own words, rewrite the paragraph as clearly and completely as you can.

   For Franklin, curiosity about the nature of lightning grew
out of his fascination with the scientific device then making
the rounds, known as the Leyden jar. It reacted with a spark
and crackle when presented with static electricity. He sent a
kite up as a storm arrived, a kite with a foot-long wire extending from it, trying to get some lightning down the silk
kite string to see whether it would set off the Leyden jar. He
succeeded, and thus demonstrated the similarity of lightning
and electricity, and went on to invent the lightning rod.
Imitators soon popped up everywhere, some of them electrocuting dogs and cats in demonstrations, others electrocuting themselves when they neglected to ground the lines.

VERB FILL-IN

Fill in each blank with the verb form that is appropriate for
each sentence.

The science of kite design is hardly _____ in the past.
                                          stick

The modern science of meteorology _____ a big lift from
                                        get

the invention of the box kite at the turn of this century by Lawrence

Hargrave, a meticulous Australian who _____ on the prob-
                                          work

lems of manned flight. One hundred and fifty years before that, two

Scotsmen _____ a train of six kites up with thermometers
            send

_____ the first high altitude temperature readings.
    take

And the ingenious design departure of a flexible kite

_____ in 1951 by a NASA engineer, whose ideas
    patent

_____ now by hang-glider enthusiasts and by aircraft engi-
    employ

neers _____ for new, simpler craft. He _____
        search   experiment

with this nonrigid kite, _____ a wind tunnel from a door-
                            improvise

way and an electric fan.

SENTENCE COMPLETION

From the column at the right, select the correct line to complete each of the numbered lines at the left. Write each sentence in its correct form.

1. All kinds of kites are available through new specialty
   stores

2. Sales are booming, but it
   seems unlikely that this
   industry

3. Fascination with the kite
   in the western world had
   peaked at

4. The Wright brothers led up
   to their historic flight by

A. the beginning of this century.

B. electrocuting cats and dogs
   in their demonstrations.

C. first testing kite gliders of
   the sort developed fifty
   years earlier.

D. that have opened in recent
   years across the country.

E. with a string carried across
   by a kite.

Illustration 157

5. Alexander Graham Bell experimented feverishly and grandiosely with kites as

6. Bell's kite resembled a huge honeycomb or a

7. The man-lifting capabilities of kites had long since been tried

8. The modern science of meteorology got a big lift

9. Imitators of Ben Franklin soon popped up everywhere, some of them

10. We do not know where radio would be if Marconi

11. The first bridge across the Niagara gorge began

12. The kite's ultimate value for humans is blessedly ambivalent, skittering upward along a fine line

F. will burgeon into sidelines of kite warm-up suits and shoes.

G. between pure science and pure fun.

H. in the Orient.

I. the key to manned flight.

J. had not hoisted his antenna on a kite.

K. from the invention of the box kite.

L. free-floating football stadium light stanchion.

CLOZE EXERCISE

Fill in each blank with the best word to complete the meaning of the sentence.

That's about as sadistic as the _____ of the kite ever

became, although _____ hear some claims that medieval

kites _____ rigged to dump fireballs on siege _____.

Right before World War I a _____ kite was perfected that

could haul _____ observer up to 3,500 feet into

_____ air, along with the firearm, telephone, _____

spyglass, but the airplane made that _____ before it was

widely used.

So _____ kite is one of the few _____ inventions to be spared infamy, a _____ which should only add

to its _____ pleasure as it rises in popularity _____

again in forms that currently range _____ large tetrahedral

wedges to postage-stamp-size models _____ like sylphs on

silken thread.

SENTENCE COMBINING

Combine each pair of sentences into a single grammatical
sentence.

1. The Chinese used kites for thousands of years.
   They used the kites on their farms.

2. The Pacific islanders used kites made of fronds.
   The fronds were attached to fishing lines.

3. The Wright brothers first used kite gliders.
   This use became the prototype of the first airplane wing.

4. Alexander Graham Bell used a tetrahedral kite.
   This kite resembled a huge honeycomb.

5. The science of kite design was not completed in the past.
   The modern science of meteorology used the kite as late as the
   turn of this century.

6. An aeronautical engineer patented a design for a flexible kite.
   The flexible kite is now used by hang-glider enthusiasts.

PUNCTUATION

Read the following paragraph. Write in the capital letters
and place commas, periods, colons, semicolons, dashes, and
quotation marks where needed.

Illustration 159

for history reveals no way to cheapen the naive charm of flying

a kite an inventive act of mankind that goes back at least 2500 years

to a time when a chinese warlord wrote of hoisting a soldier high

into the sky on a giant kite to spy down on an embattled castle this

was a time when chinese farmers tethered night kites equipped with

hummer strings whose sound warnings would increase with crop

threatening winds equally clever pacific islanders used kites made of

fronds to drop their fishing lines far offshore for the richer catches

WORD-FORM CHART

Use your dictionary to complete the following table. Follow the example shown with item 1, *specialty*. If there is no commonly used form for a particular part of speech, write the symbol XXX.

Noun	Verb	Adjective	Adverb
1. specialty	specialize	special	specially
2. writer			
3.		windy	
4. history			
5. fever			
6.		capable	
7.	improvise		
8.	pull		
9. demonstration			
10.		perfect	

WORD-FORM EXERCISE

Using your completed Word-Form Chart, select the correct
form to fit into each sentence. Use the appropriate tense of
the verb, the singular or plural form of the noun, and the
passive voice where necessary.
Follow the sequence of numbers from the Word-Form Chart
to select the correct form.

1. Custom-built kites are available in new kite _____

    stores.

2. A Chinese warlord _____ of hoisting a soldier into

    the sky on a giant kite.

3. The "hummer" strings were used to warn of crop threatening

    _____.

4. Kite gliders were used by the Wright brothers in testing for their

    _____ flight.

5. Bell was experimenting _____ with kites as the key to

    manned flight.

6. The man-lifting _____ of kites had been tried in the

    Orient.

7. Rogallo experimented with the nonrigid kite, _____

    a wind tunnel from a doorway and an electric fan.

8. Franklin experienced the _____ power of a kite across

    a pond.

9. Franklin succeeded in his experiment and thus _____

    the similarity of lightning and electricity.

10. Right before World War I a military kite _____ that

    could haul an observer 3,500 feet into the air.

Illustration   *161*

QUESTIONS FOR DISCUSSION

1. See if you can find any information about Alexander Graham Bell's Cygnet Kite and Howard Hughes's Spruce Goose plane. Look in newspaper indexes, biographies, and encyclopedias.

2. Clines says that kite flying combines "pure science and pure fun." Can you think of any other diversions that combine these two elements?

3. While Clines is pleased about "the Americanization of the kite," he is also concerned about its commercial aspect. What sports have become "industries" as they became popular? What happened to them as a result of their popularity?

TOPICS FOR WRITING

1. Choose a diversion, sport, or game that you are familiar with and, by using examples as Clines does, show how it has a practical application to life. For example, what does it teach about sportsmanship, competition, dedication, team spirit, self-confidence?

2. Clines suggests that the popularization of a sport brings commercialism. Choose a sport, diversion, or game and illustrate how it has become "big business."

3. Clines says that "the kite is one of the few marvelous inventions to be spared infamy." Write a theme discussing three inventions that developed bad reputations because of the negative ways in which they were used (examples include dynamite and pesticides).

4

Comparison and Contrast

The Form

When Shakespeare wrote, "Shall I compare thee to a summer's day?" he was indicating a comparison between the virtues of his patron and those of a beautiful day in summer. The patron was clearly judged the superior of the two, which showed Shakespeare's good sense. We still use comparisons—both in our daily lives and in our writing. We compare food brands, car models, and clothing styles. Almost every time that we make a choice, we base our selection on comparison. Strictly speaking, the word *compare* means to find both similarities and differences, but, more often, we use the word *comparison* to examine similarities and *contrast* to look at differences.

When writing a comparison, the author usually determines that the items being compared belong to the same class: two foods, two sports, two cities, two relatives. Next, he must decide if he wants simply to inform the reader of the similarities and differences or if he wants to argue the superiority of one item over the other. His thesis will reflect this decision. After he selects the points of comparison, the final decision is choosing the method of presenting the material. He can discuss all the characteristics of A and then go on to B, or he can alternate—speaking of one characteristic as it applies first to A and then to B. The alternating method is preferable when several points are being compared, so that the reader can easily follow the areas of comparison. However, both methods can be used in an essay.

Here is an excerpt from an essay comparing and contrasting two musical giants: Sir Arthur Sullivan and Leonard Bernstein. Sullivan was a nineteenth-century English composer and was half of the famous team of Gilbert and Sullivan, renowned for their numerous operettas such as *Pirates of Penzance* and *H.M.S. Pinafore*. Leonard Bernstein is well known as a conductor, author, lecturer, and composer of the music for *West Side Story* and *Candide*.

> Both Bernstein and Sullivan made their marks on the musical world as very young men who possessed obvious talents for composing and conducting. Moreover, the early career of each was imbued with chauvinistic overtones: Sullivan was thought of as the first great British composer since Handel (who was not British) or Purcell; Bernstein became the first American-born and trained musician to be appointed as music director of a major American symphony orchestra. Both men were expected to produce "serious" works such as symphonies, chamber pieces and religious music. Both men did. But when it comes to music-drama, we find almost no operas among their compositions; what we find instead are operettas and musical comedies. In fact, the most striking similarity between the two men is that, in spite of the large quantities of "serious" music each wrote, the greater part of their fame rests, and probably always will rest, on works written for the popular musical theatre.

The Student Reader

When you read a comparison and contrast, notice whether the author is simply comparing A and B or whether he is trying to prove that A is better than B. For example, if an author is planning to compare two cities, he might include the following categories:

Area
Population
Climate
Transportation
Industry
Cultural attractions

If the paper is going to be a short one and the author is not stating a preference for one city over the other, he might write entirely about city 1 and then about city 2. However, if his essay will be long or if he is trying to show his preference for one city, he might arrange the paper category by category, like this:

    I. Area
        A. City 1
        B. City 2
    II. Population
        A. City 1
        B. City 2

Placing the preferred city second gives it emphasis.

It is essential to provide transitions (connecting links) between the categories, especially if the author is using the alternating method. After he compares the areas of the two cities, for example, he might move to the next category by saying something like this: "In addition to the area, the population defines (the city of) _____." Other transitional expressions include *similarly* and *in the same way* (to show similarities) and *in contrast* and *on the other hand* (to show differences).

As you read, see if the author is clear about whether he is comparing (finding similarities) or contrasting (finding differences). At all times, he should make his categories clear, see that his method of presentation is well organized, and connect the sections of the essay smoothly.

The Professional Writer

A well-constructed comparison and contrast is offered by Bruce Catton in his essay "Grant and Lee." Here the author explores the differences and similarities between these two great Civil War generals. First, he speaks only of Robert E. Lee: his aristocratic background and charismatic personality. Then he turns to Ulysses S. Grant, discussing his democratic background and self-reliant personality. When Catton comes to their allegiances, he goes back to Lee, who defended his own region, and contrasts him with Grant, who defended the expanding nation as a whole.

Here Catton ends his discussion of the differences between the men. As he shifts the discussion to their similarities, Catton also changes his method. Now he presents his comparison point by point. He finds Grant and Lee similar as fighters, as men of daring and resourcefulness, and, finally, as generals capable of moving from war to peace.

Catton concludes by stating that similarities as well as differences can exist in men as diverse as Grant and Lee. In sum, the essay is a model of careful design as the author gracefully moves his discussion from one hero to the other.

GRANT AND LEE: A STUDY IN CONTRASTS

Bruce Catton

[1]   When Ulysses S. Grant and Robert E. Lee met in the parlor of a modest house at Appomattox Court House, Virginia, on April 9, 1865, to work out the terms for the surrender of Lee's Army of Northern Virginia, a great chapter in American life came to a close, and a great new chapter began.

[2]   These men were bringing the Civil War to its virtual finish. To be sure, other armies had yet to surrender, and for a few days the fugitive Confederate government would struggle desperately and vainly, trying to find some way to go on living now that its chief support was gone. But in effect it was all over when Grant and Lee signed the papers. And the little room where they wrote out the terms was the scene of one of the poignant, dramatic contrasts in American history.

[3]   They were two strong men, these oddly different generals, and they represented the strengths of two conflicting currents that, through them, had come into final collision.

[4]   Back of Robert E. Lee was the notion that the old aristocratic concept might somehow survive and be dominant in American life.

[5]   Lee was tidewater Virginia, and in his background were family,

(Courtesy of U.S. National Park Service.)

culture, and tradition . . . the age of chivalry transplanted to a New World which was making its own legends and its own myths. He embodied a way of life that had come down through the age of knighthood and the English country squire. America was a land that was beginning all over again, dedicated to nothing much more complicated than the rather hazy belief that all men had equal rights and should have an equal chance in the world. In such a land Lee stood for the feeling that it was somehow of advantage to human society to have a pronounced inequality in the social structure. There should be a leisure class, backed by ownership of land; in turn, society itself should be keyed to the land as the chief source of wealth and influence. It would bring forth (according to this ideal) a class of men with a strong sense of obligation to the community; men who lived not to gain advantage for themselves, but to meet the solemn obligations which had been laid on them by the very fact that they were privileged. From them the country would get its leadership; to them it could look for the higher values—of thought, of conduct, of personal deportment—to give it strength and virtue.

[6] Lee embodied the noblest elements of this aristocratic ideal. Through him, the landed nobility justified itself. For four years, the Southern states had fought a desperate war to uphold the ideals for which Lee stood. In the end, it almost seemed as if the Confederacy fought for Lee; as if he himself was the Confederacy . . . the best thing that the way of life for which the Confederacy stood could ever have to offer. He had passed into legend before Appomattox. Thousands of tired, underfed, poorly clothed Confederate soldiers, long since past the simple enthusiasm of the early days of the struggle, somehow considered Lee the symbol of everything for which they had been willing to die. But they could not quite put this feeling into words. If the Lost Cause, sanctified by so much heroism and so many deaths, had a living justification, its justification was General Lee.

[7] Grant, the son of a tanner on the Western frontier, was everything Lee was not. He had come up the hard way and embodied nothing in particular except the eternal toughness and sinewy fiber of the men who grew up beyond the mountains. He was one of a body of men who owed reverence and obeisance to no one, who were self-reliant to a fault, who cared hardly anything for the past but who had a sharp eye for the future.

[8] These frontier men were the precise opposites of the tidewater aristocrats. Back of them, in the great surge that had taken people over the Alleghenies and into the opening Western country, there was a deep, implicit dissatisfaction with a past that had settled into grooves. They stood for democracy, not from any reasoned conclusion about the proper ordering of human society, but simply because they had grown up in the middle of democracy and knew how it worked. Their society might have privileges, but they would be

privileges each man had won for himself. Forms and patterns meant nothing. No man was born to anything, except perhaps to a chance to show how far he could rise. Life was competition.

[9] Yet along with this feeling had come a deep sense of belonging to a national community. The Westerner who developed a farm, opened a shop, or set up in business as a trader, could hope to prosper only as his own community prospered—and his community ran from the Atlantic to the Pacific and from Canada down to Mexico. If the land was settled, with towns and highways and accessible markets, he could better himself. He saw his fate in terms of the nation's own destiny. As its horizons expanded, so did his. He had, in other words, an acute dollars-and-cents stake in the continued growth and development of his country.

[10] And that, perhaps, is where the contrast between Grant and Lee becomes most striking. The Virginia aristocrat, inevitably, saw himself in relation to his own region. He lived in a static society which could endure almost anything except change. Instinctively, his first loyalty would go to the locality in which that society existed. He would fight to the limit of endurance to defend it, because in defending it he was defending everything that gave his own life its deepest meaning.

[11] The Westerner, on the other hand, would fight with an equal tenacity for the broader concept of society. He fought so because everything he lived by was tied to growth, expansion, and a constantly widening horizon. What he lived by would survive or fall with the nation itself. He could not possibly stand by unmoved in the face of an attempt to destroy the Union. He would combat it with everything he had, because he could only see it as an effort to cut the ground out from under his feet.

[12] So Grant and Lee were in complete contrast, representing two diametrically opposed elements in American life. Grant was the modern man emerging; beyond him, ready to come on the stage, was the great age of steel and machinery, of crowded cities and a restless burgeoning vitality. Lee might have ridden down from the old age of chivalry, lance in hand, silken banner fluttering over his head. Each man was the perfect champion of his cause, drawing both his strengths and his weaknesses from the people he led.

[13] Yet it was not all contrast, after all. Different as they were—in background, in personality, in underlying aspiration—these two great soldiers had much in common. Under everything else, they were marvelous fighters. Furthermore, their fighting qualities were really very much alike.

[14] Each man had, to begin with, the great virtue of utter tenacity and fidelity. Grant fought his way down the Mississippi Valley in spite of acute personal discouragement and profound military handicaps. Lee hung on in the trenches at Petersburg after hope itself had died. In each man there was an indomitable quality . . .

the born fighter's refusal to give up as long as he can still remain on his feet and lift his two fists.

[15] Daring and resourcefulness they had, too; the ability to think faster and move faster than the enemy. These were the qualities which gave Lee the dazzling campaigns of Second Manassas and Chancellorsville and won Vicksburg for Grant.

[16] Lastly, and perhaps greatest of all, there was the ability, at the end, to turn quickly from war to peace once the fighting was over. Out of the way these two men behaved at Appomattox came the possibility of a peace of reconciliation. It was a possibility not wholly realized, in the years to come, but which did, in the end, help the two sections to become one nation again . . . after a war whose bitterness might have seemed to make such a reunion wholly impossible. No part of either man's life became him more than the part he played in this brief meeting in the McLean house at Appomattox. Their behavior there put all succeeding generations of Americans in their debt. Two great Americans, Grant and Lee—very different, yet under everything very much alike. Their encounter at Appomattox was one of the great moments of American history.

VOCABULARY

Look up the following words in your dictionary. Use the system developed in the dictionary section in the back of the text. Be sure to write the part of speech, the pronunciation, and the meaning(s) of each word.

fu·gi·tive (fyōō′jə-tĭv) *adj.* **1.** Running or having run away; fleeing, as from justice, the law, or the like. **2. a.** Passing quickly; fleeting: *fugitive hours.* **b.** Difficult to comprehend or retain; elusive. **c.** Given to change or disappearance; perishable. **3.** Tending to wander; vagabond. **4.** Having to do with topics of temporary interest; ephemeral. —See Synonyms at **transient.** —*n.* **1.** One who flees; a runaway; refugee. **2.** Anything fleeting or ephemeral. [Middle English *fugitif,* from Old French, from Latin *fugitivus,* from adjective, "fleeing," from *fugitus,* past participle of *fugere,* to flee. See **bheug-**[1] in Appendix.*] —**fu′gi·tive·ly** *adv.* —**fu′gi·tive·ness** *n.*

Definition ©1981 Houghton Mifflin Company. Reprinted by permission from *The American Heritage Dictionary of the English Language, New College Edition.*

poignant

aristocratic

tidewater

chivalry

legends

myths

embodied

hazy

obligation

solemn

deportment

sanctified

heroism

tanner

sinewy

reverence

obeisance

surge

implicit

grooves

acute

static

tenacity

diametrically

burgeoning

lance

aspiration

reconciliation

STUDY QUESTIONS

Finding the Matter

1. Who were Ulysses S. Grant and Robert E. Lee?

2. Why did they meet on April 9, 1865, in Appomattox, Virginia?

3. Explain how the words *aristocrat*, *chivalry*, and *knighthood* refer to Lee's background.

4. How was Grant's background different from Lee's?

5. Why was Lee's philosophy "regional" and Grant's philosophy "national"?

Exploring the Manner

1. Find the thesis*. What does it tell you about Grant and Lee?

2. Does Catton alternate between the two men in his essay, or does he discuss one completely and then the other? Does it matter which man he mentions first?

3. Why isn't paragraph 4, which is only one sentence long, attached to paragraph 5?

4. Find the paragraph in which Catton stops discussing differences and begins finding similarities between the men.

5. Locate and define the six examples* Catton gives of the similar fighting qualities of both men.

SYNONYMS

From the column at the right, select the best synonym for the italicized word in each sentence. Rewrite each sentence using the appropriate synonym.

1. A society keyed to the land as the chief source of wealth and influence would have a class of men with a strong sense of *obligation* to the community.

   A. foggy

   B. debt

   C. gallantry

   D. serious

2. These were men who lived not to gain advantage for themselves but to meet the *solemn* obligations which had been laid on them by their privileged positions in society.

3. America was a land that was beginning all over again, dedicated to nothing much more complicated than the rather *hazy* belief that all men had equal rights and should have an equal chance in the world.

4. Lee personified the age of *chivalry* in the New World.

5. Lee embodied the noblest elements of the *aristocratic* ideal.

6. The Virginian lived in a *static* society which could endure almost anything except change.

7. The Westerner would fight with an equal *tenacity* for the broader concept of society.

8. Different as they were in background, in personality, in underlying *aspirations*, these two great soldiers had much in common.

9. Grant was interested in the great age of steel and machinery, of crowded cities and restless, *burgeoning* vitality.

10. Lee might have ridden down from the old age of chivalry with *lance* in hand and banner flying.

E. genteel

F. perseverance

G. growing

H. unchanging

I. hopes

J. spear

PARAPHRASE

Read this paragraph twice; then close your book. Using
your own words, rewrite the paragraph as clearly and completely as you can.

Lee embodied the noblest elements of an aristocratic ideal.
Through him, the landed nobility justified itself. For four
years, the Southern states had fought a desperate war to uphold the ideals for which Lee stood. In the end, it almost
seemed as if the Confederacy fought for Lee; as if he himself
was the Confederacy . . . the best thing that the way of life
for which the Confederacy stood could ever have to offer.
He had passed into legend before Appomattox. Thousands
of tired, underfed, poorly clothed Confederate soldiers, long
since past the simple enthusiasm of the early days of the
struggle, somehow considered Lee the symbol of everything
for which they had been willing to die. But they could not
quite put this feeling into words. If the Lost Cause, sanctified
by so much heroism and so many deaths, had a living justification, its justification was General Lee.

VERB FILL-IN

Fill in each blank with the verb form that is appropriate for
each sentence.

The westerners _____ to have a deep feeling of be-
                          seem

longing to a national community. The westerner who _____
                                                       develop

a farm, _____ a shop, or set up business as a trader could
            open

hope to prosper only as his community _____. If the land
                                          prosper

_____, with towns and highways and accessible markets, he
    settle

could better himself. He _____ his fate in the terms of the
                            see

nation's own destiny. As its horizons _____, so _____

expand   do

his. He _____, in other words, a great stake in the con-

have

tinued growth and development of his country. His interest in this

growth _____ a primary factor in his life.

be

SENTENCE COMPLETION

From the column at the right, select the correct line to complete each of the numbered lines at the left. Write each sentence in its correct form.

1. When Grant and Lee met at the Appomattox Court house,

2. These men were bringing the Civil War

3. Lee had the notion that the old aristocratic concept might somehow survive

4. Lee stood for the feeling that it was somehow of advantage to human society to

5. In the end, it almost seemed as if the confederacy fought for Lee;

6. Grant had come up the hard way and embodied nothing in particular

7. Grant's men stood for democracy, not for any reasoned conclusion about the proper ordering of human society, but simply

A. and would remain dominant in American life.

B. except the eternal toughness and sinewy fiber of the men who grew up beyond the mountains.

C. a great chapter in American life came to a close, and a great new chapter began.

D. because they had grown up in the middle of democracy and knew how it worked.

E. they could better themselves.

F. to its virtual finish.

G. have a pronounced inequality of the social structure.

H. to growth, expansion, and a constantly widening horizon.

I. was competition.

8. These men thought that life

9. These men also thought that if the land was settled with towns and highways and accessible markets,

10. The aristocrat fought to keep things the way they were; the Westerner fought because everything he lived by was tied

11. Each man was the perfect champion of his cause, drawing both his strengths

12. In each man was the born fighter's refusal to give up as long as

13. Greatest of all was their ability, at the end, to turn quickly from

14. Their encounter at Appomattox

J. as if he himself was the Confederacy.

K. and his weaknesses from the people he led.

L. war to peace once the fighting was over.

M. he could still remain on his feet and lift his two fists.

N. was one of the great moments in American history.

CLOZE EXERCISE

Fill in each blank with the best word to complete the meaning of the sentence.

So Grant and Lee _____ in complete contrast, repre-

senting _____ diametrically opposed elements in

_____ life. Grant was the _____ man emerging;

beyond him, _____ to come on the _____, was the

great age _____ steel and machinery, of _____

cities and a restless _____ vitality. Lee might have

_____ down from the old _____ of chivalry,

lance in _____, silken banner fluttering over _____

head. Each man was _____ perfect champion of his

_____, drawing both his strengths _____ his weak-

nesses from the _____ he led.

Yet, it _____ not all contrast, after _____.

Different as they were— _____ background, in personality,

in _____ aspiration—these two great _____ had

much in common. _____ everything else, they were

_____ fighters. Furthermore, their fighting _____

were really very much _____.

SENTENCE COMBINING

Combine each pair of sentences into a single grammatical
sentence.

1. They were two strong men.
   They represented the strengths of two conflicting currents.
2. Lee was in a new world.
   This new world was making its own legends and its own myths.
3. Lee was an aristocrat.
   Lee embodied the noblest elements of the aristocratic ideal.
4. Lee lived in a static society.
   The society could endure almost anything except change.
5. Grant was the son of a tanner.
   Grant had come up the hard way.
6. The Westerner would fight with tenacity.
   He was interested in the broader concept of society.
7. Out of the behavior of Grant and Lee at Appomattox came the
   possibility of a peace of reconciliation.
   This peace of reconciliation led the way to the two sections
   becoming one nation again.

8. Lee saw himself in relation to his own region.
   Grant had a deep sense of belonging to a national community.

9. The society of the frontier men might have privileges.
   They would be privileges each man had won for himself.

PUNCTUATION

Read the following paragraphs. Write in the capital letters
and place commas, periods, colons, semicolons, dashes, and
quotations marks where needed.

when ulysses s grant and robert e lee met in the parlor of a
modest house at appomattox court house virginia on april 9 1865
to work out the terms for the surrender of lees army of northern
virginia a great chapter in american life came to a close and a great
new chapter began

these men were bringing the civil war to its virtual finish to be
sure other armies had yet to surrender and for a few days the fugitive
confederate government would struggle desperately and vainly trying
to find some way to go on living now that its chief support was gone
but in effect it was all over when grant and lee signed the papers and
the little room where they wrote out the terms was the scene of one
of the poignant dramatic contrasts in american history

WORD-FORM CHART

Use your dictionary to complete the following table. Follow the example shown with item 1, *oddity*. If there is no commonly used form for a particular part of speech, write the symbol XXX.

Noun	Verb	Adjective	Adverb
1. oddity	XXX	odd	oddly
2. embodiment			
3. dedication			
4.		heroic	
5.		obeisant	
6.			competitively
7.	grow		
8.		local	
9.			elementally
10.	reconcile		

WORD-FORM EXERCISE

Using your completed Word-Form Chart, select the correct form to fit into each sentence. Use the appropriate tense of the verb, the singular or plural form of the noun, and the passive voice where necessary.

Follow the sequence of numbers from the Word-Form Chart to select the correct form.

1. These were two strong men, these _____ different generals.

2. Lee _____ a way of life that had come down through the age of knighthood and the English country squire.

3. America _____ to nothing much more complicated than the hazy belief that all men had equal rights.

4. If the Lost Cause, sanctified by so much _____ and so many deaths, had a living justification, its justification was General Lee.

5. Grant was one of a body of men who owed reverence and _____ to no one.

6. The life of the frontier men was full of _____.

7. The frontier man had an acute dollars-and-cents stake in the continued _____ and development of his country.

8. The Virginia aristocrat gave his first loyalty to the _____ in which his society existed.

9. Grant and Lee were in complete contrast, representing two diametrically opposed _____ in American life.

10. As a result of the behavior of these two great generals at Appomattox came the possibility of a peace of _____.

QUESTIONS FOR DISCUSSION

1. Choose three of America's modern "aristocrats" (e.g, Ted Kennedy). Consider the ways in which they are a privileged group and whether or not they show any "obligation to their community" as Catton said Lee did.

2. What are the advantages, disadvantages, and consequences of both the "national" and "regional" concepts of society?

TOPICS FOR WRITING

1. Write a paper comparing two living political figures who represent opposing value systems. Choose specific areas of comparison.

2. Ask a grandparent or other senior member of your family to list ideas (or values) that are important to her but that she feels are missing, ignored, or rejected in modern society. Choose one of these ideas that you feel has *no* value or validity in modern society. Write an essay comparing the attitudes of the two generations.

3. Compare two groups of people in your native country. Choose two groups who differ in religion, education, language, occupation, or political outlook. Compare their life-styles, economic and social status, and feelings toward each other.

JAPAN'S MULTITIER WAGE SYSTEM

Robert C. Wood

[1] Nippon Steel's Kimitsu works is an approved stop for Western journalists and politicians making quick surveys of the Japanese economic miracle. Close to Tokyo, it has sometimes been called the most efficient steel mill in the world. The benefits Nippon Steel employees receive there have become internationally famous.

[2] What is much less talked about is that inside the mill Nippon Steel employees do very little of the hardest work. Nippon Steel employees wear silver helmets, while subcontract workers wear yellow helmets—and yellow helmets outnumber silver ones. Men in silver helmets observe operations, check dials and operate clean, highly automated machinery. Men in yellow helmets climb under hot oxygen furnaces to clean them, bend over short shovels to recondition the tracks where hot metal will flow and work close to ear-splitting noise.

[3] Nippon Steel's public relations manager at the mill, Teruhisa Noda, told me that the subcontract workers were "part of the family

of Nippon Steel." He noted that the family pays them almost as much as it pays Nippon Steel employees and tries to give them "lifetime employment." But he admitted that in addition to the dirty, difficult work they must do, subcontract workers also work longer hours than regular employees for no extra pay. They receive few of the famous benefits Nippon Steel men get.

[4] When pressed, Noda acknowledged that subcontract workers are part of the Nippon Steel family in "an old sense of family." It is a traditional Confucian family, in which the superior members think it natural that they are richer and more powerful than their lesser relatives.

[5] Motoyoshi Arai operates a locomotive for one of the largest subcontractors. Arai is paid about 10% less than Nippon Steel men, and he does not think of the system as familylike. He feels exploited. Arai once headed the union at his company, Nittetsu Transportation, and he still works hard to strengthen it. But Arai's union has not been very successful. By now he is convinced that the exploitation is permanent.

[6] "When we started out with the union, our objective was to get our wages closer to Nippon Steel's," he says. "But after six or seven years we realize that's out of the question, so we're trying to raise the base for everybody."

[7] The difference between Nippon Steel employees in silver helmets and the men in yellow is based on something that has divided upper and lower classes in every country for thousands of years: power. As a group, regular employees of Nippon Steel could easily shut down the Kimitsu works. Subcontract workers—while not always completely powerless—can cause much less trouble.

[8] I spent more than four years in Japan trying to make sense of the Japanese economy's mysteries—the apparent generosity of big companies to their workers, the nation's rapid growth and its lack of labor strife, unemployment and poverty. I have come to a conclusion closely involved with the question of silver helmets versus yellow: The most dramatic of Japan's economic marvels depend on the way the system distributes pay and benefits in proportion to the disruption that groups could cause by withholding their services.

[9] Men in big, powerful Japanese companies, who hold strategic positions in the economy, are allowed to take most of the fruits of their companies' successes. In 1977 men in companies with 1,000 or more workers averaged Y203,700 ($980) a month plus overtime, bonuses of Y855,900 ($4,000) a year and generous fringe benefits. That's $16,000 a year without fringes. In 1980 the figure is maybe 20% higher.

[10] Most smaller companies cannot treat their workers nearly as well because competitors can be set up easily with nonunion labor. Male small-company workers averaged only 71% of big-company

men's pay. The difference in pay between big- and small-company men was bigger than the difference between college graduates and those who never finished high school. And small companies offer far inferior fringe benefits.

[11] By using small subcontractors, the biggest companies can capitalize on the wage difference. Their organized workers are not threatened because the bosses have promised—and the unions have enough power to assure—that the profits and flexibility subcontracting gives the big companies will benefit their regular employees.

[12] Nippon Steel directly employs 73,002 people—42% as many as U.S. Steel, although the Japanese company produces more steel and the two companies' dollar sales volumes are similar. More modern equipment explains part of the contrast, but subcontracting is probably a more important factor.

[13] Because companies like Nippon Steel use low-wage subcontractors, Japanese industry ultimately tends to use labor more efficiently than unionized American industries. Not only are the subcontracted workers paid less, they are less rigid in their work standards. And the jobs available with small companies and subcontractors help eliminate unemployment. Not everybody makes a top wage, but every able-bodied person can find work.

[14] All this owes much to U.S.-imposed reforms and employees' reactions to them after World War II. Our reforms forced big companies' managers to put high priority on regular employees' needs. Douglas MacArthur could not have imagined the system that would emerge, but he was the creator as much as the Japanese.

[15] MacArthur and the New Deal intellectuals who staffed America's Occupation legalized and encouraged Japan's Socialist and Communist parties, who quickly established unions in virtually all big companies. The unions enrolled even managers' key assistants.

[16] Meanwhile the Occupation was purging top industrialists, leaving the remaining managers utterly confused. "Labor almost controlled management," the president of one of Japan's conservative union federations recalled to me. "Nowadays there's a lot of talk about worker participation in management, but in those days nobody could be appointed in top management without the approval of the Communist Party."

[17] To make their companies function, managers had to promise that security and income for regular employees would be their key goals. And because unions contained so many of the companies' powerful people, they could assure that these promises were largely kept.

[18] As the postwar period progressed the new top managers consolidated their hold over their companies, but it was never worthwhile for them to change their basic commitments. Japanese law places fewer restrictions on managers than American law, and man-

agers of mature companies receive little pressure from representatives of investor owners. But they must still cope with unions. Three-quarters of all workers in firms employing more than 500 belong. Unions—which are no longer Communist-dominated but still include virtually every regular employee under the age of 35 and everyone over 35 who has no management title—probably have more influence over the managers of most large companies than any group except possibly the companies' bankers.

[19] Labor disputes still occur regularly. Each spring big-company employees cover the walls of some very staid offices and factories with big-character denunciations of management that can remind a foreigner of Peking during the Cultural Revolution.

[20] Why do these disputes so seldom end in long strikes? In good part because the regular employees—Nippon Steel's silver hats—realize that as privileged employees they have a stake in the company's health; they don't want to weaken the source of their good fortune.

[21] Thus interruptions of work are usually limited to a few hours a day, and when employees are not embroiled in the annual ritual of pay negotiations they have good incentive to work as a team to build a more efficient and more prosperous company.

[22] Outside the privileged caste of big-company employees, however, only 40% of the workers in firms employing 100 to 499, and only 10% of the workers in firms employing 10 to 99, belong to unions. In companies employing fewer than 30 the figure drops to 1½%. When they exist, subcontractors' unions lack the bargaining power to force concessions on their own. And unions at important subcontractors lack common interests with lesser contractors' unions for a united front. With no real prospects for success, few ever launch long strikes.

[23] Nittetsu Transportation's Motoyoshi Arai has direct experience with the Nippon Steel union's attitude toward subcontractor unions. Arai thinks Yoshiji Miyata, who headed the Nippon Steel union when Arai headed Nittetsu Transportation's, is an enemy of Nittetsu Transportation men.

[24] "Five years ago I was union chief, and we were fighting for a higher bonus," Arai told me disdainfully. "Miyata's elder brother—he's now in parliament—came to me and said, 'Don't do that; you're causing trouble. Don't make strikes.'"

[25] Without the Nippon Steel union's support, Arai's position was weak. Nittetsu Transportation's locomotive and truck operators could cause a lot of disruption, but Nippon Steel could replace them. And although they receive benefits dramatically inferior to those Nippon Steel men get, their benefits significantly exceed those of the less important subcontractors.

[26] Arai lives in a company-supplied apartment for Y3,500 ($17) a

month. It is ten minutes farther from the plant than the apartments supplied to Nippon Steel men and has one less room, but if Arai had to look for a new job he probably could not find a $17-a-month apartment anywhere. And although running a locomotive is harder and dirtier than operating the new, modern equipment to which most Nippon Steel men are assigned, it is cleaner and easier than other jobs that would pay as well. Nittetsu Transportation men know they have much to lose if Nippon Steel ever eliminates their jobs.

[27] Legally, Nittetsu Transportation is a wholly owned subsidiary of Nippon Steel. Its managers, who were mainly regular Nippon Steel employees dispatched to the subcontractor for a few years, refused to concede anything to Arai. When he came up for reelection to his union post, they worked to undermine his candidacy. "They said that if I was elected, Nippon Steel wouldn't give the company any more work," Arai told me. All the jobs at Nittetsu Transportation would be destroyed if that happened. Arai lost.

[28] Arai explained that the worst subcontracting conditions are outside the gates of the Kimitsu works in "grandchild subcontractors," small companies that do maintenance and any other work that can be trucked to their shops. Grandchild subcontractors can cause almost no disruption. Because entrepeneurs can set up small companies fairly easily, each one faces tough competition from others. To unionize them would be a colossal task because Nippon Steel can find a new, nonunion subcontractor if ever the workers at a particular company become overly militant. Workers at the important subcontractors have no more incentive to help grandchild subcontractors than Nippon Steel men have to help Nittetsu Transportation workers.

[29] A typical grandchild subcontractor shop is a grime-covered corrugated metal and cement building with amenities limited to perhaps a ping-pong table in a grubby recreation room. The average worker in the steel industry at companies employing 10 to 99 people works 32 hours a month more than workers in companies employing more than 1,000. He may receive overtime pay for some of those hours, but never at time-and-a-half rates.

[30] Nippon Steel officials say there are 7,400 regular employees at the Kimitsu works and something less than 9,000 subcontract workers inside the mill's gates. Arai estimates that some 10,000 people work for the grandchild subcontractors in the Kimitsu area.

[31] That means that of a total employment roster of perhaps 26,000 people, just over one in four wears the privileged silver hat.

[32] Subcontracting creates a lot of jobs for people who might simply find themselves unemployed in the U.S. because no one will pay them United Steelworkers' or United Auto Workers' wages. Tiny workshops are more common than rice stores in most neighborhoods of Japanese cities. Some 180,000 Japanese manufacture

electronic components for subcontractors in their homes. Workshops with less than 100 workers employ 51.5% of Japanese manufacturing employees, compared to 23.4% in America.

[33] Here's the paradox: Though small companies always pay less than large ones, competition among them for labor keeps wages at decent levels and gives Japan's poorest classes a larger share of the nation's income than America's poorest classes get. In one of the few Japanese neighborhoods noted for their poverty, a Japanese minister who had once worked as a missionary in Jersey City told me in the depths of Japan's last recession that he could introduce any alcoholic derelict up to age 35 or 40 to companies that would hire him for Y150,000 to Y200,000 ($700 to $950) a month or more including overtime and bonuses.

[34] This was true even though Japan's unemployment rate at the time was at its worst levels since the 1950s, (a bit over 2%). Job-placement officials in New York say that comparable Americans almost certainly could find no steady job at all—though America's per capita GNP remains about 10% above Japan's.

[35] The paradox deepens:

[36] A study by the Organization for Economic Cooperation & Development found the bottom fifth of Japanese households received more of national income than the bottom fifth of any major Western country—nearly 8%. The U.S. figure was 4.5%. Correcting for Americans' tendency to live alone and thus report lower "household" incomes, the analysis indicated the poorest fifth of Japanese received nearly one-and-one-half times the share the poorest Americans received.

[37] The conclusion is almost inescapable. The Japanese system, like the American system, creates a privileged caste of workers. But unlike the American system, the Japanese system does not institutionalize unemployment by holding wages in any industry so high that people are kept from working.

[38] You might call it scabbing; U.S. trade unions certainly would. But the multitier wage system has two overwhelming advantages. It keeps Japanese labor costs down and productivity up while, at the same time, giving job opportunities to the least advantaged segments of Japanese society.

VOCABULARY

Look up the following words in your dictionary. Use the system developed in the dictionary section in the back of the text. Be sure to write the part of speech, the pronunciation, and the meaning(s) of each word.

fur·nace (fûr′nĭs) *n.* **1.** An enclosure in which energy in a nonthermal form is converted to heat; especially, such an enclosure in which heat is generated by the combustion of a suitable fuel. **2.** Any intensely hot, enclosed place. **3.** A severe test or trial. [Middle English *furna(i)s,* from Old French *fornais,* from Latin *fornāx* (stem *fornāc-*). See **gwher-** in Appendix.*]

Definition ©1981 Houghton Mifflin Company. Reprinted by permission from *The American Heritage Dictionary of the English Language, New College Edition.*

mill

subcontract

locomotive

exploited

strife

fringe(s)

capitalize

flexibility

eliminate

priority

emerge

utterly

consolidated

staid

denunciations

embroiled	amenities
incentive	paradox
caste	derelict
concessions	scabbing
launch	segments
subsidiary	
colossal	
grime	

STUDY QUESTIONS

Finding the Matter

1. What do the silver and the yellow helmets indicate at Nippon Steel's Kimitsu Company?

2. In what way are the subcontract workers like members of a traditional Confucian family?

3. Why can't companies smaller than Nippon Steel treat their workers as well as the giant company does?

4. Why is unemployment much lower in Japan than it is in the United States?

5. Why are the infrequent strikes at Nippon Steel usually short?

6. What are "grandchild subcontractors"? Why do they have the worst conditions of all subcontractors?

Exploring the Manner

1. What are the major differences between the jobs of the employees in silver helmets and those in yellow helmets? What are the similarities?

2. Most of the time Wood discusses the steel industry in the third person* (it or they), but occasionally he changes to the first person* singular (I), as in this example: "I spent more than four years in Japan trying to make sense of the Japanese economy's

mysteries." What is the effect on the reader of the shift in the point of view*?

3. Although the article basically compares the levels of Japan's wage system, there is also a historical section showing how the unions arose in Japan after World War II. What does this section add to the article?

SYNONYMS

From the column at the right, select the best synonym for the italicized word in each sentence. Rewrite each sentence using the appropriate synonym.

1. The Nippon employees receive *advantages* that have become internationally famous.

2. Some of the men in the yellow helmets feel *used*, and they are convinced that this is a permanent state.

3. The *aim* of the workers in the yellow helmets was to get their wages closer to Nippon Steel's.

4. The jobs available with small companies and subcontractors help to *end* unemployment.

5. Although the Americans imposed reforms on Japanese industry after World War II, no one could have imagined the system that would *arise*.

6. Labor *arguments* still occur regularly in Japanese companies.

7. Once a year, Nippon Steel's employees become *involved* in pay negotiation.

A. exploited

B. disputes

C. colossal

D. scabbing

E. benefits

F. grime

G. eliminate

H. embroiled

I. objective

J. emerge

8. To unionize the minor companies would be an *enormous* task.

9. A typical grandchild subcontractor shop is made of corrugated metal and is covered with *dirt*.

10. *Strikebreaking* is taking a job that is held by a worker on strike.

PARAPHRASE

Read this paragraph twice; then close your book. Using your own words, rewrite the paragraph as clearly and as completely as you can.

I spent more than four years in Japan trying to make sense of the Japanese economy's mysteries—the apparent generosity of big companies to their workers, the nation's rapid growth and its lack of labor strife, unemployment and poverty. I have come to a conclusion closely involved with the question of silver helmets versus yellow: The most dramatic of Japan's economic marvels depend on the way the system distributes pay and benefits in proportion to the disruption that groups could cause by withholding their services.

VERB FILL-IN

Fill in each blank with the verb form that is appropriate for each sentence.

Here _____ the paradox. Though small companies al-
           be

ways _____ less than large ones, competition among them
           pay

for labor _____ wages at decent levels and _____
           keep   give

Japan's poorest classes a larger share of the nation's income than

America's poorest classes ――――――――. In one of the few Japanese

get

neighborhoods noted for their poverty, a Japanese minister who had

once ――――――― as a missionary in Jersey City ―――――――

work   tell

me that in the depths of Japan's last recession he ――――――――

introduce

any alcoholic derelict up to age 35 or 40 to companies that

――――――――― him for Y150,000 to Y200,000 ($700–$950) a

hire

month or more including overtime and bonuses.

SENTENCE COMPLETION

From the column at the right, select the correct line to complete each of the numbered lines at the left. Write each sentence in its correct form.

1. Nippon Steel employees wear silver helmets,

2. Men in silver helmets observe operations,

3. Nippon is a traditional Confucian family, in which the superior members think it natural

4. Men in big, powerful Japanese companies, who hold strategic positions in the economy,

5. Most smaller companies cannot treat their workers nearly as well

6. By using small subcontractors,

A. that they are richer and more powerful than their lesser relatives.

B. the biggest companies can capitalize on the wage difference.

C. to a few hours a day.

D. while subcontract workers wear yellow helmets.

E. because competitors can be set up easily with nonunion labor.

F. check dials, and operate clean, highly automated machinery.

G. creates a privileged caste of workers.

7. Jobs that are available
    with small companies and
    subcontractors

8. As the postwar period pro-
    gressed, the new top man-
    agers had to promise that

9. Interruptions of work are
    usually limited

10. The Japanese system, like
    the American system,

H. security and income for
    regular employees would be
    their key goals.

I. help eliminate unemploy-
    ment.

J. are allowed to take most
    of the fruits of their
    companies' successes.

CLOZE EXERCISE

Fill in each blank with the best word to complete the meaning of the sentence.

Most smaller companies cannot _____ their workers

nearly as _____ because competitors can be _____

up easily with nonunion _____. Male small-company

workers averaged _____ 71% of big-company men's

_____. The difference in pay _____ big- and small-

company men _____ bigger than the difference

_____ college graduates and those _____ never

finished high school. _____ small companies offer far

_____ fringe benefits.

SENTENCE COMBINING

Combine each pair of sentences into a single grammatical
sentence.

1. Subcontract workers wear yellow helmets.
    Yellow helmets outnumber silver ones.

2. The difference in employees' helmets is based on something special.
   That difference is based on power.

3. The bosses' promises are kept.
   The union has the power to assure that the bosses keep their promises.

4. Five years ago I was union chief.
   Five years ago we were fighting for a bonus.

5. Labor disputes occur regularly.
   These work stoppages are very short.

6. Subcontracting creates a lot of jobs.
   People who find it hard to get jobs are happy with subcontracting.

PUNCTUATION

Read the following paragraph. Write in the capital letters and place commas, periods, colons, semicolons, dashes, and quotation marks where needed.

legally nittetsu transportation is a wholly owned subsidiary of nippon steel its managers who were mainly regular nippon steel employees dispatched to the subcontractor for a few years refused to concede anything to arai when he came up for reelection to his union post they worked to undermine his candidacy they said that if i was elected nippon steel wouldnt give the company any more work arai told me all the jobs at nittetsu transportation would be destroyed if that happened arai lost

WORD-FORM CHART

Use your dictionary to complete the following table. Follow the example shown with item 1, *employer/employee.* If there is no commonly used form for a particular part of speech, write the symbol XXX.

Noun	Verb	Adjective	Adverb
1. employer employee	employ	employable	XXX
2. tradition			
3.		economic	
4. strategy			
5. inferiority			
6.	imagine		
7.			weakly
8.	disrupt		
9.		systematic	
10. segment			

WORD-FORM EXERCISE

Using your completed Word-Form Chart, select the correct form to fit into each sentence. Use the appropriate tense of the verb, the singular or plural form of the noun, and the passive voice where necessary.
Follow the sequence of numbers from the Word-Form Chart to select the correct form.

1. Subcontract workers work longer than regular _____

   for no extra pay.

2. Nippon Steel is a _____ Confucian family.

3. The author spent more than four years in Japan trying to make sense of the Japanese _____ mysteries.

4. Men in big companies, who hold _____ positions in the economy, are allowed to take most of the fruits of their companies' successes.

5. Small companies offer far _____ fringe benefits.

6. Douglas MacArthur could not have _____ the system that would emerge.

7. The workers don't want to _____ the source of their good fortune.

8. Nittetsu Transportation's locomotive and truck operators could cause a lot of _____.

9. The multitier wage _____ has two overwhelming advantages.

10. The system gives job opportunities to the least advantaged _____ of Japanese society.

QUESTIONS FOR DISCUSSION

1. What differences might there be in the author's attitude toward Japan's wage system if he were a Japanese writer instead of an American one?

2. Are there labor disputes in your native country? If so, how long do they last and what is the usual outcome?

3. Wood says that the male small-company workers earn only 71% of the pay of workers in big companies. This difference in pay is larger than the difference between the pay of college graduates and the pay of those who never finished high school. Thus a college graduate working in a small company would earn less than a high-school dropout working in a large company. What is your reaction to this situation?

TOPICS FOR WRITING

1. Write a theme comparing the traditional family unit in your native country with the family unit in America. Consider these questions in your paper: Which family members have the most power? Which ones have the least power? Do all members accept this power structure?

2. Wood says that the Japanese system "distributes pay and benefits in proportion to the disruption that groups could cause by withholding their services." With regard to the American economy, write a composition comparing two groups from the list below. Imagine that both groups have threatened to go on strike. Compare the two groups in terms of the effects each group would have on your life if it withheld its services.

hospital technicians	train conductors
policemen	bus drivers
firemen	gasoline retailers
teachers	air controllers
garbage collectors	radio and television broadcasters

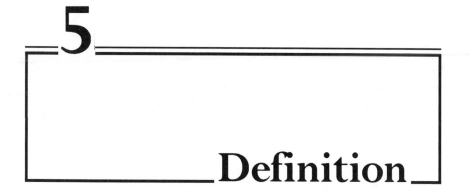

Definition

The Form

"But I've gotta use words when I talk to you," wrote the famous twentieth-century poet T. S. Eliot. This may appear to be an obvious statement, but it requires a second look. Simply using words does not guarantee communication. Before a speaker or writer can hope to transmit her message in a manner that reflects her original thought, she must select her words carefully. Moreover, the writer must try to make certain that her words will be understood as she intended them to be.

If the writer is using the common dictionary or *lexical* meaning of a word, she can expect the reader to know the word or to look it up. A dictionary definition will establish the *class* of a word and then will show how it differs from other words in the same class. For example, an elephant is a large four-footed mammal belonging to the family *Elephantidae*, but it differs from other mammals by having a trunk, five toes, and tusks.

The dictionary entry also includes synonyms (words of similar meaning), antonyms (words of opposite meaning), and etymology (the historical derivation of a word). All of this information can be useful to a writer.

Sometimes, the writer wants to give a special meaning to a word. For example, a student may wish to write a paper arguing that English is the "official language" of the United States, even though there is no law establishing this. She can propose her own definition, saying, "In this paper I am going to use the word *official* to mean the language in which the laws of the country are written." She can then present her evidence showing that, according to her definition, English is indeed the official language of the United States. This kind of personal or *stipulative* definition is useful only if the writer explains it clearly and uses it consistently.

The Student Reader

Sometimes, a definition appears within an essay merely to clarify the meaning of a particular word. At other times, the definition *is* the main point of the essay and occupies several paragraphs or even the entire essay. The second kind is called an *extended* definition, and it usually includes several kinds of supporting ideas. For example, if a writer were going to explore the meaning of the word *friendship*, she might elaborate upon the dictionary definition by including a stipulative definition, illustrated, perhaps, with an example taken from her own experience. Next, she might give examples of different forms of friendship (between men and women, women and women, children and adults). She might wish to compare two or more kinds of friendship, pointing out their similarities and differences. Any combination of methods may produce an effective definition in expository writing.

Some extended definitions may be stipulative as well. Only 35 years after the end of the American Civil War, Mark Twain wrote an essay entitled "As Regards Patriotism." In his extended definition, he rejects the standard meaning of patriotism as blind, unquestioning devotion to one's country:

> Training does wonderful things. It moved the people of this country to oppose the Mexican War; then moved them to fall in with what they supposed was the opinion of the majority—majority Patriotism is the customary Patriotism—and go down there and fight. Before the Civil War it made the North indifferent to slavery and friendly to the slave interest; in that interest it made Massachusetts hostile to the American flag, and she would not allow it to be hoisted on her State House— in her eyes it was the flag of a faction. Then by and by, training swung Massachusetts the other way, and she went raging South to fight under that very flag and against that aforetime protected interest of hers.

Opposed to the definition of patriotism as "trained" obedience, Twain argues for each citizen to formulate a personal definition of patriotism and not to accept the standard dictum "My country right or wrong."

Then men can be trained to manufacture their own Patriotism. They can be trained to labor it out in their own heads and hearts and in the privacy and independence of their own premises.

The Professional Writer

In her essay "Natural—A Word of Many Meanings," Wells explores the problems involved in establishing a definition of the word *natural* on food labels. The problem, she explains, is not the dictionary definition but the desire of manufacturers to take advantage of the consumer's interest in buying pure or uncontaminated food. The manufacturers don't want to use the impartial dictionary definition (denotation) of the word *natural*. Instead, they want to use the meanings associated with the word (connotations), including "healthful," "clean," or "nutritious." The problem arises when the manufacturers use connotative instead of denotative meaning in an attempt to persuade the consumer to buy a particular product—even if it has no nutritional value.

A different use of definition occurs in Jonathan Kozol's essay. Although it is entitled "Reinventing Childhood," what the author really wants to express is a new definition of childhood—his own. His essay is a personal (subjective) examination of what is wrong with the current concept of childhood as a "preparation for life, not a portion of it." He traces the historical changes in the concept of childhood and then argues against our modern definition. Kozol uses examples of childhood responsibility and involvement as they are practiced in Cuba and the United States to show us how we should create our new definition. Throughout the essay, Kozol evolves his personal definition of childhood, hoping that the people who read his words will change their definitions to conform to his.

NATURAL — A WORD OF MANY MEANINGS

Patricia Wells

Natural (nach er el) adj. 1. of or dealing with nature 2. produced or existing in nature, not artificial 3. innate, not acquired 4. true to nature, lifelike 5. normal n.—a person or thing sure to be successful.
—Webster's New World Dictionary

[1] To Webster, a "natural" is a sure thing. To consumers, "natural" can mean anything from organic to real to good for one's health. And to the Government agencies assigned to regulate the use of the word on food labels and in food advertising, "natural" is on its way to being defined as one big headache.

[2] Meanwhile, to food manufacturers and advertisers responding to the ever-growing obsession with a natural world, the term has indeed become synonymous with success.

[3] What everyone seems to agree upon is that there is no universally accepted definition of "natural" as applied to food, and until there is the word will float freely in the marketplace.

[4] Walk down any supermarket aisle today and "natural" shouts from the shelves. We not only have 100 percent natural cereal, natural beer and natural deodorant, but potato chips "still made in the original natural way" and artificially colored drinks boasting of natural orange, lemon and grape flavors. The proliferation continues with a dog food touted for its gravy with "natural beef flavor."

[5] While consumers may be confused over just what natural means in each of these cases, they appear to be convinced that somehow

natural means better. In a 1977 survey of consumer attitudes and behavior toward products labeled "natural," the Consumer Response Corporation of New York found that the majority of the 1,000 consumers questioned thought that, in general "natural" products were different from other products and that they were pure, free of additives, preservatives and chemicals.

[6] The survey also found that the consumers believed "natural" products had no adverse effects and were more healthful, safer and better.

[7] But the consumer who reads fineprint ingredient labels on many "natural" foods quickly finds that "natural" has literally dozens of meanings.

[8] Does the term "100 percent natural" on a box of raisins mean the same as the "naturally good, nothing artificial added" claim on a jar of baby food? Is "natural" light beer more natural than a beer without the "natural" claim? And is it misleading for a manufacturer to call a product "natural clam juice" when it contains, among other things, monosodium glutamate?

[9] While aware that the overuse and possible abuse of the term encourages consumer confusion, regulatory agencies such as the Food and Drug Administration and the Federal Trade Commission have yet to take firm stands on what manufacturers can and cannot do with the "natural" claim.

[10] In 1974, the F. T. C. staff recommended that the terms "natural" and "organic" be banned in advertising because they were misleading. The recommendations were not adopted, although, according to a commission spokesman, "the commissioner did agree there was reason to believe there was a problem concerning the terms."

[11] "They do have a potential for deception and unfairness, and can connote superiority," the spokesman noted, adding that the F. T. C. held public hearings on the subject last year and was in the process of formulating some rules regarding the use of the terms.

[12] The Food and Drug Administration, empowered to regulate truth in labeling on many food products, has not defined the term "natural," said one spokesman, "largely because it's not a term that's easy to define."

[13] Wayne Pines, deputy assistant commissioner for the F. D. A., said that the agency planned no major activity "designed to stem the use of the word natural" because it hopes to deal with the entire food labeling issue in a broader way.

[14] "We're in the process of developing a food labeling strategy and will deal with the term natural along the way, but as a specific definition I doubt it," he said.

[15] Mr. Pines did add that "The rule we go by is if a product

claimed to be natural but contained artificial additives, and we thought this was misleading, we would write a letter to the manufacturer and ask for compliance."

[16] To date, he said, he knew of no instances in which the F. D. A. wrote a manufacturer on the issue.

[17] Manufacturers, on the other hand, appear engaged in a game of one-upmanship. Sometimes the use of the word appears to be absurd, as with the soft drink that claims "Natural-Flavored" in bold letters on the front label, then lists acetic acid, artificial color and sodium benzoate in small print on the back label. Often "natural" is used in self-defense, with products such as raisins, most of which have never contained additives or preservatives. Anheuser-Busch's "Natural Light" beer is another example of self-defense labeling.

[18] "All of our beers are natural, in that they contain nothing artificial," said Jack McDonough, marketing brand manager for Natural Light, sold nationally since last June.

[19] "We played up the word natural here primarily because dietary foods are associated with artificiality, and we wanted to assure consumers we weren't playing any chemical tricks here."

[20] Quaker Oats, which has long had a reputation for product purity, has gone one step further. It's the first company to claim that its product may be natural pointing out that natural does not mean "organic." It's 100 Percent Natural Cereal label reads: "Quaker 100 Percent Natural Cereal is a natural, not organic, food product made from conventionally grown foodstuffs to which no artificial additives or preservatives have been added."

[21] A check of several large food companies and food manufacturers' trade groups found that they are no closer to a definition than consumers or Government agencies.

[22] "We have found no universally accepted definition of the term natural—we do agree the word presents a problem," said a General Foods spokesman, who added that the word "natural" is "confusing to consumers."

VOCABULARY

Look up the following words in your dictionary. Use the system developed in the dictionary section in the back of the text. Be sure to write the part of speech, the pronunciation, and the meaning(s) of each word.

nat·u·ral (năch′ər-əl, năch′rəl) *adj. Abbr.* **nat.** **1.** Present in or produced by nature; not artificial or man-made. **2.** Pertaining to or concerning nature: *natural science.* **3.** Pertaining to or produced solely by nature or the expected order of things: *a natural death; natural causes.* **4. a.** Pertaining to or resulting from inherent nature; not acquired: *"The love of power . . . and the admiration of it . . . are both natural to man."* (Christopher

Morris). **b.** Distinguished by innate qualities or aptitudes: *a natural leader.* **5.** Free from affectation or artificiality; spontaneous. **6.** Not altered, treated, or disguised: *natural coloring.* **7.** Consonant with particular circumstances; expected and accepted: *"In Willie's mind marriage remained the natural and logical sequel to love."* (Duff Cooper). **8.** Established by moral certainty or conviction: *natural rights.* **9.** In a primitive, uncivilized, or unregenerate state. **10.** Illegitimate. Said of offspring. **11.** *Mathematics.* Of or pertaining to positive integers. **12.** *Music.* **a.** Not sharped or flatted. **b.** Having no sharps or flats. —See Synonyms at **naive, normal, sincere.** —*n.* **1.** *Informal.* One seeming to have the qualifications necessary for success: *a natural for the job.* **2.** *Music.* **a.** The sign (♮) placed before a note to cancel a preceding sharp or flat. **b.** A note so affected. **3.** Yellowish gray to pale orange yellow. See **color.** **4.** In certain card and dice games, a combination that wins immediately.   [Middle English, from Old French, from Latin *nātūrālis,* from *nātūra,* NATURE.] —**nat′u·ral·ness** *n.*

Definition ©1981 Houghton Mifflin Company. Reprinted by permission from *The American Heritage Dictionary of the English Language, New College Edition.*

organic

obsession

synonymous

proliferation

touted

adverse

stem

abuse

banned

potential

compliance

one-upmanship

ingredient

STUDY QUESTIONS

Finding the Matter

1. What is misleading about placing the label *natural* on potato chips and artificially colored drinks?

2. What characteristics do consumers expect to find in "natural" food products?

3. What is the Food and Drug Administration (FDA) doing about the various meanings of *natural* on food labels?

4. What does the author mean when she says that the word *natural* on a box of raisins is used in "self-defense"?

5. Why did the Quaker Oats Company state that their product was "natural" but not "organic"?

Exploring the Manner

1. Wells lists several separate definitions of *natural*. To which definition does her opening sentence refer? Is this the most common dictionary meaning of the word? How do you know?

2. What does the author mean when she says that until there is a common definition of *natural*, the word "will float freely in the marketplace"?

3. Does the author criticize the FDA for failing to stop abuses of the label *natural*? Find the passages in which she suggests her opinion.

4. The conclusion* of an essay usually expresses the author's final comment on the subject. Why does Wells end her essay with a weak statement from a manufacturer?

SYNONYMS

From the column at the right, select the best synonym for the italicized word in each sentence. Rewrite each sentence using the appropriate synonym.

1. The Federal Trade Commission (FTC) recommended that the use of the terms "natural" and "organic" be *prohibited* in advertising.

A. potential

B. adverse

C. stem

D. touted

2. The use of these terms shows *possible* deception in advertising products.

3. The FDA does not plan to *stop* the use of the word "natural."

4. The *increase* in the use of these terms continues even with dog food.

5. The pet food was *publicized* as having "natural beef flavor."

6. The overuse and possible *misuse* of the term can encourage consumer confusion.

7. Consumers believe that "natural" products have no *bad* effects and that they are actually safer.

E. banned

F. abuse

G. proliferation

PARAPHRASE

Read this paragraph twice; then close your book. Using your own words, rewrite the paragraph as clearly and completely as you can.

While consumers may be confused over just what *natural* means, they appear to be convinced that somehow *natural* means better. In a 1977 survey of consumer attitudes and behavior toward products labeled *natural*, the Consumer Response Corporation of New York found that the majority of the 1,000 consumers questioned thought that, in general, "natural" products were different from other products and that they were pure—free of additives, preservatives, and chemicals.

VERB FILL-IN

Fill in each blank with the verb form that is appropriate for each sentence.

Quaker Oats, which _____ a reputation for product

have

purity, _____ one step further. It _____ the first

go   be

company to claim that its product may be natural while _____

point

out that natural does not mean "organic." Its 100 Percent Natural

Cereal label _____ : "Quaker 100 Percent Natural Cereal

read

_____ a natural, not organic, food product _____

be   make

from conventionally grown foodstuffs to which no artificial additives

or preservatives _____ ."

add

SENTENCE COMPLETION

From the column at the right, select the correct line to complete each of the numbered lines at the left. Write each sentence in its correct form.

1. What everyone seems to agree upon is

2. While consumers may be confused about just what *natural* means,

3. The consumer who reads the ingredients on labels

4. The FDA and FDC have yet to take firm stands

5. Regulatory groups have not yet defined the term *natural*

A. quickly finds that *natural* has literally dozens of meanings.

B. that there is no universally accepted definition of *natural*.

C. a game of one-upmanship.

D. that they were no closer to a definition than consumers or government agencies.

E. in a much broader way.

6. The FDA hopes to deal with the entire food-labeling issue

7. A check of large food companies and food manufacturers' trade groups found

8. Quaker Cereal is advertised as having

9. Manufacturers of food appear to be engaged in

10. The FDA writes letters to food manufacturers if they think a claim is made

F. they appear to be convinced that somehow *natural* means "better."

G. that is misleading to the consumer.

H. largely because it is a difficult term to define.

I. no artificial additives or preservatives.

J. on what manufacturers can and cannot do with the "natural" claim.

CLOZE EXERCISE

Fill in each blank with the best word to complete the meaning of the sentence.

Manufacturers, on the other hand, appear ＿＿＿＿＿＿ in a game of one-upmanship. Sometimes ＿＿＿＿＿＿ use of the word appears to ＿＿＿＿＿＿ absurd, as with the soft drink ＿＿＿＿＿＿ claims "Naturally Flavored" in bold letters ＿＿＿＿＿＿ the front label, then lists acetic ＿＿＿＿＿＿, artificial color and sodium benzoate in ＿＿＿＿＿＿ print on the back label. Often ＿＿＿＿＿＿ is used in self-defense, with products ＿＿＿＿＿＿ as raisins, most of which have ＿＿＿＿＿＿ contained additives or preservatives. Anheuser-Busch's "Natural ＿＿＿＿＿＿" beer is another example of self-defense ＿＿＿＿＿＿.

SENTENCE COMBINING

Combine each pair of sentences into a single grammatical sentence.

1. Consumers believed that "natural" products had no adverse effects.
   They believed these products to be healthier and safer.

2. The FDA is aware that the term *natural* encourages possible abuse.
   The FDA thinks the term *natural* leads to consumer confusion.

3. The FTC recommended that the term *natural* be banned.
   The FTC also recommended that the term *organic* be banned in advertising.

4. Wayne Pines is a deputy assistant commissioner for the FDA.
   Wayne Pines said the agency planned no major activity to stem the use of the word *natural.*

5. Sometimes the use of the word *natural* appears to be absurd.
   Some soft drinks have labels that say "naturally flavored" and then go on to list ingredients such as acetic acid, artificial color, and sodium benzoate.

6. A beer company claims its beer is "natural."
   A beer company claims its beer contains nothing artificial.

PUNCTUATION

Read the following paragraphs. Write in the capital letters and place commas, periods, colons, semicolons, dashes, and quotation marks where needed.

wayne pines deputy assistant commissioner for the fda said that

the agency planned no major activity designed to stem the use of the

word *natural* because it hopes to deal with the entire food labeling

issue in a broader way

were in the process of developing a good food labeling strategy and will deal with the term natural along the way but as a specific

definition i doubt it he said

WORD-FORM CHART

Use your dictionary to complete the following table. Follow the example shown with item 1, *obsession*. If there is no commonly used form for a particular part of speech, write the symbol XXX.

Noun	Verb	Adjective	Adverb
1. obsession	obsess	obsessional	XXX
2.	preserve		
3. ingredient			
4. container			
5.		superior	
6. label			
7.		primary	
8. synonym			
9. universe			

WORD-FORM EXERCISE

Using your completed Word-Form Chart, select the correct form to fit into each sentence. Use the appropriate tense of the verb, the singular or plural form of the noun, and the passive voice where necessary.

Follow the sequence of numbers from the Word-Form Chart to select the correct form.

1. Food manufacturers and advertisers feel the consumers have an

   ever-growing ——————— with a natural world.

2. Consumers want products that are free of additives,

   ———————, and chemicals.

3. Consumers should read the fine print on food labels so that they

   can become familiar with the ——————— in the products.

4. Is it misleading for a manufacturer to call a product "natural

   clam juice" when it ———————, among other things, mono-

   sodium glutamate?

5. The terms *natural* and *organic* have a potential for deception and

   can connote ———————.

6. The FDA is empowered to regulate truth in ———————.

7. The word *natural* is played up ——————— because dietetic

   foods are associated with artificiality.

8. The expressions *100% natural* and *naturally good, nothing

   artificial* are not necessarily ———————.

9. There is no ——————— accepted definition of the term

   natural.

QUESTIONS FOR DISCUSSION

1. How do you, as a consumer, feel about the purity of the food that you eat? What do you think of the chemicals added to our food as preservatives, coloring, or flavoring?

2. Working with your classmates, formulate a definition of *natural* that could be used by the FDA in monitoring food labeling.

TOPICS FOR WRITING

1. Write a composition entitled "Confessions of a Junk-Food Junkie." Make certain that you include your own definition of *junk food.*

2. We all differ about what a good breakfast is, depending upon what we are used to eating at this meal. Describe and define a "good breakfast" and a "poor breakfast."

3. Words may have different meanings in different situations. For example, a friendship between two males or two females is quite different from a male-female friendship. Write a basic definition of friendship and then differentiate two or three kinds of friendship. Use specific examples to illustrate the characteristics.

REINVENTING CHILDHOOD

Jonathan Kozol

[1] The invention of childhood is barely 400 years old. Until the end of the 16th century, children, once beyond the years of infancy, were treated, dressed, and permitted to act much the same as adults, with due allowance made for their frail bodies and small size.

[2] With the advent of childhood as "a unique condition," lasting generally into and sometimes even after adolescence, the role of children underwent dramatic change. Little by little, they came to be regarded as they would be viewed for the next several centuries: little packets of charming but incorrigible mischief, lovable at best, infuriating at worst, in either case requiring constant feeding and attention—contributing little and consuming much. Children were regarded as small problems patiently waiting to be big ones. Throughout this period, childhood was deprecated as a time of moral passivity; that children might have something worth contributing was never seriously entertained.

[3] Our views of children have changed dramatically in the present century. First, Freud taught us that our most profound moral and psychological dispositions are formed by childhood experience. Then such experts as Jean Piaget and Lawrence Kohlberg traced the development of moral thought through the years of childhood and youth. Finally, in only the past few decades, children have begun to be credited with the ability not only to think ethically, but to act as moral agents in a changing society.

[4] What has caused us to recognize these wasted possibilities, after attributing to children for so long the same ineptitude as the senile and insane? We may attribute this change of heart, in part, to the work of imaginative authors, including Phillip Ariès, Ivan Illich, and the late Paul Goodman; even more emphatically, to the writings as well as the living conviction of such men as Dr. Benjamin Spock. Of equal importance were the models set for us by several other nations, Cuba and Israel probably the most important and influential. Above all, perhaps, was the vivid example given to us by young men and women on their own, whether in their courageous activism in the voter-registration projects of the early Sixties or in their opposition to the war in Vietnam.

[5] For whatever reason, the definition of childhood has changed— and, with it, an unhappy role which has, for a century at least, been forced upon our public schools. The school, as Alfred North Whitehead noted, is built upon ideas that lead neither to action, nor to passion, nor to transformation, but (at most) to good term papers

and examinations. Childhood thereby becomes a moratorium on life, a time in which young people spend about one-quarter of their projected biological existence in rote drill and readiness for the three-quarters they may never live to know. Youth is thus defined as preparation *for* life, not a portion *of* it.

[6] "It doesn't seem real," one student said to me in Syracuse, New York, last spring. "Everything we do in school is like a simulation of some other thing that would be real if it weren't taking place in school."

[7] This wholesale neglect of the world outside the window is best dramatized by that insidious vehicle of scholastic alienation, "the simulation game." We close the windows, pull down the blinds, ventilate the air, deflect the light, absorb the sound, etherize the heart, and neutralize the soul. Then we bring in simulation games to try to imitate the world that we have, with such great care and at such vast expense, excluded.

[8] I witnessed this farce in a $12 million stone-and-concrete high school without walls and also without windows poised at the corner of the two most explosive streets in Harlem. Inside, the "innovative," "open-structured" "teacher-as-a-resource person" introduced to her locked-in class of black and militant, cheated and embittered eighth-grade children a simulation game called Ghetto: "Let's pretend now that we live within one of the racially impacted regions of the Northeast section of the country. . . ."

[9] The direct consequence of this perverse method is that children come to view school, university, moral struggle—indeed, all social transformation—as "not what we do, but what is done to us." The child thus comes to adopt a passive view of his relationship to history. Asking students in a suburban U.S. high school how they conceived of history, I got back the same answers that my own peers (and those of my parents, I suspect) would offer:

[10] "History is everything important that has happened in the past and now is over."

[11] "History is what is done by famous and important people."

[12] This strikes us as a more or less natural view. In fact, it is the fruit of our training, and is not duplicated everywhere. I was relieved to find at least one other country where the response was very different, for children and adults both. Visiting a junior high school, I asked the same question.

[13] "History," said one student in the ninth grade, "is what we do in the morning about the things we thought about the night before."

[14] Something is changing, and it is a very deep and sweeping change, when children, in whatever nation, dare to speak this way at least about the world in which they live.

[15] The change is real. Clearly, it has yet to filter down to all or very many of the classrooms in this nation, but there is already suffi-

cient change for us to start to dream of it on a much larger scale. In many schools of the Western world, a new definition of the whole idea of childhood has started finally to take effect.

[16] In a school outside Havana, in the fall of 1976, I watched a class of third-grade children taking small amounts of a black, powder-like substance from large wooden barrels in one corner of the room, pouring it carefully onto small square pieces of thin cloth or paper, then slowly stitching it together with needle and thread. It was a few minutes before I recognized what they were doing. They were making tea bags!

[17] I discovered that they, along with the other third-graders of Cuba, were producing all the tea bags that would be required in the next year.

[18] A modest event: 45 minutes out of the full day. The work was not unduly hard; and the children faced no threat of injuring their backs or straining their arms. They simply took a small and seemingly enjoyable role in helping to provide one of the basic needs of their society.

[19] Here in Boston, a similar movement is underfoot; not uniformly nor, for now, as official city or state policy, but simply as the spontaneous reaction of good teachers to a new, less narrow, and less crippling vision of the role of children.

[20] Students at one secondary school in Boston study Early Childhood Development in the morning, then work, for pay, with troubled youngsters in a neighborhood day-care center in the afternoon. Another group of Boston high-school pupils tutors elementary-level students in basic math and reading skills—improving their own competence while helping those 10 years their junior to make dramatic strides through one-to-one attention.

[21] A third group of ingenious high-school kids in Boston now operates a retail store out of an embellished pushcart at Boston's fashionable and historic Quincy Market.

[22] All of these efforts are for real; none is a "simulation." Whether it is tutoring in Boston or tea bags in Havana, the work of these young people is authentic and useful; in every instance, the student comes to see himself as a full-scale member and participant of the real political and economic life of his society.

[23] Now, at last, in 1979, an even more exciting possibility is in the wind. A plan is underway to introduce to Congress legislation which may make it possible for hundreds of thousands of secondary-school and college students to take leaves of absence for six months or more, in order to form the spearhead of a high-powered effort to eradicate adult illiteracy in the United States. The basic elements involve at least 5 million people 15 to 25 years old in an effort to liberate 25 million U.S. adults from the bondage of illiteracy.

[24] If legislation to empower this type of program passes House

and Senate subcommittees and the inevitable floor debates during the months ahead, our Congress will have done much more than begin the abolition of adult illiteracy. It will also have helped to redefine the role of childhood and to emancipate young people, for the first time, from the prison cells of simulation and from the school-mandated sense of uselessness, of wasted hours and exhausted years, which are the results of our archaic definition of those two words, "youth" and "childhood," in the United States.

[25] Perhaps a time is coming when schools no longer will feel the need to use their scarce funds to go out and purchase simulation games. Childhood, as we have seen, is a relatively new invention. As we struggle to outgrow what has become an outmoded concept, perhaps we can also outgrow our perception of the schools in which our children are trapped. In the Year of the Child, we might begin by re-inventing the whole idea of childhood.

[26] Children need not remain, in the words of Ivan Illich, "a consumer definition for a commodity known as school." They can also be forces to transform their schools and, with them, the societies in which they live.

VOCABULARY

Look up the following words in your dictionary. Use the system developed in the dictionary section in the back of the text. Be sure to write the part of speech, the pronunciation, and the meaning(s) of each word.

frail¹ (frāl) *adj.* **frailer, frailest. 1.** Having a delicate constitution; physically weak; not robust. **2.** Slight; weak; not strong or substantial. **3.** Easily broken or destroyed; vulnerable; fragile; uncertain. **4.** Morally weak; easily led astray or into evil. —See Synonyms at **fragile, weak.** [Middle English *frele, frail,* from Old French *frele, fraile,* from Latin *fragilis,* FRAGILE.] —**frail'ly** *adv.* —**frail'ness** *n.*
frail² (frāl) *n.* **1.** A rush basket for holding fruit, especially dried fruit. **2.** The quantity of fruit, such as raisins or figs, contained in a frail, usually from 50 to 75 pounds. [Middle English *fraiel,* from Old French *fraiel†.*]

Definitions with permission, From *Webster's New World Dictionary*, Second College Edition. Copyright © 1980 by Simon & Schuster, Inc.

advent

incorrigible

infuriating

deprecated

passivity

profound

moral

ethically

ineptitude

authentic

spearhead

eradicate

illiteracy

bondage

senile

moratorium

rote

simulation

insidious

vehicle

abolition

archaic

commodity

absorb

etherize

poised

embittered

perverse

spontaneous

ingenious

embellished

STUDY QUESTIONS

Finding the Matter

1. How were children dressed and treated until the end of the sixteenth century?

2. Why does Kozol say that from the seventeenth century through the nineteenth century children were considered "small problems patiently waiting to be big ones"?

3. Why have our attitudes toward children changed dramatically in the present century? Find four causes.

4. How recently have adults begun to consider children capable of participating in society?

5. What was absurd about the Harlem teacher "simulating" a game called Ghetto?

6. What examples does Kozol use of children actively contributing to their society while in school?

Exploring the Manner

1. Why does Kozol entitle his article "Reinventing Childhood" instead of "Redefining Childhood"?

2. Locate Kozol's definition of what a modern American childhood should be. Is his a lexical* definition or a stipulative* one? Support your answer.

3. What method of organization* does Kozol use at the beginning of his article to lead up to his thesis*?

4. What is the nature of the audience* that Kozol is trying to reach in this essay?

5. How do his examples* help to define his ideal of modern childhood?

SYNONYMS

From the column at the right, select the best synonym for the italicized word in each sentence. Rewrite each sentence using the appropriate synonym.

1. As time went on, children were regarded as little packets of charming but *unmanageable* mischief.

2. They were considered to be lovable and *enraging* little persons who required constant care.

3. It was Freud who taught us that childhood is the time that we form our *deep* moral and psychological dispositions.

A. infuriating

B. authentic

C. perverse

D. bondage

E. incorrigible

F. eradicate

G. ingenious

H. profound

4. The example of the lesson
   in the Harlem school shows
   a *contrary* method being
   used with inner-city
   children.

5. A group of *clever* high
   school students in Boston
   operates a retail store from
   a pushcart.

6. The work of these young
   people is *real* and useful,
   for by doing this the students come to regard themselves as full-scale members
   of the society.

7. We must change our educational methods in order to
   erase illiteracy in the United
   States.

8. By changing our methods
   we will liberate millions of
   adults from the *slavery* of
   illiteracy.

PARAPHRASE

Read this paragraph twice, then close your book. Using
your own words, rewrite the paragraph as clearly and completely as you can.

With the advent of childhood as a "unique condition,"
lasting generally into and sometimes even after adolescence,
the role of children underwent dramatic change. Little by
little, they came to be regarded as they would be viewed for
the next several centuries: little packets of charming but
incorrigible mischief, lovable at best, infuriating at worst,
in either case requiring constant feeding and attention—
contributing little and consuming much. Children were regarded as small problems patiently waiting to be big ones.
Throughout this period, childhood was deprecated as a time
of moral passivity; that children might have something worth
contributing was never seriously entertained.

VERB FILL-IN

Fill in each blank with the verb form that is appropriate for
each sentence.

Our views of children _____ dramatically in the present
                          change

century. First, Freud _____ us that our most profound
                          teach

moral and psychological dispositions _____ by childhood
                                          form

experience. Then such experts as Jean Piaget and Lawrence Kohlberg

_____ the development of moral thought through the years
     trace

of childhood and youth. Finally, in only the past few decades, chil-

dren _____ to be credited with the ability not only to think
         begin

ethically, but to act as moral agents in a changing society.

What _____ us to recognize these wasted possibilities,
         cause

after attributing to children for so long the same ineptitude as the

senile and insane? We may _____ this change of heart, in
                              attribute

part, to the work of imaginative authors. Of equal importance

_____ the models set for us by several other nations, Cuba
     be

and Israel probably the most important and influential. Above all,

perhaps, _____ the vivid example _____ to us by
         be   give

young men and women on their own.

SENTENCE COMPLETION

From the column at the right, select the correct line to complete each of the numbered lines at the left. Write each sentence in its correct form.

1. I discovered that they, along with the other third-graders of Cuba,

2. The children simply took a small and seemingly enjoyable role in helping to provide

3. Students in Boston study Early Childhood Development in the morning, then work for pay

4. A group of high school students now operates

5. The student comes to see himself as a full-scale member and participant

6. Whether it is tutoring in Boston or tea bags in Havana,

7. Childhood, as we have seen,

8. As we struggle to outgrow what has become an outmoded concept,

9. In the Year of the Child, we might begin

10. Children can also be forces to transform their schools and,

A. by reinventing the whole idea of childhood.

B. were producing all the tea bags that would be required in the next year.

C. a retail store out of an embellished pushcart.

D. the work of these young people is authentic and useful.

E. perhaps we can also outgrow our perception of the schools in which our children are trapped.

F. with troubled youngsters in a day-care center in the afternoon.

G. of the real political and economic life of his society.

H. with them, the societies in which they live.

I. is a relatively new invention.

J. one of the basic needs of their society.

CLOZE EXERCISE

Fill in each blank with the best word to complete the meaning of the sentence.

For whatever reason, the definition _____ childhood

has changed—and, with _____, an unhappy role which has,

_____ a century at least, been _____ upon our

public schools. The _____, as Alfred North Whitehead

noted, _____ built upon ideas that lead _____ to

action, nor to passion, _____ to transformation, but (at

most) _____ good term papers and examinations.

_____ thereby becomes a moratorium on _____,

a time in which young _____ spend about one-quarter of

their _____ biological existence in rote drill _____

readiness for the three-quarters they _____ never live to

know. Youth _____ thus defined as preparation for

_____, not a portion of it.

SENTENCE COMBINING

Combine each pair of sentences into a single grammatical
sentence.

1. Cuba and Israel set up models for us concerning children.
   Cuba and Israel were the most important and influential countries
   in setting up models.

2. Young men and women in the sixties were active in voter
   registration.
   They were active in their opposition to the Vietnam War.

3. Schools of today lead neither to action nor to transformation. Schools lead to term papers and examinations.

4. Change has yet to filter down to all the classrooms of the nation. There is already sufficient change for us to think of it on a larger scale.

5. Cuba's third-grade children worked in class. They were producing all the tea bags for their country.

6. Children can serve as forces to transform their schools. Children can transform the societies in which they live.

PUNCTUATION

Read the following paragraphs. Write in the capital letters and place commas, periods, colons, semicolons, dashes, and quotation marks where needed.

all of these efforts are for real none is a simulation whether it is tutoring in boston or tea bags in havana the work of these young people is authentic and useful in every instance the student comes to see himself as a full scale member and participant of the real political and economic life of his society

now at last in 1979 an even more exciting possibility is in the wind a plan is under way to introduce to congress legislation which may make it possible for hundreds of thousands of secondary school and college students to take leaves of absence for six months or more in order to form the spearhead of a high powered effort to eradicate adult illiteracy in the united states the basic elements in-volve at least 5 million people 15 to 25 years old in an effort to liberate 25 million u s adults from the bondage of illiteracy

WORD-FORM CHART

Use your dictionary to complete the following table. Follow the example shown with item 1, *passiveness/passivity*. If there is no commonly used form for a particular part of speech, write the symbol XXX.

Noun	Verb	Adjective	Adverb
1. passiveness passivity	XXX	passive	passively
2. ethic			
3.		simulative	
4. relation			
5.	enjoy		
6.	trouble		
7.		legislative	
8.	abolish		
9. archaism			
10. perception			

WORD-FORM EXERCISE

Using your completed Word-Form Chart, select the correct form to fit into each sentence. Use the appropriate tense of the verb, the singular or plural form of the noun, and the passive voice where necessary.

Follow the sequence of numbers from the Word-Form Chart to select the correct form.

1. Childhood was deprecated as a time of moral _____.

2. In only the past few decades, children have begun to be credited

    with the ability to think _____.

3. One student said that everything that is done in school seems to

   be a _____ of some other thing that would be real if it

   weren't taking place in school.

4. The child comes to adopt a passive view of his _____

   to history.

5. The children in Cuba took a small and seemingly _____

   role in helping to provide one of the basic needs of their society.

6. Some secondary school students in Boston worked for pay with

   _____ children of the community.

7. A plan is under way to introduce to Congress _____

   which may make it possible for many students to take leaves of

   absence from school in order to do other work.

8. If this occurs, Congress will have done much more than begin

   the _____ of adult illiteracy.

9. We still suffer from our _____ definition of "youth"

   and childhood.

10. As we outgrow our outmoded concept of childhood, perhaps we

    can outgrow our _____ of the schools in which our

    children are trapped.

QUESTIONS FOR DISCUSSION

1. Kozol says, "Childhood . . . becomes a moratorium on life, a time
   in which young people spend about one-quarter of their existence
   in rote drill and readiness for the three-quarters they may never
   live to know. Youth is thus defined as preparation for life, not a

portion of it." Discuss the ways in which this statement is true or not true in the educational system of your native country.

2. Since Kozol is a specialist in education, he takes his examples from the school environment. In what other areas of living can one encourage children to participate in life and not simply prepare for it?

3. How realistic is it to expect secondary school teachers to change their courses to include "real" instead of "simulated" learning experiences? Explain your point of view.

4. What activities within the school day could make elementary or high school children feel that they are part of their neighborhood, city, state, or country?

5. Kozol describes a plan to give students leaves of absence for six months or more in order to initiate a "high-powered effort to eradicate adult illiteracy in the United States." Do you agree or disagree with such a plan? Give your reasons. If your native country had such a plan, would you want to participate? Explain why.

TOPICS FOR WRITING

1. Kozol says: "In the Year of the Child we might begin by reinventing the whole idea of childhood." Write a composition in which you define the concept of childhood in your native country and discuss the changes that should be made in the way children are regarded there.

2. In preparation for a theme, work out a definition of childhood that includes involvement in the home, school, and community. Explain what jobs you consider appropriate at different ages.

3. Write a composition describing the contributions that children can make to a family in which both parents are working.

4. Imagine that a high school English class had decided to develop a work-study program to help the children of new immigrants practice speaking English. Write a theme narrating the experience of one student's first meeting with the non-English speaker.

6

Analysis

The Form

Analysis is the systematic study of something, usually by breaking it down into its parts. We may analyze a painting, a poem, or a mathematical problem by examining the components of each. One form of analysis is *division*, such as separating a shopping list into dairy products, vegetables, meat, and cleaning items. Such division can lead to *classification*, whereby we place similar products into the categories listed above: milk and eggs (dairy products), carrots and peas (vegetables), chicken and lamb (meats), and detergent and scouring powder (cleaning items). Not many people take the time to classify their shopping lists this way, but think of the time and energy they could save if they did so.

Classification not only groups similar objects but also separates them from contrasting ones. The categories should not overlap if we are to understand their distinct qualities and to distinguish the items within the categories from one another. Often, division comes before classification, as in this excerpt from E. B. White's essay "Here Is New York."

> There are roughly three New Yorks. There is, first, the New York of the man or woman who was born here, who takes the city for granted and accepts its size and its turbulence as natural and inevitable. Second, there is the New York of the commuter—the city that is devoured by

locusts each day and spat out each night. Third, there is the New York of the person who was born somewhere else and came to New York in quest of something. Of these three trembling cities the greatest is the last—the city of final destination, the city that is a goal.

White follows this division with classification, as he describes in detail the kinds of people who fill each category.

The Student Reader

When you read an essay that uses the method of analysis, first be aware of the author's purpose. If, for example, he is analyzing the educational value of various kinds of television programs, he may select categories such as comedies, game shows, soap operas, documentaries, news, sports, and films. He will then evaluate the examples from each category in terms of his thesis.

Another author might write a classification essay on the same topic of television programs. He might decide to show how a single topic, baseball, can be categorized as a sports event (a televised baseball game), a news item (baseball scores announced on the television news), or a documentary ("The History of Baseball").

The writer composing a process analysis must decide whether he is going to speak directly to the reader ("How to Bake an Apple Pie") or whether he is going to inform the reader of a process or event ("How the Tides Work"). In the first instance, he would be careful to provide a clear sequence of steps so that the reader could follow his instructions. In the second instance, he would provide specific information about the moon, gravity, and the changing tide tables. In both kinds of process analysis the writer must give enough detailed information to hold the reader's interest and to explain the process.

The Professional Writer

In his process essay "How to Get Ready for Studying Abroad," Roger Cox presents a series of steps designed to aid the American student in a foreign environment. The author hopes that his program will help students to cope with the difficulties involved in studying abroad. With modifications, the advice should be applicable to any student studying in a foreign country.

Unlike Cox, John Ciardi does not give advice in his essay "Of Writing and Writers." Instead, he explains a personal theory. On the basis of his many years as a poet, editor, and literary critic, Ciardi has placed writers into four different categories. He then goes on to analyze the qualities of the writer in each category, finding one category far superior to the other three.

A different approach to analysis can be found in Vicki Goldberg's essay "What Can We Do About Jet Lag?" Here the author tries to tell travelers how to reduce the discomfort caused by long-distance flights. First she explains the actual process of jet lag, the reactions of our bodies to rapid travel across time zones: disturbed sleep patterns, changed body temperatures, and reduced performance ability. Then she presents a series of steps to be followed if one wishes to avoid or minimize jet lag. These include being well rested before the flight, avoiding heavy eating or drinking on the flight, and pacing activities after arriving at one's destination. As with any good process analysis, this essay is instructional for the reader; it is especially valuable, of course, for the long-distance traveler.

HOW TO GET READY FOR STUDYING ABROAD

Roger Cox

[1] It was all so misleadingly simple. I had studied French in college, and my university offered a year abroad in France. My scholarship would apply; credit for courses was assured; advisers were available on campus to discuss passports, visas, shots, international student IDs and drivers' licenses. A charter flight had been booked and housing had been arranged. There was even a list of suggestions for packing. What could be simpler?

[2] Of course, we *were* told at the orientation meetings that it might be difficult to adjust to a foreign language, strange customs, and the European academic system. I remember paying scant attention. *"Tout s'arrange,"* I said to myself. "Everything works out."

[3] And everything did work out—more or less—but I was in for

some big surprises. If you're planning to study overseas, let me suggest a few key points to consider before you leave the U.S.A.:

Learn the Language

[4] In France, they speak French. Why, then, did I not strive vigorously to learn the language before I arrived? The requirement of two years of college French is minimal. One of my teachers warned that I was only marginally grounded in the language.

[5] "I know," I replied. "My vocabulary isn't what it should be."

[6] "Yes," she said. "Your vocabulary is limited, your grammar faulty, your syntax eccentric, and your pronunciation unabashedly American."

[7] But learning to speak French in the U.S. was hard work, so I put it off until I got to France, where I assumed language skills could be acquired effortlessly. Unfortunately, I was so embarrassed by my poor command of the language that I was afraid to speak.

[8] Slang also posed some disheartening problems. I mean, you know, like when students hang out to rap about where their heads're at, they don't draw on the vocabulary of 17th-century literary masterpieces. Most of us were more capable of discussing metaphysics than understanding the colloquial language of everyday conversation.

[9] Help came in the form of a Gallic proverb: "In order to speak good French, you have to relax; and in order to relax, you have to drink wine."

[10] At least half of that adage proved to be true. The greatest obstacle to learning a foreign language isn't vocabulary or grammar or pronunciation; it's self-consciousness. The trick is to plunge ahead, oblivious of embarrassing and ridiculous mistakes. I eventually learned to relax while making ridiculous mistakes.

[11] The same teacher who found my French so lacking also offered one helpful suggestion: read. Not just great French literature, but newspapers, popular magazines, dime novels, children's stories, menus, timetables, weather reports, and TV guides. The less intellectual the publication, the more likely it is to be written as people actually speak.

Don't Insist on the American Way

[12] Adjusting to another country demands changes in behavior and an open mind. Daily bathing, for example, is an American way of life, while many Europeans cannot imagine why anyone would want to shower more often than once a week. Because I lived in a dorm, I could follow my hygienic habits, and the French theirs. But in some student housing, such freedom wasn't possible, either because the

proprietors considered daily showers extravagant or because there were no showers on the premises.

[13] Social interactions can be a lot more complex. In France, for instance, a woman will not let a man pay for so much as a cup of espresso—to do so would be tantamount to inviting amorous advances. American women were assumed to play by the same rules, whether they *knew* the rules or not.

[14] On the other hand, the French see absolutely nothing wrong with a group of young men dancing together. We male Americans were not about to dance without women—until one night when I went out on the town with several French friends, and the lot of them took to the dance floor. Whenever such cultural customs conflicted, I had to choose to remain aloof and risk offending, or embrace their ways. I danced.

[15] Some of these rules and customs can be learned in advance; others are picked up easily abroad. Remaining flexible is the key.

Be Prepared for Independent Study

[16] The cultural difference that jolted me the most was in the university system itself. In Europe, the professor is a man on a pedestal, expecting and receiving deference. His contact with students is minimal. Even in the classroom, students neither question nor discuss the material presented.

[17] Attendance at the once-a-week classes is entirely voluntary. No assignments are given. The final exam does not consist of material presented in lectures. The course is defined not by how much material a professor covers but by a syllabus which lists the texts, periods, or literary works the student is expected to be familiar with. The classroom is supplemental, a model for the kind of preparation the student should be doing.

[18] Classroom discussion, midterm exams, threats of pop quizzes, an occasional paper—in short, all those methods of coercing students to do the work—are missing.

[19] The directors of my study-abroad program recognized that this was, in fact, too much to ask of educationally spoon-fed Americans. They arranged for graduate students to discuss the material presented in lectures, to answer our questions, and to give and correct homework assignments.

[20] Nevertheless, since classes began in November and exams were not until May, many of us didn't begin to study in earnest until April. Such procrastination had a necessarily detrimental effect on my grades. More significant, however, is that my spoken French vastly improved only after I started preparing for exams. A more disciplined approach would have been to begin in November, establishing my own schedule and sticking to it. But old habits die hard.

Go the Tourist Route in Moderation

[21] When classes meet infrequently, wanderlust is hard to resist. Living abroad meant that I could usually take short excursions—a week here, four days there. At Easter I splurged with a 25-day swing (two weeks were a school holiday) through seven European countries. After three weeks, churches, museums, historic sites, even country-sides and people began to run together. I can still recall Florence, one of the first stops on that marathon, in great detail; Munich, one of the last stops, is hazy, indistinct. All in all, the brief trips I made were far more satisfying than my longer expeditions.

[22] Moreover, all that art and history can become a blur if you don't know what you're seeing. When touring Notre Dame, Sacré Coeur and Montmartre, the Louvre, Ile de la Cité (the ancient heart of Paris), Versailles, and the châteaux of the Loire Valley, I could respond to their beauty with considerable awe but not much understanding. I wished I had taken a general course in art history before going to Europe.

Stay Loose

[23] Because we had come for an extended stay and spoke (at least haltingly) the language, many opportunities for making friends were opened up to us. We met French undergraduates in university classes and at the student restaurants where we ate all our meals. Others came to the meetings of a Franco-American club, which also arranged parties, dances, evenings of entertainment, and sporting events to bring Americans and French together.

[24] Some strong attachments were formed, but we naturally met with some anti-American sentiment as well. The best course was to ignore it, but discussions with fellow students about American political actions and policies were inevitable. We became adept at skirting volatile issues with ambassadorial diplomacy.

[25] One incident summed up our status as aliens with strong local ties. Late one afternoon I sat around a sidewalk cafe with some French students, who eventually departed for an anti-American demonstration. Out of genuine concern for my welfare, one of them warned me not to go near the rally. "Don't be offended," he said, "It's not you we don't like, it's the Americans."

[26] Whatever the complications of language, customs, and politics, my fondest memories are of the people I met. One man in particular stands out. Several of us were invited to dinner at his home, a simple dwelling in a small village. A laborer by trade, he was enormously proud to have Americans visit, yet humbled by what he considered the inadequacy of what he offered. Dinner consisted of homemade soup, vegetables fresh from his garden, local fish, steak (clearly a

concession to supposed American tastes) grilled over embers of grape-vine wood, his wife's special cake, fruit, and cheese. The host apologized throughout the evening for the poverty of the fare, while wine flowed freely. He could not do enough to make us feel welcome. He was one of the warmest, most genuinely hospitable people I have ever met.

[27] Yet he was not uncommon. Traveling about the countryside, staying in small hotels and *pensiones,* I met many like him. Learning French was the key to receiving an outpouring of kindness. We were a rare species, in a way—Americans who didn't expect the world to speak English. And our efforts to learn the language were almost universally met with warmth and old-world graciousness.

VOCABULARY

Look up the following words in your dictionary. Use the system developed in the dictionary section in the back of the text. Be sure to write the part of speech, the pronunciation, and the meaning(s) of each word.

strive (strīv) *intr.v.* **strove** (strōv) or *rare* **strived, striven** (strĭv'-ən) or **strived, striving, strives.** 1. To exert much effort or energy: *"She strove to make him moral, religious"* (D.H. Lawrence). 2. To struggle; contend: *"Good nature now and passion strive/Which of the two should be above"* (Suckling). [Middle English *striven,* from Old French *estriver,* perhaps from *estrif,* STRIFE. Strove, striven; Middle English *stroof, streven,* analogous formations, from *striven.*] —**striv′er** *n.*

Definition ©1981 Houghton Mifflin Company. Reprinted by permission from *The American Heritage Dictionary of the English Language, New College Edition.*

vigorously

marginally

eccentric

unabashedly

disheartening

Gallic

proverb

adage

obstacle

plunge

oblivious

hygienic

proprietors

extravagant

premises

interactions

tantamount

amorous

aloof

deference

supplemental

coercing

procrastination

wanderlust

excursions

splurged

marathon

expeditions

awe

inevitable

adept

skirting

volatile

rally

concession

species

STUDY QUESTIONS

Finding the Matter

1. What warnings were the students given about differences between French and American cultures?

2. Why did French slang present a special problem for the author?

3. Why does self-consciousness present an obstacle to learning a foreign language?

4. How can reading newspapers, menus, and children's stories be as valuable in learning a second language as studying grammar and literature?

5. What cultural differences did the author discover in France? How did he adapt to the new customs?

6. In what way is the student-professor relationship different in France?

Exploring the Manner

1. Although the essay is written in the first person* (*I*), the audience* is addressed in the section headings and elsewhere. Who is the intended audience?

2. If you use the section headings as an outline, how valuable is the article as a guide to studying abroad? What hints can you add?

3. Why does the author use American slang* in paragraph 8 when he presents the problem of French slang?

SYNONYMS

From the column at the right, select the best synonym for the italicized word in each sentence. Rewrite each sentence using the appropriate synonym.

1. I did not *attempt* to learn the language before I went to France.

2. This French *proverb* proved to be true: "In order to speak good French, you have to relax, and in order to relax, you have to drink wine."

3. The greatest *obstruction* to learning a foreign language is self-consciousness.

4. The trick in learning the language is to plunge ahead and try to be *unaware* of ridiculous mistakes.

5. I lived in a dorm, and so it made it easier for me to follow my own *sanitary* habits.

6. The *owners* of French housing considered daily showers extravagant.

7. Rules and customs of a foreign country cannot always be learned in advance; therefore one must be *adaptable*.

8. Some of us met with anti-American *feelings* from French students.

9. Political discussions with fellow students were *unavoidable*.

10. The students' efforts to learn the language were always met with warmth and *kindness* by the Europeans.

A. obstacle

B. hygienic

C. oblivious

D. adage

E. graciousness

F. strive

G. proprietors

H. flexible

I. sentiments

J. inevitable

PARAPHRASE

Read this paragraph twice; then close your book. Using your own words, rewrite the paragraph as clearly and completely as you can.

Adjusting to another country demands changes in behavior and an open mind. Daily bathing, for example, is an American way of life, while many Europeans cannot imagine why anyone would want to shower more often than once a week. Because I lived in a dorm, I could follow my hygienic habits, and the French theirs. But in some student housing, such freedom wasn't possible, either because the proprietors considered daily showers extravagant or because there were no showers on the premises.

VERB FILL-IN

Fill in each blank with the verb form that is appropriate for each sentence.

1. A charter flight _____ and housing _____
                                    book   arrange

   for my trip to France.

2. If you _____ to study overseas, let me give you some
                    plan

   advice.

3. I _____ French for two years in college.
            study

4. I assumed language skills _____ more easily in France.
                             acquire

5. I eventually _____ to relax while making ridiculous
                  learn

   mistakes.

6. The French see absolutely nothing wrong with a group of young

   men ───────── together.
       dance

7. The cultural difference that jolted me the most ─────────
                                                        be

   in the university system.

8. The course ───────── not by how much material a professor
        define

   covers but by a syllabus.

9. Since classes ───────── in November and exams were not
           begin

   until May, many of us didn't ───────── to study in earnest
                                   begin

   until April.

10. A more disciplined approach ───────── to begin a schedule
                                    be

    of study in November.

SENTENCE COMPLETION

From the column at the right, select the correct line to complete each of the numbered lines at the left. Write each sentence in its correct form.

1. Whatever the complications of language, customs, and politics my fondest memories

2. I could respond to the beauty of what I saw on my trip with considerable awe

3. Our French host apologized throughout the evening

4. The brief trips I made were far more satisfying

5. The directors of my study-abroad program recognized that the work planned

6. Classes met only once a week and attendance

7. The same teacher who found my French lacking offered

8. We students were a rare species, in a way, Americans who didn't expect

9. They arranged for graduate students to discuss materials presented in lectures.

A. than my longer expeditions.

B. was entirely voluntary.

C. but not with much understanding.

D. was too much to ask of educationally spoon-fed Americans.

E. for the poverty of the fare.

F. one helpful suggestion: read.

G. are the people I met.

H. the world to speak English.

I. to answer our questions, and to give and correct homework assignments.

CLOZE EXERCISE

Fill in each blank with the best word to complete the meaning of the sentence.

The cultural difference that jolted me _____ most was

in the university system _____. In Europe, the professor is a

_____ on a pedestal, expecting and receiving _____.

His contact with students is minimal. _____ in the class-

room, students neither question _____ discuss the material

presented.

Attendance at _____ once-a-week classes is entirely

voluntary. No _____ are given. The final exam does

_____ consist of material presented in lectures.

_____ course is defined not by how _____ mate-

rial a professor covers but by _____ syllabus which lists the

texts, periods, _____ literary works the student is expected

_____ be familiar with. The classroom is _____,

a model for the kind of _____ the student should be doing.

SENTENCE COMBINING

Combine each pair of sentences into a single, grammatical
sentence.

1. The requirement of two years of college French is minimal.
   I had two years of college French.

2. The students were capable of discussing metaphysics.
   The students could not understand the colloquial language of
   everyday conversation.

3. The trick is to plunge ahead.
   The trick is to be oblivious of embarrassing mistakes.

4. I was told to read popular magazines, children's stories, and
   weather reports.
   I was told to read the less intellectual publications.

5. A Frenchman does not usually pay for a woman's food.
   A Frenchman assumes that American women play by the same
   rules.

6. Students do not have to attend classes.
   Attendance is voluntary.

PUNCTUATION

Read the following paragraphs. Write in the capital letters
and place commas, periods, colons, semicolons, dashes and
quotation marks where needed.

in france they speak french why then did i not strive vigorously

to learn the language before i arrived the requirement of two years

of college french is minimal one of my teachers warned that i was

only marginally grounded in the language

i know i replied my vocabulary isnt what it should be

yes she said your vocabulary is limited your grammar faulty your

syntax eccentric and your pronunciation unabashedly american

WORD-FORM CHART

Use your dictionary to complete the following table. Follow
the example shown with item 1, *deference*. If there is no commonly used form for a particular part of speech, write the
symbol **XXX**.

Noun	Verb	Adjective	Adverb
1. deference	defer	deferential	deferentially
2.			vigorously
3.	interact		
4. conflict			
5.		supplemental	
6.	procrastinate		
7.		enormous	
8. coercion			
9.	awe		
10.	skirt		

WORD-FORM EXERCISE

Using your completed Word-Form Chart, select the correct form to fit into each sentence. Use the appropriate tense of the verb, the singular or plural form of the noun, and the passive voice where necessary.

Follow the sequence of numbers from the Word-Form Chart to select the correct form.

1. The European professor is a man on a pedestal who expects to receive _____ treatment.

2. I should have made a _____ effort to learn the language before I went to France.

3. Social _____ in France are complex for a newcomer to understand.

4. Whenever cultural customs _____ , I had to choose between remaining aloof or embracing foreign ways.

5. The classroom serves as a _____ to the preparation that the student should be doing.

6. I always used to _____ when it came to doing my schoolwork.

7. The Frenchman who invited us to his home was _____ proud to have Americans visit him.

8. By using various threatening methods, the French colleges always _____ the students to do their work.

9. I was really _____ by the beauty of the European cities I had visited.

10. In order not to become involved in arguments, we _____ political issues.

QUESTIONS FOR DISCUSSION

1. What are the daily concerns of a person who has recently arrived in a foreign country and has to adjust to a new language and a new culture?

2. Discuss some of the customs that differ in America and in your native culture. (Some examples are dating, manners, holiday customs.)

3. Describe the "culture shock" that you experienced when you first arrived in the United States.

4. Is a second language easier to learn before or after one arrives in a foreign country? How effective is foreign language study in your native country?

TOPICS FOR WRITING

1. Make a list of the ways in which foreign students planning to study in the United States can prepare themselves for the difficulties ahead. Then write a theme describing the process.

2. Write a paper explaining the ways in which foreign students can adjust to the problems of studying at American colleges after they have arrived in the United States.

3. Examine the ways in which the school that you are now attending can help the nonnative student to feel more relaxed and therefore (according to Cox) better able to learn.

4. Write an article for your native high school's newspaper telling the students of your problems studying in another country. Like Cox, explain each problem and its cause(s); then suggest the steps required to overcome the problem. Choose one or more of these problem areas: (a) language acquisition, (b) culture shock, (c) anti- _____ feeling, (d) educational differences.

OF WRITING AND WRITERS

John Ciardi

[1] There is no formula by which a man can become a writer, and there is no end to the number of ways in which a man can be one. Writing can be an art, a trade, a craft, or a hobby. The artist writes compulsively, as a way of knowing himself, or of clarifying what he does not know about himself. He writes, let us say, for those glimpses of order that form can make momentarily visible. But add that he writes in about the way a drunkard drinks. His passion springs not from reason, but from thirst.

[2] The artist-writer and the drunkard are both aware—if only in moments of painful sobriety—that there are consequences to what they do, but for both of them the doing itself is the real conse-

(Courtesy of U.P.I.)

quence. The happy difference between the writer's compulsion and the drunkard's is that the drunkard hopes to lose himself in his bottle, whereas the writer hopes to find himself on his page. In his act of writing, the writer finds himself wiser, more sentient, more pertinent to his own life, perhaps more confused by it, but more meaningfully confused. He is a language-haunted man and a cadence-haunted man and a form-haunted man and an image-haunted man, and he knows that whatever ghosts he gathers about him in the writing are, finally, his best sense of himself. And he knows that those ghosts are the shadowy tribesmen of every man's first-and-last identity. The writer as artist does say things, but he does not write for the sake of saying. The saying is inevitable but secondary. He writes to be in the company of his necessary ghosts, much as a man will trek halfway round the world to get back home to the company of what names him.

[3] The man who writes as a trade is simply an employed person, a wage-earner. He may be more or less serious about his trade. He may be good or bad at it. He may, at times, confuse his own motives and try to write as an artist does. He may even refuse easy assignments that could produce fat checks. Still, as a man practicing a trade, he must write, finally, to make a living. That is to say he must write not for himself (compelled) but for the check his writing will bring.

[4] The difference between the craftsman and the hobbyist is, as I see it, a matter of intensity. Or perhaps there is no real difference except that the word "craft" implies at root an agonizing exertion, whereas the word "hobby" carries no feeling with it but the sense of idle play. The craftsman works at his writing harder than does the hobbyist, whether for pay or not, and is likely to be more self-demanding without ever quite achieving the passion and the compulsion of the artist. I am tempted to think of Dr. Samuel Johnson, lexicographer, as practicing the craft of writing without quite managing to make a trade of it. But who would dare call him a hobbyist? The hobbyist simply amuses himself. The center of what he does with his life is somewhere else. The writing, like a stamp collection, is a way of passing a quiet evening in a room somewhere off the center of the house.

[5] In writing, trade blurs into craft, and craft blurs into hobby, but there can be no blurring of the line between the artist-writer and every other kind of writer. Except, perhaps, that it is possible to write well on any of these four levels. Even the hobbyist might turn out an enduring if slight fragment—say, a memorable piece of light verse. Even a craftsman or a man plying a trade—say, a Daniel Defoe—might turn out a piece of real or imagined journalism so firmly marshaled upon itself that it stays memorable and firm. But only the writer-as-artist, I believe, can write in a way that burns forever.

[6] Combustion is, of course, the heart of it. And combustion in art can be produced only by the passion of compulsive men. The artist is once more like the drunkard in that he cannot stop to count the cost of his compulsion. The writer may write himself (as the drunkard may drink himself) out of employment, family, social acceptance, and out of health and life itself. There is no help for it: the man *must* do what he does. There is no mercy in it: no page cares what it has cost the writer.

[7] All writing is measured, in the long run, by its memorableness. A man either writes in forms that cling to human memory, and so become unforgettable; or he writes forgettably and is soon forgotten—with, perhaps, the temporary exception that the American school system often seems to be a conspiracy to keep some unflaggingly forgettable writing in student memory by forced feeding.

[8] The fact is that language supremely used will survive the death of its own mother tongue. Latin and Greek are both dead languages, but the high moments of Greek and Latin writing are still alive in men's minds. Man needs language because he lives by it and knows himself by it, and because he lives in it and knows himself in it without recourse to logic, but as an act of identity he can never hope to reason out or do without. He will store great acts of language for the simple reason that he lives by them.

[9] The combustion of the artist-writer springs from the passion with which he engages that mysterious act of identity, losing himself in it as his only hope of finding himself. The writer may be wrong, of course. And there is no mercy for the wrong. If a man ruins himself in his compulsion to write a dull book, I am left with no compulsion to read it. Another man may write, no, not easily, but joyously, thriving on his difficulties because he has an appetite for them, and that man may come in a glow of well-being to write a good book. The page has treated him kindly.

[10] But the reader does not care what it costs the man. Why should he? The library is full of books, and he owes no duty to any but those that please him. He reads joyously through the happy man's good book without a thought for the self-ruined failure whose volume continues to gather dust until it becomes itself dust. Or, finished with the happy man's good book, the reader may lose himself next in the good book another man killed himself to write. What should the reader care? He does not so much as see the corpse. There is no corpse in good writing: the writing is always a life. It is the writer who becomes the corpse, but never in his writing—not if it is of the memorable and burning.

[11] And add one thing more about the writing—on whatever level, the success of the writing is measured by the most democratic process in human experience. Whoever you are as a person, whoever you were, the writing lives or dies outside of you and apart from you.

Whether you write from a throne or a dungeon, and whether or not you deserve to be on the one or in the other, the reader does not know you and does not care and has no reason to care. Take a piece of paper, put a life on it or a piece of a life, make that life burn to reality (that is to say, to the illusion of a reality) in the act of language in which you summon it—and the reader (always the unknown reader) is yours without a thought of who you are in yourself on the other side of that page.

VOCABULARY

Look up the following words in your dictionary. Use the system developed in the dictionary section in the back of the text. Be sure to write the part of speech, the pronunciation, and the meaning(s) of each word.

for·mu·la (fôr′myə-lə) *n., pl.* **-las** or **-lae** (-lē′). **1.** An established form of words or symbols for use in a ceremony or procedure. **2.** An utterance of conventional notions or beliefs; a hackneyed expression; cliché. **3.** *Chemistry.* **a.** A symbolic representation of the composition, or of the composition and structure, of a chemical compound. **b.** The chemical compound so represented. **4.** A prescription of ingredients in fixed proportion; recipe. **5.** A liquid food prescribed for an infant and containing most required nutrients. **6.** A mathematical statement, especially an equation, of a rule, principle, answer, or other logical relation. [Latin *fōrmula*, diminutive of *fōrma*, FORM.] **—for′-mu·la′ic** (fôr′myə-lā′ĭk) *adj.*

Definition ©1981 Houghton Mifflin Company. Reprinted by permission from *The American Heritage Dictionary of the English Language, New College Edition.*

compulsively

clarifying

glimpses

sobriety

consequence

sentient

pertinent

haunted

cadence

trek

intensity

implies

idle

lexicographer

exertion

combustion

conspiracy

unflaggingly

STUDY QUESTIONS

Finding the Matter

1. What similarity is there between the artist-writer and the drunkard? What difference can you find between them?

2. What kinds of ghosts haunt the artist-writer?

3. How does a person who writes for a living differ from the artist-writer?

4. How does Ciardi distinguish between writing as a "craft" and writing as a "hobby"?

5. Why doesn't every artist-writer produce a great work of literature?

Exploring the Manner

1. Since he is a poet, Ciardi like to use words on a figurative* as well as a literal* level. For example, when he speaks of the "combustion" of the artist-writer, he does not really mean fire. What is he referring to?

2. How do you know that Ciardi is not talking about physical thirst when he says that the artist-writer, like the drunkard, has a passion that "springs not from reason, but from thirst"?

3. Does Ciardi treat his four categories seriously, or is he really using them to glorify the artist-writer? Support your answer by finding Ciardi's thesis*.

4. What kind of audience* would be most interested in this essay? What meaning could the essay have for people in business or science as well as the arts?

SYNONYMS

From the column at the right, select the best synonym for
the italicized word in each sentence. Rewrite each sentence
using the appropriate synonym.

1. The artist writes *obsessively*
   as a way of knowing himself.

2. The artist-writer and the
   drunkard are both aware
   that what they do has *results*.

3. In his act of writing, the
   writer finds himself more
   relevant to his own life.

4. Because he is concerned with
   language and expression, the
   writer cannot help but be
   haunted by the *rhythm* of
   his tools.

5. The artist-writer is like a
   man who will *travel* halfway
   round the world to get back
   home to the environment
   that defines him.

6. The word "hobby" carries
   no feeling with it but the
   sense of *inactive* play.

7. The word "craft" *suggests*
   agonizing exertion.

8. I am tempted to think of
   Dr. Samuel Johnson, lexicographer, as practicing the
   craft of writing without
   quite managing to make a
   business out of it.

9. Even the hobbyist might
   turn out a fragment that is
   lasting.

A. pertinent

B. trek

C. idle

D. consequences

E. trade

F. enduring

G. compulsively

H. cadence

I. implies

PARAPHRASE

Read this paragraph twice; then close your book. Using
your own words, rewrite the paragraph as clearly and completely as you can.

The man who writes as a trade is simply an employed
person, a wage-earner. He may be more or less serious about
his trade. He may be good or bad at it. He may, at times,
confuse his own motives and try to write as an artist does.
He may even refuse easy assignments that could produce
fat checks. Still, as a man practicing a trade, he must write,
finally, to make a living. That is to say he must write not for
himself (compelled) but for the check his writing will bring.

VERB FILL-IN

Fill in each blank with the verb form that is appropriate for
each sentence.

The fact _____ that language supremely used _____
          be

_____ the death of its own mother tongue. Latin and Greek
  survive

_____ both dead languages, but the high moments of Greek
    be

and Latin writing _____ in men's minds. Man _____
              alive   need

language because he _____ by it and _____ himself
                  live   know

by it, and because he _____ in it and _____
                 live   know

himself in it without recourse to logic, but as an act of identity he

_____ never hope to reason out or do without. He
    can

_____ great acts of language for the simple reason that he
   store

_____ by them.
   live

SENTENCE COMPLETION

From the column at the right, select the correct line to complete each of the numbered lines at the left. Write each sentence in its correct form.

1. Writing can be an art, a trade,

2. The artist-writer and the drunkard are both aware that there are consequences to what they do,

3. The writer by trade may even refuse easy assignments

4. For a hobbyist, the writing, like a stamp collection, is a way of passing a quiet evening

5. Only the writer-as-artist

6. All writing is measured, in the long run,

7. If a man ruins himself in his compulsion to write a dull book,

8. The library is full of books and

9. Whether you write from a throne or a dungeon,

10. Make a piece of paper burn with reality

A. I am left with no compulsion to read it.

B. in a room somewhere off the center of the house.

C. but for both of them, the doing itself is the real consequence.

D. the reader owes no duty to any books but those that please him.

E. by its memorableness.

F. and the reader is yours without a thought of who you are in yourself on the other side of the page.

G. can write in a way that burns forever.

H. that could produce fat checks.

I. a craft, or a hobby.

J. the reader does not know you and does not care.

CLOZE EXERCISE

Fill in each blank with the best word to complete the meaning of the sentence.

In writing, trade blurs into _____, and craft blurs into

hobby, _____ there can be no blurring _____

the line between the artist-writer _____ every other kind of

writer. _____, perhaps, that it is possible _____

write well on any of _____ four levels. Even the hobbyist

_____ turn out an enduring if _____ fragment—

say, a memorable piece _____ light verse. Even a craftsman

_____ a man plying a trade—_____, a Daniel

Defoe—might turn _____ a piece of real or _____

journalism so firmly marshalled upon _____ that it stays

memorable and _____. But only the writer-as-artist, I

_____, can write in a way _____ burns forever.

SENTENCE COMBINING

Combine each pair of sentences into a single, grammatical sentence.

1. The man who writes as a trade is simply an employed person.
   The man who writes as a trade is simply a wage earner.

2. There is no formula by which a man can become a writer.
   There is no end to the number of ways in which a man can be a writer.

3. In writing, trade blurs into craft.
   In writing, craft blurs into hobby.

4. Latin and Greek are both dead languages.
   The high moments of Greek and Latin writing are still alive in men's minds.

5. Man needs language because he lives by it and knows himself by it.
   Man needs language because he lives in it and knows himself in it without recourse to logic.

6. Whether you write from a throne or a dungeon the reader does not know you.
   Whether you deserve to be on one or in the other the reader does not care.

PUNCTUATION

Read the following paragraph. Write in the capital letters and place commas, periods, colons, semicolons, dashes, and quotation marks where needed.

but the reader does not care what it costs the man why should

he the library is full of books and he owes no duty to any but those

that please him he reads joyously through the happy mans good

book without a thought for the self ruined failure whose volume

continues to gather dust until it becomes itself dust or finished with

the happy mans good book the reader may lose himself next in the

good book another man killed himself to write what should the

reader care he does not so much as see the corpse there is no corpse

in good writing the writing is always a life it is the writer who

becomes the corpse but never in his writing not if it is of the

memorable and burning

WORD-FORM CHART

Use your dictionary to complete the following table. Follow the example shown with item 1, *visibility*. If there is no commonly used form for a particular part of speech, write the symbol XXX.

Noun	Verb	Adjective	Adverb
1. visibility	XXX	visible	visibly
2. passion			
3.			pertinently
4.	identify		
5. artist			
6.		employable	
7.		memorable	
8.	survive		
9.		merciful	
10. democrat			

WORD-FORM EXERCISE

Using your completed Word-Form Chart, select the correct form to fit into each sentence. Use the appropriate tense of the verb, the singular or plural form of the noun, and the passive voice where necessary.

Follow the sequence of numbers from the Word-Form Chart to select the correct form.

1. The author writes for those glimpses of order that form can

   make ＿＿＿＿＿＿＿＿.

2. The dedicated writer is usually a _____ man.

3. In the act of writing, the writer finds himself more

   _____ to his own life.

4. The ghosts of writing serve to make the author's self

   _____.

5. Writing, in its highest form, is an _____ endeavor.

6. A serious writer who uses his craft to earn his living is

   simply an _____ person.

7. A hobbyist might write a piece that will stay in your

   _____.

8. The partial _____ of Greek and Latin is the result of

   writing, not speech.

9. One must not feel _____ toward the writer who writes

   a dull book.

10. The success of a book is measured by the most _____

    process in human experience.

QUESTIONS FOR DISCUSSION

1. Ciardi says that the artist-writer writes compulsively. Do you have any artistic compulsions? Explain how they affect you.

2. In what ways does writing teach people about themselves?

3. Ciardi comments that the American school system keeps "forgettable writing" in students' memories by making it required reading. What single book made the greatest impression on you before you entered college? Did you think it was great literature at the time? What do you think of its literary merit now?

TOPICS FOR WRITING

1. Write a composition explaining what you can learn about yourself by writing. Choose and discuss three categories of self-discovery (such as fears, strengths, goals).

2. Analyze your present job or future career as it fits into one or more of Ciardi's categories.

3. Ciardi says that writing is a democratic process because success is measured by the writing itself, not by the origins of the writer. Choose another field in which the background of the person is not involved with his or her achievement. Discuss three categories that do determine success in this field.

WHAT CAN WE DO ABOUT JET LAG?

Vicki Goldberg

[1]   After 17 years in the Senate, Hiram Fong retired because of jet lag. The Hawaii senator, who made the 9,700-mile trip to Washington and back nine times a year, told a reporter it took him nearly a week to recover from each leg of the journey—18 weeks a year "in purgatory, trying to get back to normal."

[2]   It's not the first time travel has undone a lawmaker. The signers of the Declaration of Independence complained that King George III "has called together legislative bodies at places unusual, uncomfortable and distant for the sole purpose of fatiguing them into compliance with his measures."

[3]   Now the British and French claim to have the ultimate in traveler convenience, the Concorde. Because the traveler will spend less time on board with supersonic flight, there should be some easing of the general fatigue of air travel. But jet lag will remain even if the FAA prediction of crossing the Atlantic in 45 minutes by 1988 holds true. The Concorde no longer advertises that it can cut down on jet lag, because it can't; a doctor pointed out the time shift is the same no matter how fast you make it.

[4]   Jet lag after rapid travel across time zones is a malaise devised by this century. We don't yet have a pill to prevent it, but various scientific studies are at least beginning to explain precisely how it affects our bodies. By understanding how it works, we may at least learn to mitigate its worst symptoms.

[5]   Standard time zones themselves are fairly new. Before 1883, there were 100 time zones in America, with 27 local times in Michigan alone. Individual towns set their clocks by the best local estimate of noon. The railroads adopted the present four zones to make scheduling less of an acrobatic feat; the government made them legal for the whole country in 1918. Now jets keep slipping across time faster than bodies can shift gears.

[6]   When the plane arrives in London at 9:00 in the morning from New York, body time is still 4:00 A.M.: temperature and hormones are behaving as if the passenger were still in New York—and asleep. People can reset their watches in seconds, but not their bodies, which are slow to adapt. Different body functions will adjust to London time at different rates. Daily activity rhythms may slip into place fairly soon, but sleep patterns struggle to find the proper city for two days or more, and normal temperature rhythms can require over a week to adjust. The body is internally desynchronized, which probably accounts for much of the fatigue of jet travel.

[7]   After crossing several time zones, sleep rhythms undergo marked

(Courtesy of U.P.I.)

changes during the first night: in laboratory and flight studies, Rapid
Eye Movement (REM) sleep, during which most dreaming deemed
essential to mental well-being occurs, was delayed and severely
cut back. By the second night, the normal pattern began to reassert
itself, but sleep tended to be interrupted and shortened by early
morning waking for up to five days. Most subjects in such research
have been in their 20s; the few in their 40s had particularly depressed
REM sleep and were more likely to wake up early for an extended
period.

[8] Body temperature won't follow the new clock for some time.
Karl E. Klein and Hans-Martin Wegmann, German scientists, studied
eight young American residents who flew from the U.S. to Germany
and then back again 18 days later. They found that body temperature
dropped significantly at certain hours and rose at others on the first
postflight day in either direction, and did not return to preflight

levels until the third day. (It is known that a temperature depression often follows stress.) More than three days are needed to shift the *phase* of temperature rhythm, that normal curve from low in the morning to highest in the late afternoon and lowest in the early morning sleeptime hours. In this study, phase adjustment took 11 to 12 days after the westward flight, 14 to 15 after going east. Earlier studies had found three to five days sufficient.

[9] Temperature and performance are probably related. Studies show highs and lows in both occur at roughly the same hours. Not surprisingly, the clock that regulates efficiency on complicated performance tasks seems as reluctant as temperature rhythms to reset after long flights. And there's the rub for businessmen and diplomats, as well as others, who must be capable and efficient after travel.

[10] Volunteers given performance tests before and after flights across time zones had significantly decreased capacity at certain hours for several days after travel. In time-shift experiments, performance on relatively simple tests such as reaction time, grip strength, and easy mathematical problems fell off for two or three days after flights. The loss in capacity was greater in the morning after eastward flights, in the afternoon after going west. As with temperature, the adjustment of the phase of performance rhythms took a long while. Resynchronization was relatively rapid for the simple tests, but efficiency on complex psychomotor performance tasks—like piloting a supersonic flight simulator—took at least five, and up to 10, days to adapt. Kissinger's Middle Eastern diplomacy looks almost miraculous in this light.

[11] But travelers may have a peculiar advantage over the natives if they watch their time carefully. Performance follows a daily curve similar to that of temperature, with a peak in the afternoon and a trough at night. A study by Klein and others published in 1970 stated that the old schedule persisted in the body for up to three days at the new destination, even as adjustment to the new schedule was proceeding. Thus the subjects studied had *two peaks and two troughs* each day, one on European and one on American time. Travelers from Europe to the U.S. performed more efficiently for the first three nights at late night hours, when they had an extra peak, than people already adapted to American time. That information may be useful only to someone who needs to do business at 3:00 A.M., but a little clever figuring might make the trip more productive.

[12] Hormonal rhythms are also disturbed by skipping across time zones, and since some rhythms take five, others six, seven, or eight days to shift to the new schedule, the body remains internally desynchronized for some time. No one knows whether we suffer lasting harm from such desynchronization. Time-shift experiments with blow flies, simulating repeated time-zone crossings, found that

flies subjected to such shifts lived shorter than normal lives. In 1976, Juergen Aschoff, an expert on biological rhythms, wrote, "These data cannot be applied to man, but they should serve as a warning not to underestimate the possible deleterious effects of frequent air travel eastward or westward."

[13] Circadian, or 24-hour, rhythms probably confer some advantage or they would not have evolved; disturbing them with the means available to modern technology is likely to be disadvantageous. Recent experiments on coddling moths, on the other hand, turned up certain time shifts—changes in 24-hour light-dark cycles—that did not alter the life span and one that even prolonged it slightly. Once more, the data do not fit human beings; rather, they indicate how little we really know about the legacy of the jet age.

[14] Evidence strongly suggests that jet travel is easier on the system going west than going east. After westward flights, it usually takes a shorter time to resynchronize, and performance loss is generally less. Klein and Wegmann reported that during the first 30 to 40 hours after a westbound flight, biological rhythms shifted between 20 to 80 percent more in phase than after an eastbound flight. Even if the traveler's home is in the east, adaptation tends to be faster after westward flight, overriding the psychological effects of returning home. (It is easiest of all to fly north and south. All clocks along the way are in agreement, and though fatigue sets in, desynchronization does not.)

[15] Westbound travel may be easier than eastbound for two reasons. Studies of people in environments devoid of any time cues have shown that the natural rhythms of most people tend to run slightly longer than 24 hours; so it is not surprising that it is easier to adapt to a longer day on a westward flight than to a shorter one heading east. But a more important reason may be that many passengers simply find it more convenient to leave in the evening after work; going east, they therefore arrive in the morning and, without a night's sleep, find it hard to stay awake. Clearly, it is better to leave at an hour that lets you see a pillow before you sightsee on another continent.

[16] Of course, individual reactions differ. We do not know yet whether people who are by nature early risers adjust at rates different from late-night, late-morning types. Experience and some experimental evidence indicate that older people suffer more from jet lag than the young. One interesting suggestion is that people who stay relatively isolated on arrival, with few time cues and little physical activity, seem to take longer to adjust than those who travel in groups, go outdoors more, and get more social stimulus. Research in this area is still patchy, but social cues and influences are generally thought to be important in setting human circadian rhythms.

[17] The airlines refer to jet lag as "travel dysrhythmia," to indi-

cate it's not the airplane's fault but the human being's for boarding it. Whatever it's called, jet travelers are learning ways to beat it. On short hops, watches need never be changed. The corporate medical director of American Airlines claims he saved the job of a California executive who had to commute often to New York, leaving at 9:00 A.M., arriving at 6:00 P.M., and barely slogging his way through the next morning's meeting. "Insist the meeting be at 7:00 the night you arrive," the doctor advised. "It's 4:00 in the afternoon for you, and you're still fresh." It worked. It is also useful to find out if the airport hotel has 24-hour food service and a room away from the street noise so you can dine at 10:00 P.M. local time and sleep till 10:00 in the morning. The Russians are experimentally keeping pilots on Moscow time for short layovers; special hotels in Havana and elsewhere stay on Russian light-dark schedules and mealtimes.

[18] On longer trips, careful planning cuts losses. Be well rested before leaving—this means no last-minute, frantic dash to the airport—as your sleep may not be complete for a couple of nights. (Some TWA European flights have a quiet zone, without movies, and with meals served soon after takeoff for those who wish to sleep on board.) Try to arrive at an hour close to your regular bedtime. If sleep is elusive, get up and exercise or take a warm bath, but avoid alcohol, tranquilizers, or hypnotics, all of which can interfere with REM sleep, already jeopardized by the time shift. If possible, avoid major tasks and decisions for the first day or two, and continue to pace yourself for at least one day for every time zone crossed. A rule of thumb for adjustment is one day for every hour's change, but it doesn't quite work, since the body stubbornly refuses to realign every function at the same rate.

[19] To minimize the stress of flight, airlines recommend wearing loose-fitting clothing and comfortable shoes to keep circulation unrestricted. Moving around, or at least flexing the different muscle groups, during the flight helps stave off muscle fatigue and blood clots. (Lufthansa offers an isometric exercise program, based on NASA's fitness program for astronauts, on one of its inflight music channels.) Since jet lag cannot be avoided, heavy eating and drinking should be, both during the flight and for a couple of days afterward, as they place an additional stress on the system. If you add alcohol to altitude, the total can be greater than the sum of the parts: in the air, two or three cocktails are the equivalent of three or four at sea level (for complex reasons having to do with the lower air pressure in the cabin, which means less oxygen is available for the body, and with the slower rate of alcohol metabolism at high altitudes).

[20] If you cannot avoid an important meeting shortly after arrival, it may be useful to preadapt to the local time of your destination. Mealtimes and bedtime can be gradually changed over a period of

several days before departure. In 1931 Wiley Post flew around the world in a record-breaking eight days, having first readjusted his biological clock so that he was out of phase when he left New York, in phase over Russia with his trip half done. Post said that preadapting had enabled him to stay alert without stimulants.

[21] Almost the only other option is to be an Eskimo. *The New York Times* once reported that "the perpetual darkness of the Eskimos' winters and the lightness of their summers prevent their establishing deep-seated rhythmic patterns of bodily functions easily thrown out of kilter by time-zone changes." The rest of us have deep-seated rhythmic patterns; we had best pay heed to them, for we have not evolved at the same speed as the mighty engine of a jumbo jet.

VOCABULARY

Look up the following words in your dictionary. Use the system developed in the dictionary section in the back of the text. Be sure to write the part of speech, the pronunciation, and the meaning(s) of each word.

> **pur·ga·to·ry** (pûr'gə-tôr'ē, -tōr'ē) *n., pl.* **-ries. 1.** *Roman Catholic Church.* A state in which the souls of those who have died in grace must expiate their sins. **2.** Any place or condition of expiation, suffering, or remorse. —*adj.* Tending to cleanse or purge. [Middle English *purgatorie,* from Medieval Latin *purgātōrium,* from Late Latin *purgātōrius,* from Latin *purgāre,* to PURGE.]

> Definition ©1981 Houghton Mifflin Company. Reprinted by permission from *The American Heritage Dictionary of the English Language, New College Edition.*

legislative — Law making bodies

compliance - in agreement

ultimate

fatigue

malaise

mitigate

acrobatic

temperature

hormones

phase

synchronized

efficiency

reluctant

psychomotor

miraculous

peaks

troughs

deleterious

evolved

legacy

isolated

patchy

dysrhythmia

frantic

tranquilizers

hypnotics

stave

metabolism

perpetual

kilter

heed

STUDY QUESTIONS

Finding the Matter

1. What American industry adopted the present four time zones, and why was it done?

2. How are sleep rhythms disturbed after a traveler crosses several time zones?

3. What happens to the body temperature after a trip across time zones?

4. How are body temperature and performance related?

5. Why doesn't the traveler suffer jet fatigue when traveling north and south?

6. Why is westbound travel less of a strain on the traveler than east-bound travel?

Exploring the Manner

1. Although the essay is a process analysis, it begins with two examples* of jet lag. What is their function in the essay?

2. In her thesis, the author divides her essay into two analyses of jet lag. What are they?

3. The author lists nine methods of minimizing jet lag. Is there any reason for the order in which she presents these ideas? Has she saved the best ones for last? Explain your reasons.

4. The author ends the essay, as she began it, with an example. This time she discusses the Eskimos, who would suffer little or no jet lag because of their climate-related body rhythms. How does this example* relate to her thesis? How effective is the ending of the essay?

SYNONYMS

From the column at the right, select the best synonym for the italicized word in each sentence. Rewrite each sentence using the appropriate synonym.

1. With the new Concorde plane, there will be a shorter flight to Europe, so travelers will suffer less *fatigue* in air travel.

A. mitigate

B. trough

C. exhaustion

D. high point

2. Jet lag results in a general feeling of *malaise* among most airplane travelers.

3. By understanding how jet lag works, we may be able to *relieve* some of its worst symptoms.

4. Travelers show a daily curve, with a *peak* in the afternoon.

5. In this daily curve, travelers also show a *low point* at night.

6. Frequent plane travel can prove to be *deleterious* to most people.

7. It is recommended that travelers be well rested before a flight and that they avoid a last-minute, *desperate* dash to the airport.

8. Eskimos' rhythmic patterns of bodily functions are affected by the *perpetual* darkness of their winters.

E. frantic

F. sickness

G. continuous

H. harmful

PARAPHRASE

Read this paragraph twice; then close your book. Using your own words, rewrite the paragraph as clearly and completely as you can.

Individual reactions differ. We do not know yet whether people who are by nature early risers adjust at rates different from late-night, late-morning types. Experience and some experimental evidence indicate that older people suffer more from jet lag than the young. One interesting suggestion is that people who stay relatively isolated on arrival, with few time cues and little physical activity, seem to take longer to adjust than those who travel in groups, go outdoors more, and get more social stimulus. Research in this area is still patchy, but social cues and influences are generally thought to be important in setting human circadian rhythms.

VERB FILL-IN

Fill in each blank with the verb form that is appropriate for each sentence.

Volunteers _____ performance tests before and after
                    give

flights across time zones _____ decreased capacity at
                                  have

certain hours for several days after travel. In time-shift experiments,

performance on relatively simple tests _____ off for two or
                                              fall

three days after flights. The loss in capacity _____ greater in
                                                        be

the morning after eastward flights, in the afternoon after going west.

As with temperature, the adjustment of the phase of performance

rhythms _____ a long while. Resynchronization
              take

_____ relatively rapid for the simple tests, but efficiency
      be

on complex psychomotor performance tasks _____ at least
                                                  take

five and up to ten days to adapt. Kissinger's Middle Eastern diplo-

macy _____ almost miraculous in this light.
          look

SENTENCE COMPLETION

From the column at the right, select the correct line to complete each of the numbered lines at the left. Write each sentence in its correct form.

1. Jet lag after rapid travel across time zones is

2. By understanding how jet lag works,

3. After crossing several time zones,

4. Researchers found that body temperature dropped significantly at certain hours

5. People can reset their watches

6. The subjects studied had two peaks and two troughs each day,

7. No one knows whether we suffer lasting harm

8. Westbound travel is usually easier

9. Experience and experimental evidence indicate that older people

10. Moving around, or at least flexing the different muscle groups during the flight,

11. If you cannot avoid an important meeting shortly after arrival,

12. Most of us have deep-seated rhythmic patterns; we had best pay heed to them,

A. but not their bodies.

B. than eastbound travel.

C. a malaise devised by this century.

D. one on European time and one on American time.

E. sleep rhythms undergo marked changes.

F. it may be useful to preadapt to the local time of your destination.

G. suffer more from jet lag than the young.

H. for we have not evolved at the same speed as the mighty engine of a jumbo-jet.

I. and rose at others on the first postflight day in either direction.

J. from desynchronization.

K. helps stave off muscle fatigue and blood clots.

L. we may at least learn to mitigate its worst symptoms.

CLOZE EXERCISE

Fill in each blank with the best word to complete the meaning of the sentence.

Scientists found that body temperature _____ significantly at certain hours and _____ at others on the first _____ day in either direction, and _____ not return to preflight levels _____ the third day. (It is _____ that a temperature depression often _____ stress.) More than three days _____ needed to shift the phase _____ temperature rhythm, that normal curve _____ low in the morning to _____ in the late afternoon and _____ in the early-morning sleep time _____. In this study, phase adjustment _____ 11 to 12 days after _____ westward flight, 14 to 15 _____ going east. Earlier studies had _____ three to five days sufficient.

SENTENCE COMBINING

Combine each pair of sentences into a single grammatical sentence.

1. Senator Hiram Fong retired because of jet lag.
   Senator Fong made the 9,700-mile trip from Washington to Hawaii nine times a year.

2. The body is internally desynchronized by jet lag.
   Desynchronization accounts for much of the fatigue of jet travel.

3. Daily activity rhythms may slip into place fairly soon.
   Normal temperature rhythms can require over a week to adjust.

4. Alcohol, tranquilizers, and hypnotics can interfere with REM
   sleep.
   REM sleep is essential to mental well-being.

5. Heavy eating and drinking should be avoided during the flight.
   An additional stress on the system is caused by heavy eating and
   drinking.

6. Many people are by nature early risers.
   Early risers adjust at rates different from late-night types.

PUNCTUATION

Read the following paragraph. Write in the capital letters
and place commas, periods, colons, semicolons, dashes, and
quotation marks where needed.

the airlines refer to jet lag as travel dysrhythmia to indicate its not

the airplanes fault but the human beings fault for boarding it what-

ever its called jet travelers are learning ways to beat it on short hops

watches need never be changed the corporate medical director of

american airlines claims he saved the job of a california executive

who had to commute often to new york leaving at 900 am arriving

at 600 pm barely slogging his way through the next mornings meeting

insist the meeting be at 700 the night you arrive the doctor advised

its 400 in the afternoon for you and youre still fresh it worked it is

also useful to find out if the airport hotel has 24 hour food service

and a room away from the street noise so you can dine at 1000 pm

local time and sleep till 1000 am in the morning

WORD-FORM CHART

Use your dictionary to complete the following table. Follow
the example shown with item 1, *ultimateness.* If there is no
commonly used form for a particular part of speech, write the
symbol XXX.

Noun	Verb	Adjective	Adverb
1. ultimateness	XXX	ultimate	ultimately
2.			scientifically
3.		efficient	
4. relative			
5.	adjust		
6. day			
7. psychology			
8.	experiment		
9.			frantically
10. hypnotism			

WORD-FORM EXERCISE

Using your completed Word-Form Chart, select the correct
form to fit into each sentence. Use the appropriate tense of
the verb, the singular or plural form of the noun, and the
passive voice where necessary.
Follow the sequence of numbers from the Word-Form Chart
to select the correct form.

1. Now the British and the French claim to have the

   _____ in traveler convenience, the Concorde.

2. We don't yet have a pill to prevent jet lag, but various

   _____ studies are at least beginning to explain pre-

   cisely how it affects our bodies.

3. The body clock that regulates _____ on complicated

   performance tasks seems as reluctant as temperature rhythms to

   reset after long flights.

4. Resynchronization was _____ rapid for the simple tests.

5. As with temperature, the _____ of the phase of perfor-

   mance rhythms took a long while.

6. Performance follows a _____ curve similar to that of

   temperature, with a peak in the afternoon and a trough at night.

7. Even if the traveler's home is in the east, adaptation tends to be

   faster after westward flight, overriding the _____

   effects of returning home.

8. Experience and some _____ evidence indicate that

   older people suffer more from jet lag.

9. Always try to avoid a _____ dash to the airport.

10. Avoid alcohol, tranquilizers, and _____, all of which

    can interfere with sleep.

QUESTIONS FOR DISCUSSION

1. Think about and explain the professional problems that jet lag
   can cause the businessperson, the diplomat, the pilot, or the
   flight attendant.

2. What problems might be faced by a tourist experiencing jet lag?

3. What might happen if our entire country were in a single time zone?

4. Why is *jet lag* an appropriate name for this disturbance?

TOPICS FOR WRITING

1. Describe the first day after you arrive in a European city from America. Mention three ways in which you will adapt your sight-seeing schedule to allow for symptoms of jet lag.

2. Pretend that you will be attending a major business meeting shortly after your arrival in an Asian city. Write an essay narrating the events of the week before you leave home as you adapt your daily routine to the time schedule of your destination.

3. Plan and write a theme giving examples of the facilities you would want at a foreign hotel to ease your adjustment to a new time zone.

4. Discuss the jet lag experienced by you or a relative. Analyze the ways in which it affected sleeping patterns, eating patterns, and behavior.

7

Cause and Effect

The Form

Most of us tend to simplify causes and effects in our daily lives. If a woman living on our street gets divorced, for instance, one neighbor may say that the reason was money, another that it was selfishness, and still another that it was conflicting careers. The truth is that none or all of these reasons may have caused the divorce. Another possibility is that only one reason or two of the reasons mentioned may have been causes of the divorce. In writing, as in life, causes and effects are difficult to analyze, and they require clear thinking and logic.

When looking for causes and effects in an essay, you should follow certain guidelines:

1. Know how many causes and effects you are dealing with. (For example, a fire can be caused by a faulty oil burner or by oil-soaked rags ignited by the burner.)
2. Do not assume that because event A *happened* before event B that event A *caused* event B. (For example, washing one's car does not cause rain, despite the common complaint.)
3. Make certain that you distinguish between causes and effects. (For example, a missing front tooth could be the cause of a fight or the result of one.)

4. Be aware that conditions can exist which are not causes. (For example, a child who is sneezing with a bad cold may be in a room with a cat to which she is allergic. Although the cat may be contributing to the girl's sneezing, it is not the original cause of it.)

Analyzing causes and effects requires clarity of purpose and the ability to separate reasons from results.

The Student Reader

When you read a cause-and-effect essay, notice whether the author is discussing causes, effects, or both. If the paper is short, she will probably concentrate either on causes or on effects. The longer paper allows a more extensive analysis and may include both causes and effects. As you read the essay, you can ask yourself certain questions in order to check the soundness of the writer's reasoning:

1. Has the author included all the causes or effects related to the topic?
2. Are they really causes (or effects), or are they just accompanying conditions?
3. Has the author followed a logical progression of ideas in order to convince you that her thesis is correct?
4. Is the author's conclusion the logical outcome of her supporting evidence?

An effective essay will provide affirmative answers to these questions.

The Professional Writer

In his essay "The System Worked," Anthony Lewis celebrates the twenty-fifth anniversary of the *Brown vs. Board of Education* decision which effectively ended school segregation in the United States. He begins by giving some background of racial prejudice in America before 1954. Then he explains how the decision was reached by the Supreme Court. Finally, he comes to the effects of the decision:

1. The "whole attitude of the Southern whites changed."
2. Legal and social changes resulted (in particular, civil rights legislation).
3. Whites were freed from the "burden of racism."

4. America's position in the world concerning human rights was changed.

Although he does not say that this single decision was the only cause of the listed effects, it was clearly the immediate cause.

In contrast to Lewis, Edward Fiske analyzes causes in his essay "Found! A Cure for Math Anxiety." He gives numerous examples of this fear of math and several causes of this national problem:

I. The way math is taught
   A. Rigid methods
   B. Time pressure on the student
   C. The embarrassing of weak students
II. The stereotyping of girls as possibly weak math students
   A. By teachers
   B. By parents
   C. By textbooks

Fiske mentions several courses and workshops that have been set up to deal with the unfortunate effects of math anxiety, but his primary aim is to analyze the principal causes. As we read the article, we can see the problem more clearly and try to figure out how we can help in our communities, schools, and families.

THE SYSTEM WORKED*

Anthony Lewis

[1] One of the transforming events in American history occurred 25 years ago today. The decision of the Supreme Court in *Brown v. Board of Education* has changed the American landscape to an extent unanticipated even in the drama of that time.

[2] It is hard to remember, now, what this country was like before May 17, 1954. More than a third of America's public schools were segregated by law. And not just schools: In the Southern and Border states, black men and women and children were kept out of "white" hospitals and parks and beaches and restaurants. Interracial marriage

(Courtesy of the Courier-Journal and Louisville Times; Louisville, Ky.)

*The Brown v. Board of Education decision specifically answered the question, "Does racial segregation in school deprive minority groups of equal educational opportunities?" The answer was, "Yes." The Supreme Court decided that separate educational facilities are inherently unequal. This landmark decision had widespread effects, much broader than the narrow issue of education. In effect, the decision marked the end of the entire Jim Crow system, which involved segregation in public places, public vehicles, and employment.—Eds.

was forbidden. In the Deep South, law and brutal force kept blacks from voting.

[3] Washington, D. C., was as segregated a town then as Pretoria, South Africa, is today. When I first came here, in 1950, no black person could enter a theater, or sit at a lunch counter in downtown Washington, or try on clothes in a department store. Schools were separate and unequal. The United States had fought World War II with strictly segregated armed forces.

[4] Nor was the North an exemplar of racial justice. There were no black salespersons in Macy's then, or black tellers in banks. In the great cities of the North it was just about impossible for a black family to rent an apartment outside of Harlem. There were few if any notable black politicians or journalists or members of corporate boards.

[5] Suppose, in 1954, the decision had gone the other way. Suppose the Supreme Court had said that the Constitution allowed governments in America to keep citizens apart on account of their color—allowed blacks to be confined in ghettos, to be excluded from most decent public facilities, to be branded effectively a subject race. Could we have lived with such a constitutional judgment?

[6] No, the idea of a decision legitimizing racial segregation seems unimaginable. But we must not slip into thinking that it was easy for the Court to decide as it did in 1954. In the circumstances of that time it took vision and courage on the part of the justices to reach the unambiguous judgment they did, and most of all to do so unanimously.

[7] What the justices did was to interpret the open-ended words of the Constitution—"the equal protection of the laws"—in terms of the understanding of our day. In 1896, when the Court found segregation lawful, it said that there was nothing unfriendly or invidious in the practice unless Negroes "chose to put that construction upon it." After Hitler, it was not possible to pretend that racism was benevolent.

[8] It took years of struggle and suffering to enforce the school decision. But in time not just schools but the whole attitude of Southern whites changed. Today the South is often called the most integrated part of the country. The legal and social changes there have been the most sweeping accomplished peacefully, by law, anywhere in the world in these decades.

[9] The moral momentum of the Supreme Court's decision led to the first civil rights legislation in 80 years. Southern blacks finally could vote; that changed the area's politics and ended its separation from the national political mainstream. Without *Brown* and the changes that flowed from it, a Georgia governor could not conceivably have succeeded in national politics.

[10] To say that is to indicate another fundamental consequence of the decision. It liberated not just blacks but whites from the burdens of racism. Those who control a racist society are injured, too—their values distorted, their sensibilities blunted, their energy so often given over to maintaining their supremacy.

[11] Of course, paradise has not arrived. Black Americans continue to suffer economically and in innumerable ways compared to whites —especially in the cities of the North and West. To mention one example, black unemployment is double that of whites. The legacy of those centuries of slavery, discrimination and blindness will not disappear without much more effort.

[12] But no sensible American would want to go back to things as they were before 1954. There was a telling comment the other day by James Jackson Kilpatrick, the columnist, who as a Virginia editor in the 1950's and 1960's was a leading critic of the school decision. He still disagreed with its legal reasoning, he said, but its "moral force" had freed the South from a "prison of law and custom."

[13] Finally, the decision changed the position of the United States in the world. If compelled segregation were still the law of the land, this country could hardly make concern for human rights an outspoken part of its foreign policy.

[14] For Americans and people abroad, a crucial fact is that change came through the legal system. A noted Indian lawyer, Soli Sorabjee, told the NAACP Legal Defense Fund at a commemoration of the decision: "In my country many people were cynical about the usefulness of laws and constitutions. But *Brown* enhanced their faith in the judicial process: in the rule of law."

VOCABULARY

Look up the following words in your dictionary. Use the system developed in the dictionary section in the back of the text. Be sure to write the part of speech, the pronunciation, and the meaning(s) of each word.

seg·re·gate (sĕg′rə-gāt′) *v.* **-gated, -gating, -gates.** —*tr.* **1.** To separate or isolate from others or from a main body or group. **2.** To impose the separation of (a race or class) from the rest of society. —*intr.* **1.** To become separated from a main body or mass. **2.** To practice a policy of racial segregation. —See Synonyms at **separate.** —*adj.* Separated; isolated. [Latin *sēgregāre*, "to separate from the flock" : *sē*, apart (see **seu-²** in Appendix*) + *grex* (stem *greg-*), flock (see **ger-¹** in Appendix*).] —**seg′re·ga′tive** *adj.* —**seg′re·ga′tor** (-gā′tər) *n.*

Definition ©1981 Houghton Mifflin Company. Reprinted by permission from *The American Heritage Dictionary of the English Language, New College Edition.*

Jim Crow

brutal

exemplar

brand

invidious

benevolent

supremacy

crucial

cynical

enhance

STUDY QUESTIONS

Finding the Matter

1. What was decided by the Supreme Court in *Brown vs. Board of Education*, May 17, 1954?

2. How many of America's schools were legally segregated before the *Brown* decision?

3. In addition to school segregation, what other kinds of segregation were common in the South before 1954?

4. Describe the segregation that was common in Washington, D.C., when the author arrived there in 1950.

5. What segregation was occurring in the North at the same time?

6. What consequences of the *Brown* decision does Lewis mention?

Exploring the Manner

1. What is the author's thesis*, expressed in the first paragraph? When he refers to the change in the American "landscape," does he really mean physical change in the countryside? Explain.

2. Why does Lewis spend the next three paragraphs giving examples* of racial discrimination before 1954?

3. How do paragraphs 5 through 7 function as a major transition* in the essay?

4. The final consequence mentioned is the effect of the decision on the United States' position in the world. Why has the author mentioned this effect last?

SYNONYMS

From the column at the right, select the best synonym for the italicized word in each sentence. Rewrite each sentence using the appropriate synonym.

1. It was *important* that Congress vote on the issue today.

2. The girls were *separated* from the boys in their physical education classes.

3. The mugger was *cruel* when he hit his victim on the head.

4. The architect tried to *beautify* the building with outstanding sculptures.

5. He was a *kind* man who was always considerate and friendly with his neighbors.

6. A person should not be in any way *marked* because of his race, creed, or color.

7. As president, he was in a position of *superiority* in his company.

A. supremacy

B. branded

C. crucial

D. benevolent

E. enhance

F. segregated

G. brutal

PARAPHRASE

Read these paragraphs twice; then close your book. Using your own words, rewrite the paragraphs as clearly and completely as you can.

It is hard to remember, now, what this country was like before May 17, 1954. More than a third of America's public schools were segregated by law. And not just schools: In the Southern and Border states, black men and women and children were kept out of "white" hospitals and parks and beaches and restaurants. Interracial marriage was forbidden. In the Deep South, law and brutal force kept blacks from voting.

Washington, D.C., was as segregated a town then as Pretoria, South Africa, is today. When the author first came here in 1950, no black person could enter a theater or sit at a lunch counter in downtown Washington, or try on clothes in a department store. Schools were segregated and unequal. The United States had fought World War II with strictly segregated armed forces.

VERB FILL-IN

Fill in each blank with the verb form that is appropriate for each sentence.

It _____ years of struggle and suffering to enforce the
          take

school decision. But in time not just schools but the whole attitude

of Southern whites _____. The South _____
                              change   become

the most integrated part of the country. The legal and social changes

there _____ peacefully, by law.
          accomplish

The moral momentum of the Supreme Court's decision

_____ to the first civil rights legislation in 80 years. Southern
     lead

blacks _____. That _____ the area's politics and
              vote   alter

ended its separation from the national political mainstream. Without

Brown and the changes that ———————— from it, a Georgia gov-
                                    flow

ernor could not conceivably ———————— in national politics.
                              succeed

SENTENCE COMPLETION

From the column at the right, select the correct line to complete each of the numbered lines at the left. Write each sentence in its correct form.

1. One of the most transforming events in American history

2. More than a third of America's public schools

3. The United States had fought World War II

4. In the great cities of the North it was just about impossible

5. After Hitler, it was not possible

6. In the circumstances of that time it took vision and courage

7. The decision liberated not just blacks but also whites

8. Black Americans continue to suffer economically,

9. The legacy of those centuries of slavery, discrimination and blindness

10. No sensible American would want to go back

A. were segregated by law.

B. on the part of the justices to reach the unambiguous judgment they did.

C. that change came through the legal system.

D. occurred twenty-five years ago today.

E. will not disappear without much more effort.

F. this country could hardly make concern for human rights part of its foreign policy.

G. for a black family to rent an apartment outside of Harlem.

H. to things as they were before 1954.

I. to pretend that racism was benevolent.

J. from the burdens of racism.

K. especially in the cities of the North and West.

11. If compelled segregation were still the law of the land,

    L. with strictly segregated armed forces.

12. For Americans and people abroad, a crucial fact is

CLOZE EXERCISE

Fill in each blank with the best word to complete the meaning of the sentence.

The decision liberated not just _____ but whites from

the burdens _____ racism. Those who control a

_____ society are injured, too—their _____ dis-

torted, their sensibilities blunted, their _____ so often given

over to _____ their supremacy.

Of course, paradise _____ not arrived. Black Americans

continue _____ suffer economically and in innumerable

_____ compared to whites—especially in _____

cities of the North and _____. To mention one example,

black _____ is double that of whites. _____

legacy of those centuries of _____, discrimination and

blindness will not _____ without much more effort.

SENTENCE COMBINING

Combine each pair of sentences into a single grammatical sentence.

1. The Supreme Court made a decision.
   The decision changed the educational system in the U.S.

2. In the deep South, blacks were kept from voting.
   Blacks were kept from voting by law and brutal force.

3. It took vision and courage for the justices to make this judgment.
   The judgment was made unanimously.

4. The Supreme Court decided that separate educational facilities are inherently unequal.
   This led to the first civil rights legislation in 80 years.

5. The decision liberated blacks from the burdens of racism.
   The decision liberated whites from the burdens of racism.

6. Georgia had many racial problems.
   Georgia is a southern state.

7. In the South the schools were segregated.
   They were supposed to be equal.

8. The decision was important.
   The importance of it changed the position of the U..S. in the world.

9. Americans believed in the U.S. judicial process.
   They had faith in the rule of law.

PUNCTUATION

Read the following paragraphs. Write in the capital letters and place commas, periods, colons, semicolons, dashes, and quotation marks where needed.

suppose in 1954 the decision had gone the other way suppose the supreme court had said that the constitution allowed governments in america to keep citizens apart on account of their color allowed blacks to be confined in ghettos to be excluded from most decent public facilities to be branded effectively a subject race could we have lived with such a constitutional judgment

no the idea of a decision legitimizing racial segregation seems unimaginable but we must not slip into thinking that it was easy for the court to decide as it did in nineteen fifty four in the circum-

stances of that time it took vision and courage on the part of the

justices to reach the unambiguous judgment they did and most of

all to do so unanimously

WORD-FORM CHART

Use your dictionary to complete the following table. Follow the example shown with item 1, *lawyer*. If there is no commonly used word form for a particular part of speech, write the symbol XXX.

Noun	Verb	Adjective	Adverb
1. lawyer	XXX	lawful	lawfully
2.	segregate		
3.		political	
4. vision			
5.			yearly
6.	integrate		
7.		moral	
8. nation			
9. racism			
10.			legally

WORD-FORM EXERCISE

Using your completed Word-Form Chart, select the correct
form to fit into each sentence. Use the appropriate tense of
the verb, the singular or plural form of the noun, and the
passive voice where necessary.
Follow the sequence of numbers from the Word-Form Chart
to select the correct form.

1. Before May 17, 1954, more than a third of America's public

   schools were segregated by ＿＿＿＿＿＿.

2. Washington, D.C., at that time, was as ＿＿＿＿＿＿ then as

   Pretoria, South Africa, is today.

3. There were few, if any, notable black ＿＿＿＿＿＿ or

   journalists.

4. It took ＿＿＿＿＿＿ and courage on the part of the justices

   to reach the decision they did.

5. It took ＿＿＿＿＿＿ of struggle and suffering to enforce

   the school decision.

6. Today the South is often called the most ＿＿＿＿＿＿ part of

   the country.

7. The ＿＿＿＿＿＿ momentum of the Supreme Court's decision

   led to the first civil rights legislation in 80 years.

8. Southern blacks finally could vote; that changed the area's

   politics and ended its separation from the ＿＿＿＿＿＿

   political mainstream.

9. Those who control a ＿＿＿＿＿＿ society are in

10. For Americans and people abroad, a crucial fact is

    came through the ＿＿＿＿＿＿ system.

QUESTIONS FOR DISCUSSION

1. How do you account for the fact that segregation was found constitutional (lawful) by the Supreme Court in 1896 but unconstitutional (unlawful) in 1954?

2. Discuss the ways in which the *Brown* decision helped Jimmy Carter to be elected President of the United States.

3. Lewis says that the *Brown* decision "liberated not just blacks but whites from the burdens of racism." Discuss what some of these burdens might be.

4. Has the *Brown* decision given the United States the right to speak out on discrimination in other countries? Support your opinion.

TOPICS FOR WRITING

1. Although Lewis discusses the effects of the *Brown* decision, there were certainly causes as well. Write a theme analyzing the incidents that led to the 1954 Supreme Court decision to see how they contributed to the final outcome. Look up newspaper accounts for background information.

2. Write a composition discussing the effects that racial discrimination has had on you either in your native country or in America.

3. Analyze the effects of the *Brown* decision on the current relations between blacks and whites in your neighborhood. Choose one area among social, religious, educational, or business relations.

4. Write a theme based upon a situation in which you or a person you know well experienced discrimination. Describe the circumstances or background of the incident, the incident itself, and your reaction to it. What effect did the incident have on your view of yourself, on your attitude toward others, and on your political or religious views?

FOUND! A CURE FOR MATH ANXIETY

Edward B. Fiske

[1] One night recently a coed at Wesleyan University went out to the local pizza parlor with six friends. At the end of the meal, when the waiter arrived with a check that looked like the formula for nuclear fission, she was the only one at the table who could figure out how much each person owed—including the tip.

[2] The following morning the same student was confronted with a routine algebra problem in math class. She froze and could not handle it.

[3] This student had a classical case of "math anxiety"—an irrational and often debilitating fear of math that is also known as "mathophobia." It ranges from a simple distaste for such tasks as balancing the checkbook to a paralyzing dread of more complex mathematical tasks.

[4] Until recently, most people have acquiesced in the assumption that some people "just can't handle figures" or "don't have a mathematical mind." Now, however, with mathematical "literacy" be-

coming an increasingly important part of coping with modern life, educators, psychologists, and others are beginning to ask why numbers should be any more terrifying than letters and why students should not be expected to do just as well in math as they do in other subjects.

[5]   Researchers say that most Americans appear to experience some degree of low-level "math avoidance," part of which may be due to the mysteries of the subject itself. However, in all likelihood, this mathophobia is more fundamentally rooted in the way the subject is taught.

[6]   "Math classes are often places where you aren't supposed to ask a lot of questions and challenge a lot of assumptions," says Stanley Kogelman, who runs a New York City therapy workshop known as "Mind Over Math." And Kogelman is right. In contrast to other subjects, where teachers routinely solicit the thoughts and feelings of students, respect their intuition, and allow for trial and error, mathematics is most frequently presented as a rigid, authoritarian discipline in which the teacher has the one and only answer and rote memorization is the only road to success.

[7]   While most people may have some negative memories of math, some experience math anxiety in the extreme. Sheila Tobias, who has recently written a book entitled *Overcoming Math Anxiety* (published by Norton), describes a 33-year-old professional woman who became nauseated every time she had to balance her checkbook. Kogelman tells of another woman who ran a small chain of clothing stores and lived in daily terror that her employees would find out she couldn't work the cash registers or handle tally sheets.

[8]   As these examples may suggest, math anxiety is more prevalent among women. This should not be too startling. For years, "Don't bother your pretty little head with numbers" has been the all too common attitude toward women's struggle with mathematical problems. And we are all familiar with the stereotype of the bungling housewife who has to get her husband to balance the checkbook, even though that afternoon she has probably gone through elaborate mental calculations while shopping at the supermarket.

[9]   Yet studies show that girls generally do better at math than do boys up through elementary school, and it is only when they reach junior high that their performance begins to slip. By high school, most girls are taking far fewer math courses than are boys.

[10]   No wonder, then, that Lucy Sells, a sociologist at the University of California at Berkeley, was alarmed by her 1973 survey, which revealed that while 57 percent of the first-year male students had had four years of high school math, only 8 percent of the first-year females had had similar mathematical training. This means that the day they set foot on campus, more than nine out of ten women students had already disqualified themselves from three-quarters of the major fields offered at Berkeley.

[11] In another study, Sells concluded that a knowledge of algebra and geometry contributes to the ability of high school graduates to get upwardly mobile positions instead of unskilled clerical jobs. This means that the tendency for young women to give themselves only minimal training in math has a very limiting effect, even for those who do not go on to college.

[12] The most compelling explanation of girls' shying away from math is the very power of its stereotype as a "male" subject, one associated with "male" professions like engineering, chemistry, and physics. "The truth is that girls are actually discouraged from excelling in math," says Elizabeth Fennema, professor of education at the University of Wisconsin at Madison. "They are conditioned from childhood to feel that doing well in math is somehow unfeminine. Since they won't need it anyway, they are told, why bother?"

[13] As if to illustrate the point, Carol Lambert, a graduate student now catching up with calculus for the first time recalls, "I was functionally illiterate in math because I never saw any use for it. I never thought I would end up in chemistry."

[14] Tobias argues that such socialization regarding math begins well before the early teenage years. She notes that while a girl may play Monopoly or "store" and get plenty of practice in basic calculating, a boy following his favorite baseball hero's batting average, for example, gets valuable insights into the far more sophisticated concepts of ratios and percentages.

[15] With better understanding of the causes and consequences of math anxiety, numerous steps are being taken to combat it. During the course of five two-hour sessions, Kogelman's "Mind Over Math" workshops allow math-anxious adults to talk about their experiences with math and to work through their negative feelings—many of which evaporate the moment they come to realize that they have plenty of company and no longer need to be embarrassed by the temptation to count on their fingers.

[16] A similar group, led by Tobias, Bonnie Donady, and Susan Auslander, is now being organized in Washington, D.C., under the name "Overcoming Math Anxiety." Additional math-help groups of this type are being established in many other parts of the country as well.

[17] Wellesley College and Wesleyan University have received grants to develop methods for helping college students overcome their mathophobia, and Sarah Lawrence College ran a math-help clinic for adults not presently in school. Clinics are also beginning to appear at community colleges, which find a high frequency of math anxiety occurring among adults returning to school after several years away from the classroom.

[18] On a precollege level, Lawrence Hall of Science, a public-service research and teacher-training center at the University of California at Berkeley, has sponsored eight-week courses called

"Math for Girls," aimed at six- to fourteen-year-olds. The task of this program is to explore basic math concepts in a nonthreatening way and to make use of female mathematics students from the university as teachers and role models.

[19] At The Dalton School, in New York City, which is one of the first secondary schools in the country to run a math-anxiety clinic, teachers have made use of last year's feedback and altered their teaching styles to include more dialogue with students. Dominique Baudry, a junior who went through the workshops during her freshman year, notices that her teachers have started asking more questions. "We're beginning to understand our mistakes," she said. "You don't just accept that the answer is wrong. You can see why. In fact, they've even begun giving partial credit on problems." Michael Sturm, head of the math department at Dalton, reports that test scores have gone up and that teachers "accept the fact that students have needs we weren't aware of before." Several years of experience with Dalton's program have produced significant insights into the handling and prevention of the students' math anxiety.

[20] Schools can follow Dalton's lead and take their own measures to reduce the tension and pressure that unnecessarily surround the teaching of math. Besides running math-anxiety clinics, one obvious step is to cut out "time tests" that force students to race the clock while computing answers. "They never told us to spell faster," one male student complains. "Why do they do this in math?" Tobias suggests another innovation that is already being tried in some schools: allowing the use of an abacus or calculator to "diminish the nervousness that comes from fear of forgetting," because this fear in itself can become an obstacle to mastering the subject.

[21] Another anxiety-provoking practice that could be abandoned is putting students at the blackboard with the eyes of the class on them. Why not substitute what one teacher calls "math by committee," and allow students to work out problems on a cooperative basis, the way they might in social studies?

[22] It is also important to take the focus off the idea that in math there is a single "right" answer and a single "correct" way of arriving at it. There are often several correct approaches to word problems, and what matters is not whether the student reproduces the reasoning of the teacher, but whether he or she is able to develop—through intuition, approximation, and the capacity to "play around" with the problem—a series of logical steps that lead to a solution.

[23] Schools can do much to alleviate the particular problem of math anxiety among girls by taking a frank look at teachers' attitudes. John Ernest, professor of mathematics at the University of California at Santa Barbara, has identified what he calls the "Pygmalion effect," according to which students perform to a large extent in response to teachers' expectations. In a survey of one small group of teachers, for example, he found that, "Almost half the

teachers expect their male students to do better in mathematics, while *none* of them expect the female students to do better."

[24] But this kind of negative projection in the classroom is not confined solely to teachers. Lenore Weitzman, in her 1975 study, *Images of Males and Females in Elementary School Textbooks,* found that two-thirds of the textbook illustrations depicting scientific and mathematical activities featured males, and that the "examples given of females doing math were insulting and designed to reinforce the worst stereotypes."

[25] Schools can avoid using such texts and, as Ernest suggests, they can also produce a significant effect by upgrading high school counseling "to make women aware of the full range of career opportunities and of the courses they must take in high school in order to keep all their options open."

[26] Finally, much can be done to remove the stigma of mathematics as a "pure" or "theoretical" subject—which makes it seem abstract and hard to grasp—and to show how it relates to everyday life. In keeping with this, a 1977 policy statement issued by the National Council of Supervisors of Mathematics declared that, "the role of computational skills in mathematics must be seen in the light of the contributions they make to one's ability to use mathematics in everyday living. In isolation, computational skills contribute little to one's ability to participate in mainstream society."

[27] Changing children's attitudes toward math can't all be left up to the schools, however. Parents, too, must take an active role in preventing the development of math anxiety in their children—especially their daughters.

[28] Bonnie Donady, who hops between Washington, D.C., and the Wesleyan program, suggests playing number games as a way of showing that numbers can be enjoyable. In the car, for instance, "Take license plates and see if you can add up the numbers," she says. "And don't worry if your kids count on their fingers. It's not speed or being able to do it in your head that counts. It's being able to think it through."

[29] Also, parents should encourage girls, as well as boys, to take things apart and see how they are put together, an activity that gives them practice with shapes and spaces, increasing their ability to "see" two- and three-dimensional objects in the mind's eye, a skill that is useful in geometry and applied math.

[30] Parents of children in elementary school should satisfy themselves that teachers are not simply teaching math by rote but are teaching strategies for problem solving. Parents of girls should press for formal instruction in areas such as mapmaking and knot tying, which will also help with spatial visualization, and encourage participation in sports, such as soccer, that involve running toward specific targets and controlling the movement of a ball through space.

[31] At the secondary-school level, it's probably a good idea to look

at the male-female ratio in advanced math courses. If boys pre-
dominate, the principal ought to be asked to explain why this is so.

[32] Perhaps most important, parents should examine their own
attitudes toward math because, as Tobias says, they are the ones who
often "unwittingly foster the idea that a mathematical mind is something one either has or does not have." Kogelman suggests that
parents make it clear that they do not view their deficiencies in math
as "something that has to be passed from generation to generation."

[33] In one of his studies, Ernest found that, up through the sixth
grade, mothers were the ones who usually helped with homework.
From then on, mothers helped with English, but fathers were called
in to assist with math. If this is true in your house, it is necessary to
make sure your children, especially daughters, don't see this as the
inevitable division between men and women. Kogelman emphasizes
that parents should be "sure they expect their daughters to do as
well in math as in every other subject. They shouldn't offer too
much understanding about not doing well."

[34] We all know by now that parents' attitudes influence those of
their children; in a field such as mathematics, however, we have to be
especially careful, because math will most likely play a much more
important role in our children's lives and careers than it has in ours.
That is why it is important for us to become aware of our prejudices,
so that we can help our children to develop their potential in all
areas, even those in which we ourselves have problems.

VOCABULARY

Look up the following words in your dictionary. Use the
system developed in the dictionary section in the back of
the text. Be sure to write the part of speech, the pronunciation, and the meaning(s) of each word.

anx·i·e·ty (ăng-zī′ə-tē) *n., pl.* **-ties.** **1.** A state of uneasiness and
distress about future uncertainties; apprehension; worry. **2.** A
cause of such uneasiness; a worry. **3.** *Psychiatry.* Intense fear or
dread lacking an unambiguous cause or a specific threat.
4. Eagerness. [Latin *anxietās,* from *anxius,* ANXIOUS.]
   Synonyms: *anxiety, worry, care, concern, solicitude.* These
nouns express troubled states of mind. *Anxiety* suggests feelings
of fear and concern detached from objective sources, feeding
themselves, as it were. *Worry* implies persistent doubt or fear
that produces strong mental agitation. *Care,* often in the plural,
implies mental oppression of varying degree arising from heavy
responsibilities. *Concern* has more to do with serious thought
than with emotion, and stresses personal involvement in the
source of mental unrest. *Solicitude* is active concern for the
well-being of another person or persons.

Definition ©1981 Houghton Mifflin Company.
Reprinted by permission from *The American
Heritage Dictionary of the English Language,
New College Edition.*

irrational

debilitating

acquiesced

assumptions

solicit

intuition

rigid

authoritarian

nauseated

prevalent

stereotype

calculations

minimal

illiterate

evaporate

feedback

insights

approximation

capacity

alleviate

depicting

stigma

abstract

STUDY QUESTIONS

Finding the Matter

1. Why might common methods of teaching math cause people to fear it?

2. Why is math anxiety more common among women than among men?

3. What workshops have been formed for adults with math anxiety? What groups are there for college students? How are six- to fourteen-year-olds being helped?

4. How can math textbook illustrations and examples create math anxiety in women?

5. How can parents encourage their children to have healthy attitudes toward math?

Exploring the Manner

1. What does the author's use of the word *math* instead of the more formal word *mathematics* suggest about his audience*?

2. What are the two major causes of math anxiety?

3. Why does the author explain the second cause more fully than the first? What method of organization* does he use?

4. Fiske mentions different effects of math anxiety throughout the first part of the essay. Is this method successful, or would it have been better to group them?

5. The author presents fourteen ways in which math anxiety can be combatted. How does the final suggestion bring the author close to his audience*?

6. Is this essay of equal interest to males and females? Explain your answer.

SYNONYMS

From the column at the right, select the best synonym for the italicized word in each sentence. Rewrite each sentence using the appropriate synonym.

1. The student showed great *distress* when she had to do math problems.

    A. acquiesced

    B. evaporate

2. Her debilitating fear of math was really *illogical*.

3. Until recently most people have *agreed* that some people are just not capable of handling figures.

4. Teachers usually *seek* the thoughts and feelings of students in classes other than math.

5. Math teachers usually expect a *rigid* and authoritarian discipline in their classes.

6. Some people become *nauseated* when they have to deal with situations that require mathematics.

7. It is still visible today that math anxiety is more *common* among women.

8. By taking a frank look at teachers' attitudes, schools can do something to *ease* math anxiety among girls.

9. We find that most math textbooks *show* males in illustrations of mathematical activities.

10. Some people's fears of math *disappear* when they realize that many other people have the same problems.

C. strict

D. solicit

E. anxiety

F. sickened

G. alleviate

H. irrational

I. prevalent

J. depict

PARAPHRASE

Read these paragraphs twice; then close your book. Using your own words, rewrite the paragraphs as clearly and completely as you can.

Math anxiety is more prevalent among women. This should not be too startling. For years, "Don't both your pretty head with numbers" has been the all too common attitude toward women's struggle with mathematical problems. And we are all familiar with the stereotype of the bungling housewife who has to get her husband to balance the checkbook, even though that afternoon she has probably gone through elaborate mental calculations while shopping at the supermarket.

Yet studies show that girls generally do better at math than do boys up through elementary school, and it is only when they reach junior high that their performance begins to slip. By high school, most girls are taking far fewer math courses than are boys.

VERB FILL-IN

Fill in each blank with the verb form that is appropriate for each sentence.

Wellesley College and Wesleyan University _____
                                        receive

grants to develop methods for helping college students

_____ their mathophobia, and Sarah Lawrence College
   overcome

_____ a math-help clinic for adults not presently in
    run

school. Clinics also _____ to appear at community
                    begin

colleges, which _____ a high frequency of math anxiety
             find

_____ among adults _____ to school after
   occur   return

several years away from the classroom.

On a precollege level, Lawrence Hall of Science, a public-

service research and teacher-training center at the University of

California at Berkeley, _____ eight-week courses,
                          sponsor

_____ "Math for Girls," _____ at six- to
    call   aim

fourteen-year-olds. The task of this program _____
                                           be

to explore basic math concepts in a nonthreatening way and

_____ female math students from the university as
    use

teachers and role models.

SENTENCE COMPLETION

From the column at the right, select the correct line to complete each of the numbered lines at the left. Write each sentence in its correct form.

1. Studies show that girls generally do better at math

2. The tendency for young women to give themselves only minimal training in math

3. The most compelling explanation of girls' shying away from math is

4. The truth is that girls

5. With better understanding of the causes and consequences of math anxiety,

6. Workshops allow math-anxious adults

A. the very power of its stereotype as a "male" subject.

B. allowing the students to use an abacus or calculator.

C. than do boys up through elementary school.

D. as something that has to be passed from generation to generation.

E. are actually discouraged from excelling in math.

F. while none of them expects their female students to do better.

7. Teachers have made use of student feedback and

8. Schools can follow Dalton's lead and take their own measures

9. 'An innovation that is being tried in some schools is

10. Almost half the teachers expect their male students to do better in math,

11. Parents should make it clear that they do not view their own deficiencies in math

12. It is important for us to become aware of our prejudices

G. has a very limiting effect, even for those who do not go on to college.

H. so that we can help our children to develop their potential in all areas.

I. to talk about their experiences with math and to work through their negative feelings.

J. to reduce the tension and pressure that unnecessarily surround the teaching of math.

K. have altered their teaching styles to include more dialogue with students.

L. numerous steps are being taken to combat it.

CLOZE EXERCISE

Fill in each blank with the best word to complete the meaning of the sentence.

In one of his studies, Prof. Ernest _____ that, up through

the sixth grade, mothers _____ the ones who usually

helped with homework. _____ then on, mothers helped

with English, but _____ were called in to assist with math.

_____ this is true in your house, it _____ necessary

to make sure your children, especially _____, don't see this

as the inevitable division _____ men and women. Mr.

Kogelman emphasizes that _____ should be "sure they

expect their daughters _____ do as well in math as in

———————— other subject. They shouldn't offer too much

———————— about not doing well."

SENTENCE COMBINING

Combine each pair of sentences into a single grammatical sentence.

1. "Mathophobia" is an irrational and often debilitating fear of math.
   "Mathophobia" is fundamentally rooted in the way the subject is taught.

2. Math anxiety is more prevalent among women.
   Girls generally do better at math than do boys up through elementary school.

3. Only 8 per cent of women students at Berkeley have had four years of high school math.
   The others have already disqualified themselves from three-quarters of the major fields offered at Berkeley.

4. Math clinics are beginning to appear at many community colleges.
   Community colleges find a high frequency of math anxiety occurring among adults returning to school.

5. There is not always a single correct answer and way of arriving at it.
   Students must develop the ability to see the series of logical steps that lead to a solution.

6. Many textbook illustrations depict mathematical activities performed by males.
   Examples of males doing math reinforce stereotypes.

7. Math-anxious adults can work through their negative feelings about math.
   Negative feelings about math often disappear when adults realize they have plenty of company.

8. Parents must examine their own attitudes toward math.
   Parents must take an active role in preventing math anxiety in their children.

PUNCTUATION

Read the following paragraph. Write in the capital letters and place commas, periods, colons, semicolons, dashes, and quotation marks where needed.

the most compelling explanation of girls shying away from math is

the very power of its stereotype as a male subject one associated

with male professions like engineering chemistry and physics the

truth is that girls are actually discouraged from excelling in math

says elizabeth fennema professor of education at the university of

wisconsin at madison they are conditioned in childhood to feel that

doing well in math is somehow unfeminine since they wont need it

anyway they are told why bother

WORD-FORM CHART

Use your dictionary to complete the following table. Follow the example shown with item 1, *debility*. If there is no commonly used form for a particular part of speech, write the symbol XXX.

Noun	Verb	Adjective	Adverb
1. debility	debilitate	debilitating	XXX
2.	acquiesce		
3.		intuitive	
4.		stereotypical	
5.	alleviate		
6. encouragement			
7.			simply
8. deficiency			
9. capacity			
10.		anxious	

WORD-FORM EXERCISE

Using your completed Word-Form Chart, select the correct
form to fit into each sentence. Use the appropriate tense of
the verb, the singular or plural form of the noun, and the
passive voice where necessary.
Follow the sequence of numbers from the Word-Form Chart
to select the correct form.

1. An irrational and _____ fear of math is known as

   "mathophobia."

2. Most people have _____ in the assumption that some

   people just can't handle figures.

3. Teachers usually respect a student's _____ and allow

   for trial and error.

4. When we think of a bungling housewife who has to get her

   husband to balance her checkbook, we are thinking of a

   _____.

5. Schools are now aware of the necessity of _____ the

   problem of math anxiety.

6. Parents should _____ girls as well as boys to take

   things apart and put them together.

7. Teachers must not _____ teach math by having students

   memorize; they must use problem-solving strategies.

8. Parents should not think that because they are _____

   in math, their children must be too.

9. We all have the _____ to deal successfully with math

   problems.

10. We can easily overcome our _____ with regard to math.

QUESTIONS FOR DISCUSSION

1. Why is a knowledge of algebra and geometry often necessary to qualify a person for a desirable job in modern society?

2. The author says that math is, unfortunately, taught in a "rigid" and "authoritarian" manner, whereas other subjects are not taught this way. Name three college subjects where students are encouraged to develop individual ideas and are not afraid to make errors. Support your answers.

3. Name some traditional "girls'" and "boys'" games for preteen-agers. How are these stereotypes changing? What changes could prepare both sexes for success in mathematical skills?

4. What number games can parents play with their children to encourage a positive attitude toward math?

TOPICS FOR WRITING

1. Write a theme relating an experience in which someone was unable to perform simple addition (a waitress, a salesperson). Describe the reactions of the people involved.

2. Pretend that you are an elementary-school principal observing a third-grade class. At the board is a terrified child who is unable to solve a mathematical problem. He begins to cry and slowly returns to his seat. Write a report of the teacher's lesson, suggesting ways in which the child could be spared future "math anxiety."

3. Write a theme describing an anxiety more common to males than to females. Discuss the causes, effects, and possible cures.

4. Fiske's article mentions several anxiety-provoking school situations (e.g., "time-tests that force students to race the clock," "putting students at the blackboard with the eyes of the class on them"). Describe a school situation that you have found anxiety-provoking. Discuss your feelings about it, its effect on you, and possible cures.

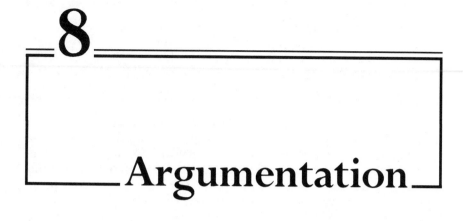

Argumentation

The Form

When one writes a narrative or descriptive essay, the purpose is usually to inform the reader. Similarly, a definition or process paper seeks to explain something. An argument, however, is intended to persuade the reader that the writer's point of view is the best one. An argument's method of persuasion is not like that of a fight or quarrel; it does not involve screaming or brawling. Instead, an argument depends upon a reasoned body of evidence to convince the reader that the writer is most probably correct.

Some arguments are directed primarily to the emotions of the reader, but the highest form of argument appeals to reason. Of course, some topics are emotionally charged. The question of whether or not abortions should be supported by federal funds has created considerable debate. If one were to argue against abortion on the basis that babies are adorable and that every pregnant woman could learn to love her prospective infant, one would be creating an emotional appeal. But if one were to say that she believed life to begin at conception for biological rather than for sentimental or religious reasons, then the reader could begin to examine an argument based on evidence rather than feelings alone.

One method of presenting evidence is called the *inductive* method. Here, the writer compiles specific facts, clues, instances, or examples and then generalizes a conclusion based on the evidence.

This is the way Sherlock Holmes worked in the Conan Doyle stories and the way that the modern police detective works: by accumulating clues which ultimately point to the criminal. Of course, the fictional Holmes was always successful and the modern detective is not as fortunate.

A person uses inductive reasoning when he chooses to eat at a restaurant at which he has enjoyed many delicious meals or when he decides not to wear woolen sweaters because they cause itching every time he puts them on. Although we use the inductive method frequently, we should be aware of its limitations. We risk being disproven when we generalize from specific instances because we have examined only a sampling. Therefore, the examples that we choose must constitute a large and representative sampling before the generalization is made.

Unlike the inductive method, the *deductive* method begins with a general statement and then narrows to a conclusion. The traditional pattern is called a *syllogism* and consists of a major premise, a minor premise, and a conclusion. Here is the classical example:

$$
\begin{array}{lll}
& \quad A & \quad B \\
\textbf{Major premise:} & \text{All men are mortal.} \\
& \quad C & \quad A \\
\textbf{Minor premise:} & \text{Socrates is a man.} \\
& \quad C & \quad B \\
\textbf{Conclusion:} & \text{Socrates is mortal.}
\end{array}
$$

A formula for the syllogism might look like this:

Major premise: $A = B$
Minor premise: $C = A$
Conclusion: $C = B$

The syllogism is valid only if the form is correct, and it is sound only if the premises are true. Sometimes, a syllogism can be valid but unsound. Here is an example:

$$
\begin{array}{lll}
& \quad A & \quad B \\
\textbf{Major premise:} & \text{All students are industrious.} \\
& \quad C & \quad A \\
\textbf{Minor premise:} & \text{I am a student.} \\
& \quad C & \quad B \\
\textbf{Conclusion:} & \text{I am industrious.}
\end{array}
$$

This is a valid syllogism because the form is correct, but it is unsound (and untrue) because the major premise is not universally true, as it should be. In order for a syllogism to be valid and sound, the form has to be correct and the premises must be true.

The Student Reader

When you read an argument, you should be able to recognize inductive or deductive techniques. Remember that the writer using the inductive method will build his case by including examples, observations, or personal experience. He should have a sufficient number of these supporting items to convince you, the reader, that the conclusions is based on a body of evidence, not just a few isolated instances. For example, a scientist does not conclude that all white mice become aggressive after being injected with a particular substance until he has seen this reaction repeated numerous times under precisely the same test conditions. Even then, his conclusion may be disproved in the future.

When you read an essay using the deductive method, look for the hidden syllogism. That is to say, examine the writer's conclusion and then supply the two premises that led to it, even if they are suggested and not stated. For example, if a writer is arguing that "Capital punishment is wrong," he may have reached this conclusion by following steps that can be expressed in the following syllogism:

Major premise: Killing a human being is wrong.
Minor premise: Capital punishment is killing a human being.
Conclusion: Capital punishment is wrong.

Whichever method or combination of methods is used, remember that the argument must be as well organized as any other kind of essay. The writer may choose to build his case by using induction alone, or he may wish to follow inductive reasoning with a deductively reached conclusion. He should also answer the opposition's arguments by showing the superiority of his own. If there is a single opposing view, he may choose to deal with it in a single paragraph. A point-by-point refutation may be necessary if each of his arguments has an opposing point of view.

Finally, the writer may rest his case, having attempted to convince you that his conclusion is correct; or he may suggest a course of action that you can take if you are in agreement with him. Either way, the writer's purpose is always to persuade.

The Professional Writer

Isaac Asimov is a famous writer of science fiction and science fact. In his essay "Designing the Superman," he develops an argument to prove that a robot may very well be the highest form of existence man can desire. He builds an inductive list of reasons to support his thesis, hoping that the reader will accept each one of them and reach the same conclusion that he has:

1. Personal aids help weak parts of our bodies (glasses, hearing aids), but they do not replace worn-out or nonfunctioning parts.
2. Artificial replacement organs are better than personal aids because they *do* replace worn-out or nonfunctioning parts.
3. Cyborgs (artificial bodies with human brains and central nervous systems) are superior to isolated replacement organs.
4. Cybs (robots) are the highest form of life because nothing wears out and the mechanical brain is at least as good as the original.

After Asimov leads the reader along this path of inductive reasoning, he shifts to the deductive method. His article contains a hidden syllogism which takes the following form:

Major premise: Things that don't wear out are better than things that do (people).

Minor premise: Cybs don't wear out.

Conclusion: Cybs are better than things that wear out (people).

The two premises seem to be acceptable, but we don't necessarily accept the conclusion. Therefore, Asimov's argument may be valid, but not every reader will find it sound (or desirable).

In his article "Your Money *and* Your Life," Cook argues that television steals the viewer's cash and time. First he gives a detailed example of a "free" evening that he spent watching television commercials and pilot programs for a market research firm. He was bored by the programs, irritated by the long forms he had to fill out, and angered by the token gifts that had been advertised as rewards. Cook felt that he had wasted a great deal of his time as well as the money he was obliged to pay for gasoline and a babysitter.

In a further attempt to convince the reader that he is paying for so-called free television, Cook explains the cost of advertising products on television:

1. The companies wishing to advertise pay advertising agencies to "produce and place commercials before the appropriate television audience."
2. The advertising agencies buy television time from the networks in order to present their clients' commercials.

3. The companies include the cost of commercial advertising in the price of the product.
4. The consumer pays for the cost of the advertising agency and the television time when he buys a product advertised on television.

Cook's personal experience and his analysis of the passing along of advertising costs are examples of the inductive method. He builds his argument step by step until he feels that the reader will agree with him that—unlike the thief who says, "Your money *or* your life"—television steals both.

DESIGNING THE SUPERMAN

Isaac Asimov

[1] Steve Austin, the hero of the TV show "The Six-Million-Dollar Man," is Superman born again.

[2] Austin, however, hits closer to home. Superman's great talents are there only because he was born on Krypton. Since Krypton is purely mythical, none of us can be born there, and Superman can only remain a dream.

[3] Austin, however, is a superman because a barely living bodily remnant was stitched together, and to it were added mechanical parts of great durability and power and with the capacity for delicate control. It cost (in the fictional world of the show) six million dollars.

[4] What about real life, then? Can millionaires have themselves made into supermen? If not now, ten years from now, perhaps? And will the price be lowered to the point where someday the average junior executive, construction worker, and housewife can afford it?

[5] It's not at all a strange thought, since it is only the culmination of what mankind has been doing for a few hundred thousand years. Improving this fragile and ultradestructible body of ours is, in fact, the name of the game we call mankind.

[6] Every tool we have represents an improved body part. The stone ax is an improved fist, and the stone knife is an improved fingernail. The armor of the medieval knight was an improved skin, and gunpowder is an improved biceps for throwing missiles.

[7] These are all external to the body, though. The tools are faithless mercenaries who will work for anyone who seizes them and who will destroy today the person they were helping yesterday.

[8] There are personal aids, designed to improve the parts of one particular person. There are spectacles to help the eyes, hearing aids to help the ear, chemicals to help the immunity mechanisms.

[9] Such things only help established organs. They supplement but do not replace. And if the organ fails altogether, that's it. Spectacles won't help a blind man.

[10] Still closer and more intimate is the pacemaker, which can be implanted in the heart and which can keep the ailing organic pump beating properly by the pacemaker's rhythmic electrical discharges.

[11] But then why not an artificial heart altogether, and artificial kidneys, and artificial lungs? Why shouldn't devices of metal and plastic and polymer be made that are more durable and more reliable than the soft and precarious tissue parts that now exist within our skins?

[12] Actually, you can build devices that will do what our various individual organs will do, but the problem is to control them. Once in the body, how do you make artificial parts work to suit one's personal convenience? How can you become aware of the light patterns an artificial eye is recording? How can you make an artificial muscle contract by a mere effort of will? How can you make a heartbeat adjust automatically to your level of activity?

[13] There we have to call in the modern electronic capacities of science. We have to insert tiny electronic devices that can be hooked to the nerves and that can be controlled by the altering nerve impulses in such a way as to duplicate the natural controls of the natural body. It is something we can't quite do yet, but toward which scientists are working with considerable success.

[14] A body can, in other words, control its mechanical parts by means of feedback. Their activity will adjust to the information brought in by the various sensory parts.

[15] The study of methods for control by feedback is called "cybernetics." If a man's organs are replaced by mechanical devices that are

cybernetically controlled, what we have is a "cybernetic organism" or, taking the first syllable of each word, a "cyborg."

[16] In order to make a cyborg possible, we must depend on the brain. This is natural, since the brain is the essence of an individual. We have no difficulty in deciding that John Smith with a wooden leg or a glass eye is still John Smith. Part after part of the body could be replaced by a durable, versatile mechanism, and the person is *still* John Smith, as long as the brain is left untouched and as long as all those mechanical parts are responsive to the commands of that brain. John Smith will still feel himself to be "I," as much "I" as he ever was.

[17] The ultimate cyborg, then, will consist of a man's brain, spinal cord, and as much of his nerves as are necessary, placed within an utterly mechanical body that it controls.

[18] Such a cyborg can be visualized as a superman indeed, if the parts are properly designed. He can be incredibly strong by ordinary human standards, incredibly quick, incredibly versatile. As long as the brain is protected, he would be able to endure hard environments. He could explore other worlds with little in the way of life-supporting equipment. With nuclear energy for power, such a cyborg would have to supply oxygen only for the brain, and could remain in outer space far more easily than he could now.

[19] In fact, come to think of it, the brain is a serious drawback. It *does* require protection from heat, cold, vacuum, and so on. It *must* be supplied with oxygen and glucose (and quite a bit of it, too, for the brain consumes a third as much oxygen as the rest of the body put together).

[20] Worse yet, the brain dies. You are born with 100 billion or so brain cells, and that is your total lifetime supply. Some of them will die; in fact, some of them are constantly dying, but no new ones will be formed. Even if all other forms of death are precluded, a century of life will find you far gone on the road to senility.

[21] Can we conquer senility someday? Perhaps, but there is as yet no hint that we will be able to do so; and there is a lot more than a hint that we can do something else—replace the brain altogether.

[22] We are building computers that are more and more elaborate and versatile and that are more and more compact. Clearly, we will some day be able to build a computer that is as complex (or even more complex) than the human brain and that is as compact (or even more compact). There are no theoretical reasons why we can't, although there are, of course, considerable engineering difficulties in the way.

[23] The time will come, then, when a cyborg's brain will become useless and, instead of discarding a perfectly useful body, there will be inserted a mechanical brain that is just as good as, or better than, the organic one had been in its prime. Now the cyborg is all cyb and no org.

[24] And if that can be done, why not make cybs to begin with?

[25] That, perhaps, is the natural route of evolution. First, there is the hit-and-miss blindness of natural evolution, which takes billions of years to produce some species that is intelligent enough to begin a directed evolution, making use of advanced biochemical and cybernetic knowledge. The intelligent species then deliberately evolves itself into a cyborg and then into a cyb (or "robot," to use another term).

[26] Perhaps all over the universe there are many millions of intelligent species that have evolved into cybs and that are waiting, with considerable excitement, to see if Homo sapiens, here on Earth, can manage it, too.

[27] And then, when we have gone from org to cyborg to cyb, from man to robot, we may finally be allowed to join the great universal brotherhood of mind that (for all we know) represents the peak and acme of what life has striven for since creation.

VOCABULARY

Look up the following words in your dictionary. Use the system developed in the dictionary section in the back of the text. Be sure to write the part of speech, the pronunciation, and the meaning(s) of each word.

myth·i·cal (mĭth′ĭ-kəl) *adj.* Also **myth·ic.** **1.** Having the nature of a myth. **2.** Existing only in myth: *the mythical unicorn.* **3.** Imaginary; fictitious; fancied. —**myth′i·cal·ly** *adv.*

Definition ©1981 Houghton Mifflin Company. Reprinted by permission from *The American Heritage Dictionary of the English Language, New College Edition.*

barely

remnant

durability

capacity

culmination

fragile

medieval

biceps

mercenaries

immunity

precarious

artificial

cybernetics

organism

versatile

vacuum

glucose

senility

theoretical

species

STUDY QUESTIONS

Finding the Matter

1. According to Asimov, what are the advantages and drawbacks of external tools, personal aids, and artificial organs?

2. What techniques are scientists working on "to duplicate the natural controls of the natural body"?

3. What do these terms mean: *cybernetics, cyborg, cyb, org*?

4. What human parts will the ultimate cyborg retain? What are the disadvantages of the cyborg?

5. If man goes from org to cyborg to cyb, what will he have become?

Exploring the Manner

1. Identify the features that create Asimov's casual style. Comment on the length of his sentences and paragraphs, his use of questions, and his colloquial* expressions.

2. What does Asimov's style indicate about the relationship that he intends to establish with his reading audience*?

3. Following a logical path of argument, including induction* and deduction*, Asimov concludes by suggesting that perhaps we ought to create robots to replace human beings in the future. Do you think he is serious? Reread the last two paragraphs and decide.

SYNONYMS

From the column at the right, select the best synonym for the italicized word in each sentence. Rewrite each sentence using the appropriate synonym.

1. Superman was born on the planet of Krypton, which is an *imaginary* place in space.

2. Millionaires, with the same *delicate* bodies as the rest of us, hope they will be able to use their money to have themselves made into supermen.

3. In *olden* times, knights wore armor to protect their bodies from harm.

4. People hope to live longer when the time comes that scientists will be able to implant *man-made* hearts, kidneys, and lungs in the human body.

5. The procedures of implantation can prove to be quite *risky*.

6. We can *scarcely* imagine the great differences that the use of cybernetics will make in the future.

7. It is not a strange idea to think that people with money will someday be able to have themselves made

A. medieval

B. artificial

C. culmination

D. mythical

E. precarious

F. fragile

G. barely

into supermen, for this idea
is the *high point* of new inventions that have been
going on for thousands of
years.

PARAPHRASE

Read these paragraphs twice; then close your book. Using
your own words, rewrite the paragraphs as clearly and completely as you can.

Every tool we have represents an improved body part. The
stone ax is an improved fist, and the stone knife is an improved fingernail. The armor of the medieval knight was an
improved skin, and gunpowder is an improved biceps for
throwing missiles.
    These are all external to the body, though. The tools are
faithless mercenaries who will work for anyone who seizes
them and who will destroy today the person they were
helping yesterday.

VERB FILL-IN

Fill in each blank with the verb form that is appropriate for
each sentence.

A cyborg _____ as a superman indeed if the parts are
        see

properly designed. He _____ incredibly strong by ordinary
        seem

human standards. He _____ incredibly quick and incredibly
        be

versatile. Since scientists _____ capable of protecting the
        be

brain, the cyborg _____ able to endure hard environments.
        be

He _____ other worlds with little in the way of life-
     explore

supporting equipment.

    The ultimate cyborg _____ of a man's brain and spinal
                       consist

cord. He _____ as many of his nerves as necessary. But the
         have

brain _____ a serious drawback. It _____ from
      be   protect

heat, cold and vacuum. It _____ with oxygen and glucose.
                 supply

SENTENCE COMPLETION

    From the column at the right, select the correct line to complete each of the numbered lines at the left. Write each sentence in its correct form.

1. Since Krypton is purely mythical, none of us can be born there, and

2. Trying to improve this fragile and ultradestructible body of ours is, in fact,

3. The armor of the knight

4. There are spectacles to help the eyes, hearing aids to help the ear,

5. Why shouldn't devices of metal and plastic be made that are more durable and more reliable

6. It is something we can't do yet, but toward which

A. the name of the game we call mankind.

B. chemicals to help the immunity mechanisms.

C. than the soft and precarious tissue parts that now exist within our skins?

D. Superman can only remain a dream.

E. was an improved skin.

F. endure hard environments.

G. scientists are working with considerable success.

H. and that is your total lifetime supply.

7. As long as the brain is
   protected, a cyborg would
   be able to

8. You are born with 100
   billion or so brain cells,

CLOZE EXERCISE

Fill in each blank with the best word to complete the meaning of the sentence.

The study of methods for _____ by feedback is called

"cybernetics." _____ a man's organs are replaced

_____ mechanical devices that are cybernetically

_____, what we have is a "_____ organism," or

taking the first _____ of each word, a "cyborg."

_____ order to make a cyborg _____, we must

depend on the _____. This is natural, since the

_____ is the essence of an _____. We have no

difficulty in _____ that John Smith with a _____

leg or a glass eye _____ still John Smith. Part after

_____ of the body could be _____ by a durable,

versatile mechanism, _____ the person is still John

_____, as long as the brain _____ left untouched

and as long _____ all those mechanical parts are

_____ to the commands of that _____. John

Smith will still feel _____ to be "I," as much _____

as he ever was.

SENTENCE COMBINING

Combine each pair of sentences into a single grammatical sentence.

1. Tools are faithless mercenaries.
   Mercenaries will work for anyone who seizes them.

2. Still closer and more intimate is the pacemaker.
   The pacemaker can be implanted in the heart to make it beat properly.

3. Man's organs can be replaced by mechanical devices.
   The mechanical devices can be cybernetically controlled.

4. In order to make a cyborg possible, we must depend on the brain.
   The brain is the essence of an individual.

5. Protection from heat, cold, and vacuum is required by the brain.
   The brain must also be supplied with oxygen and glucose.

6. The "I" will still be John Smith.
   John Smith will have his own brain, despite having other mechanical parts.

7. We may finally be allowed to join the great universal brotherhood of mind.
   This brotherhood represents the peak and acme of what life has striven for since creation.

PUNCTUATION

Read the following paragraphs. Write in the capital letters and place commas, periods, colons, semicolons, dashes, and quotation marks where needed.

the study of methods for control by feedback is called cybernetics if a mans organs are replaced by mechanical devices that are cybernetically controlled what we have is a cybernetic organism or taking the first syllable of each word a cyborg

in order to make a cyborg possible we must depend on the brain this is natural since the brain is the essence of an individual we have no difficulty in deciding that john smith with a wooden leg or a glass

eye is still john smith part after part of the body could be replaced

by a durable versatile mechanism and the person is still john smith as

long as the brain is left untouched and as long as all those mechanical

parts are responsive to the commands of that brain john smith will

still feel himself to be i as much i as he ever was

WORD-FORM CHART

Use your dictionary to complete the following table. Follow the example shown with item 1, *myth*. If there is no commonly used form for a particular part of speech, write the symbol XXX.

Noun	Verb	Adjective	Adverb
1. myth	mythicize	mythical	mythically
2.	culminate		
3. improvement			
4. establishment			
5. rhythm			
6.		automatic	
7.		essential	
8.			ultimately
9.	protect		
10.		senile	
11.	allow		
12.	strive		

WORD-FORM EXERCISE

Using your completed Word-Form Chart, select the correct form to fit into each sentence. Use the appropriate tense of the verb, the singular or plural form of the noun, and the passive voice where necessary.

Follow the sequence of numbers from the Word-Form Chart to select the correct form.

1. Since Krypton is purely ⎯⎯⎯⎯⎯⎯⎯⎯⎯, Superman can only remain a dream.

2. It is not strange to think of a person being made into a super-man, since it is only the ⎯⎯⎯⎯⎯⎯⎯⎯⎯ of what mankind has been doing for a few hundred thousand years.

3. Every tool we have represents an ⎯⎯⎯⎯⎯⎯⎯⎯⎯ body part.

4. Personal aids such as spectacles and hearing aids help already ⎯⎯⎯⎯⎯⎯⎯⎯⎯ organs.

5. A pacemaker can keep the ailing organic heart beating properly by ⎯⎯⎯⎯⎯⎯⎯⎯⎯ electrical discharges.

6. Soon man will be able to make a heartbeat adjust ⎯⎯⎯⎯⎯⎯⎯⎯⎯ to the appropriate level of activity.

7. The brain is the ⎯⎯⎯⎯⎯⎯⎯⎯⎯ of an individual.

8. The ⎯⎯⎯⎯⎯⎯⎯⎯⎯ cyborg, then, will consist of a man's brain, spinal cord, and as many of his nerves as necessary, placed within an utterly mechanical body that it controls.

9. As long as the brain ⎯⎯⎯⎯⎯⎯⎯⎯⎯, the cyborg would be able to endure hard environments.

10. Even if all other forms of death are precluded, a century of life will find you far gone on the road to ⎯⎯⎯⎯⎯⎯⎯⎯⎯.

11. When we have gone from man to robot, we may finally

    _____ to join the great brotherhood of mind that

12. life _____ for since creation.

QUESTIONS FOR DISCUSSION

1. Asimov speaks of controlling artificial parts of the body by means
   of mechanical feedback or "cybernetics." What do you know
   about a modern technique called "biofeedback," by which people
   can learn to measure and control their own bodily responses?
   Look up the word and compare the purposes of these two
   methods.

2. What ethical and spiritual qualities would be missing from
   Asimov's robot? Could these be programmed?

3. Think about what would happen if a real Steve Austin were
   created in the future. How would he fit into normal society
   (family life, business, sports, etc.)?

TOPICS FOR WRITING

1. In developing his argument, Asimov builds up to his conclusion
   by showing how man is in the process of "evolving" from his
   natural state (org or organism) into a cyb (robot). Write an
   argument opposing Asimov's conclusion that the "brotherhood of
   mind" may represent the highest achievement of life. Argue
   against each of his reasons and show the superiority of man in
   his human condition.

2. If mechanical parts are limited in number, who should have
   priority? If you were a doctor who had one artificial heart to
   implant, would you give it to a priest, a thirty-year-old mother,
   a brilliant scientist, or a five-year-old boy? Support your choice in
   a well-reasoned argumentative essay.

3. If human life could be prolonged indefinitely, what kind of a
   world would we have? Argue for or against such a world.

YOUR MONEY *AND* YOUR LIFE

David A. Cook

[1] Most Americans believe that television entertainment comes to them free of charge, and that the only price they pay is having to endure the commercials—of which they see an average of nine-and-one-half minutes during each prime-time hour and up to sixteen minutes out of sixty the rest of the day. The notion that television is free is based upon the misconception that networks and stations are in the business of selling products to viewers.

[2] In fact, as Les Brown of *The New York Times* has pointed out, the business of commercial television—the only business—is selling potential consumers to advertisers, in lots of one thousand, for between $2 and $12 per program minute.

[3] Since the costs of television advertising are passed along to consumers in the price of the advertised goods, television programming is hardly free. Dividing the $5.9 billion industry revenues for 1977 by the nation's seventy-four-and-one-half million television homes produces an average annual cost per home of $79. And this, as we shall see, is but the beginning of what the medium extracts.

[4] In the 1950s and early 1960s, all viewers were assumed to be

potential consumers for the purpose of this transaction, and the networks sold them to advertisers as an undifferentiated mass. Today,
thanks to modern demographic research, viewers whose age, race, or
class makes them poor consumers can be effectively eliminated from
the equation. Far from determining what viewers want to see, therefore, the strategic mission of the TV industry today is to deliver
precisely the audience the advertisers want to sell.

[5] Before 1968, networks sold time to national advertisers based
on statistical projections of each program's audience size provided by
rating services like those of the A. C. Nielsen Company and the
American Research Bureau, or Arbitron. As television became
ubiquitous in the 1970s, however, extending its reach into 98 percent of American homes and delivering the entire mass market on a
nightly basis, advertisers discovered that it was too expensive, and
unnecessary, to buy such undifferentiated mass audiences.

[6] As the cost of network commercial time began to climb—at an
average rate of 21 percent a year beginning in 1961 and between
1961 and 1978 by a total of more than 340 percent—the one-minute
commercial gradually gave way to short spots. By 1968, 80 percent
of all commercials were thirty, twenty, or ten seconds long. Although
the time devoted to advertising remained constant, the number of
commercial messages increased dramatically, so that a viewer in 1968
could have been exposed to as many as thirty in a typical daytime
hour. Paying high rates for their time, and also fearing that their
messages would be lost in the clutter, advertisers and agencies began
to demand more specific information about each program's viewers
so that they could target those consumers most likely to buy their
products.

[7] With prime-time rates now averaging over $100,000 per com-
mercial minute and with commercial production costs averaging
$50,000 per spot, advertisers want to be more certain than ever that
the right people see their messages. Thus, the producers and syndicators of television programs run full-page advertisements in *Broadcasting* and *Variety* describing the character of their audiences to
potential buyers. "See how much bigger our crowd is?" Archie
admonishes Edith, referring to the demographic dimensions of the
audience that watches *All in the Family*. A series of *Laverne and
Shirley* ads which ran in *Variety* last fall successively claimed "Dominance with Upper Income Viewers" (October), "Dominance with
Higher Educated Viewers" (November), and both "Dominance in
Households with Youngsters" and "Dominance in Households with
No Youngsters" (December).

[8] Since market research reveals that 80 percent of all goods and
services are purchased in the 300 largest metropolitan areas by adults
between the ages of eighteen and forty-nine, the networks and most
advertisers are seeking programs that appeal to an audience which is

demographically urban or suburban, affluent, and relatively young. "In the past, there was a kind of democratic one-man, one-vote thing," said CBS Broadcast Group research director Jay Eliasberg in 1971, speaking of the changing effect of viewer preferences on programming. "Now we're saying that some people are more equal than others, on a demographic basis: if they buy more, they vote more."

[9] The task of American commercial television, then, is to create an electronically synthesized marketplace in which the ideal consuming populace is brought together with the nation's largest purveyors of consumer goods and services. Obviously, only the very largest corporations can afford to purchase network advertising time, and only persons with a certain level of discretionary income can afford to purchase enough of the advertised goods to make the advertisers' efforts worthwhile. This, in turn, means that the scores of millions of viewers who have little discretionary income and the 400,000 incorporated American businesses which can't afford network time have little voice in contemporary American television. This situation would be disturbing even if television were free, as popular belief has it; but the irony is that the medium is subsidized by every viewer on a daily and nightly basis.

[10] Not long ago, a well-mannered telephone solicitor invited my wife and me to go to Preview House on Sunset Boulevard, where pilots for television series and commercials are market-tested, for some "free" entertainment. The caller implied that the "free gifts and prizes" to be distributed at the end of the evening would be compensation for our time.

[11] Waiting in line on the night of the screening, we noticed that our 408 fellow previewers seemed to comprise a remarkably homogeneous group. All were white, well-dressed, and relatively youthful; and I subsequently learned that Audience Studies Incorporated, the market research firm which owns Preview House, recruits selectively so that each night's audience will represent a distinct demographic test market. Inside the theater, we surrendered our invitations and were asked to fill out a number of mimeographed questionnaires meant to elicit demographic data and our entertainment preferences, brand loyalties, and habits of consumption. Finished at last, we were marched into an auditorium where a professional actor explained our mission.

[12] The arm of every seat in Preview House is wired with an electronic device called an "audimeter," he told us. It consists of a module, which fits into the palm of one hand, surmounted by a metered dial, which is controlled with the other. The dial has 360° calibration from "Very Dull" to "Very Good" and we were told to use it "precisely" to register our reactions to what we were about to see. A computer at the back of the auditorium would record and tabulate the responses.

[13] The program that night included the rough cut of an episode from *Operation Petticoat* and two animated shorts, interspersed, as on television, with commercials for new, nationally branded products. After each projection the lights came on, and we were asked to fill out questionnaires which tested our response to what we had just seen. A few were ten pages long and required some effort to complete, but the announcer kept assuring us that filling them out was prerequisite to the distribution of the free gifts and prizes.

[14] At the end of the evening, in a period corresponding roughly to prime time, my wife and I had spent more time supplying market data to the proprietors of Preview House than we had spent watching the "free entertainment" which had brought us there. I began to suspect that we had been exploited; as the gifts were distributed I became certain of it. There were four of them, all products from the test commercials: a six-box case of soap powder, an assortment of cheese snacks, a box of felt-tipped pens, and a month's supply of dry-spray deodorant.

[15] I had just wasted three hours of my time on "free entertainment" that no one would have paid to see. I had spent the time producing something saleable for the owners of Preview House and had let my growing irritation be soothed by the promise of getting something for nothing at the end. (I later learned that Audience Studies charges its clients between $2,500 and $5,000 per pilot—on our night the take must have been at least $17,000.) Worse, I had voluntarily spent my own money on gasoline, parking, and a babysitter in order to put myself in this position.

[16] I felt cheated and full of self-contempt, but when I noticed the bemused smiles on the faces in the audience around me, I couldn't help but admire the mastery of the deception. And I realized then that the whole Preview House episode was a paradigm for the experience of American commercial television. We are drawn to the theater of television by the promise of "free" entertainment; once we enter by turning on our sets, we usually find that the entertainment has quotation marks around it, too. Such is our fascination with the medium that we barely notice the shabbiness of the experience—the barely adequate production values, the one-dimensional scripts and characterizations.

[17] We give the networks our time at the rate of more than four hours a day and they sell it to advertisers at net profits of millions of dollars a year. In the end, we are left very much in the condition of the Preview House audience: diverted but unfulfilled, deceived but never quite aware of the deception.

[18] Where do these hours come from that 98 percent of us spend with our sets on? And where do they go?

[19] A recent UNESCO study concluded that television has increased the amount of time Americans spend with mass media by

40 percent, and that three-fourths of the total is now devoted to TV. At the same time, television has reduced the amount of sleep per day by thirteen minutes. It has similarly reduced the time devoted to social gatherings, radio listening, magazine- and book-reading, film-going, conversation, household tasks, and religion. In short, television has come to dominate all of our time—and thus all of our experience—not spent in work or sleep.

[20] The networks sell that time to advertising agencies at a profit. In their profit-taking, the networks, as well as the stations, naturally pass the costs of programming and overhead along to the agencies.

[21] Advertising agencies buy audience time from the networks on behalf of their clients in order to expose particular groups of consumers to the commercial messages they have prepared. They receive a commission based on the cost of this time, which they apply, in turn, to cover their expenses and produce a profit.

[22] Finally, corporate advertisers engage the services of advertising agencies to produce and place commercials for their products before the appropriate television audiences. They then build the cost of advertising (which now includes the costs of commercial production and placement, the costs of network programming, and the overhead of both networks and ad agencies) into the price of the advertised goods and pass it on to the consumer, who presumably buys the product, at least in part, as a result of TV advertising.

[23] So, when the consumer-viewer buys the products advertised on television, he or she contributes to the total subsidization of the networks, the ad agencies, and the sponsors. In effect, the national audience *gives away* what the networks provide to the agencies at a huge net profit annually and what the agencies procure for the sponsors at a huge net profit annually—its *time*. And this same audience is then charged for what it has lost in the retail price of goods and services.

[24] Television, then, not only robs us of our time, but it makes us foot the bill for every aspect of the theft. Through this medium advertisers not only command our leisure time in our homes at night, but they sell it back to us in the shopping malls on the weekends at a profit.

[25] Except that we can't really buy it back. Like American Indians trading their land to the colonists for trinkets, we are selling off our most precious and nonrenewable resource—the time of our lives—for a handful of electronic gimcracks and colored beads.

[26] But there's more—one last cruel twist to the electronic shell game we call free television. It's that dirty little secret of the American product environment called planned obsolescence, where *we* are the product. Because the product life of an audience is finite, no less so than that of an automobile. And, like automobiles, audiences

depreciate rapidly with age until they no longer have a market value. And that's television's final joke on us all: that, as we grow older, we must eventually enter that land of shades where consumerism becomes a rather slow-pulsed affair of purchasing food, medical care, and an occasional patent remedy. Only now, since we are no longer in possession of our youth and its wordly appetites, does the attention of American advertising and American television finally desert us.

[27] Then, perhaps, when the time is short, we will find that we have given the tube the best years of our lives, bought the products, and gotten little in return but a certification of our own obsolescence. then, perhaps, we will be forced to confront the cruelest indignity of all: that having stolen the time of our lives, American television casts us on the rubbish heap when there's nothing left to steal.

VOCABULARY

Look up the following words in your dictionary. Use the system developed in the dictionary section in the back of the text. Be sure to write the part of speech, the pronunciation, and the meaning(s) of each word.

mis·con·cep·tion (mĭs'kən-sĕp'shən) *n.* An incorrect interpretation or understanding; a delusion.
Definition ©1981 Houghton Mifflin Company. Reprinted by permission from *The American Heritage Dictionary of the English Language, New College Edition.*

potential

revenues

extracts

mass

demographic

strategic

ubiquitous

constant

clutter

syndicators

affluent

synthesized

purveyors

discretionary

ironic

homogeneous

recruits

elicit

tabulate

animated

interspersed

exploited

bemused

paradigm

gimcracks

obsolescence

STUDY QUESTIONS

Finding the Matter

1. According to Cook, what two misconceptions do most viewers have about American television?

2. What is the age span that describes the biggest purchasers of goods and services in America? Where do these consumers live? What qualities besides age might classify a television viewer as a poor consumer?

3. What three factors caused the advertisers and advertising agencies to seek more specific information about each program's viewers? To what use do they put this information?

4. How did the author feel after he had spent three hours watching television and then had to fill out several pages of marketing questionnaires? What reasons does he give for his feelings? How did other members of the audience react?

Exploring the Manner

1. How does the title suggest the thesis*?

2. How would you describe the author's tone* in this article? Does the fact that he is a professor of English have anything to do with his attitude* toward television? Explain.

3. After the networks receive the statistical information from the research firms, the author shows how the costs are passed along. Trace the process (paragraphs 20–23) that leads to his thesis in paragraph 24.

4. What kinds of evidence does Cook accumulate to support his thesis? Does he use deduction* as well as induction*? Use specific examples* to support your answer.

SYNONYMS

From the column at the right, select the best synonym for the italicized word in each sentence. Rewrite each sentence using the appropriate synonym.

1. The advertisers tried for programs that were *lively* and appealing.

2. In 1968, the time devoted to advertising remained *unchanged* even though the number of commercial messages increased.

3. The advertisers were seeking programs that would appeal to an audience that was relatively *rich* and young.

4. Advertisers began to demand more specific information about each program's

A. constant

B. animated

C. affluent

D. interspersed

E. strategic

F. clutter

viewers because they feared
their messages would be lost
in the *disorder* of the
agency's work.

5. Television commercials are
scattered throughout a half
hour's program.

6. The *critical* mission of the
TV industry today is to
deliver precisely the audience that the advertisers
want to sell.

PARAPHRASE

Read this paragraph twice; then close your book. Using your
own words, rewrite the paragraph as clearly and completely
as you can.

    Waiting in line on the night of the screening, we noticed
that our 408 fellow previewers seemed to comprise a remarkably homogeneous group. All were white, well-dressed,
and relatively youthful; and I subsequently learned that
Audience Studies Incorporated, the market research firm
which owns Preview House, recruits selectively so that each
night's audience will represent a distinct demographic test
market. Inside the theater, we surrendered our invitations
and were asked to fill out a number of mimeographed
questionnaires meant to elicit demographic data and our
entertainment preferences, brand loyalties, and habits of
consumption. Finished at last, we were marched into an
auditorium where a professional actor explained our mission.

VERB FILL-IN

Fill in each blank with the verb form that is appropriate for
each sentence.

I _____ three hours of my time on "free entertainment"
      waste

that no one would _____ to see. I _____ the time
               pay   spend

producing something saleable for the owners of Preview House and

_____ my growing irritation be soothed by the promise
          let

of getting something for nothing at the end. (I later _____
                                                          learn

that Audience Studies _____ its clients between $2,500
                    charge

and $5,000 per pilot—on our night the take must _____
                                                        be

at least $17,000.) Worse, I _____ my own money on gaso-
                          spend

line, parking, and a baby-sitter in order to put myself in this position.

SENTENCE COMPLETION

From the column at the right, select the correct line to complete each of the numbered lines at the left. Write each sentence in its correct form.

1. Most Americans believe that television comes to them free of charge,

2. The business of commercial television, the only business,

3. Far from determining what viewers want to see,

4. As the cost of network commercial time began to climb,

5. Since market research reveals that 8 per cent of all goods are purchased in the largest metropolitan areas

A. the networks and most advertisers are seeking programs that appeal to an audience which is demographically urban or suburban, affluent, and relatively young.

B. the one minute commercial gradually gave way to shorter spots.

C. pass the costs of programming and overhead along to the agencies.

D. until they no longer have a market value.

by adults between the ages of eighteen and forty-nine,

6. In their profit taking, the networks, as well as the stations,

7. When the consumer-viewer buys the products advertised on television,

8. Television not only robs us of our time, but it makes us foot the bill

9. Like automobiles, audiences depreciate rapidly with age

10. And that's television's joke on us all: that, as we grow older,

E. and that the only price they have to pay is to endure commercials.

F. we must eventually enter that land of shades where consumerism becomes a rather slow-pulsed affair.

G. the strategic mission of the TV industry today is to deliver precisely the audience the advertisers want to sell.

H. for every aspect of the theft.

I. he or she contributes to the total subsidization of the networks, the ad agencies, and the sponsor.

J. is selling potential consumers to advertisers.

CLOZE EXERCISE

Fill in each blank with the best word to complete the meaning of the sentence.

A recent UNESCO study _____ that television has increased _____ amount of time Americans _____ with mass media by _____ per cent, and three-fourths _____ the total is now _____ to TV. At the _____ time, television has reduced _____ amount of sleep per _____ by 13 minutes. It _____ similarly reduced the time _____ to social gatherings, radio _____, magazine- and book-reading, film-going,

_____, household tasks, and religion. _____ short,

television has come _____ dominate all of our

_____—and thus all of _____ experience—not

spent in _____ or sleep.

SENTENCE COMBINING

Combine each pair of sentences into a single grammatical
sentence.

1. There is a notion that television is free.
   The notion is based on a misconception that networks sell products to viewers.

2. Television advertising costs are passed along to the consumer.
   Television advertising is not free.

3. The television industry does not determine what the viewer wants to see.
   The industry delivers precisely the audience the advertisers want to sell.

4. The producers of television run full-page advertisements in *Broadcasting* and *Variety*.
   The advertisements describe the character of their audiences to potential buyers.

5. Each night's audience was a special group.
   Each special group represented a distinct demographic test market.

6. After each projection the lights were turned on.
   When the lights came on the people were asked to fill out questionnaires.

PUNCTUATION

Read the following paragraph. Write in the capital letters
and place commas, periods, colons, semicolons, dashes, and
quotation marks where needed.

after operation petticoat at the end of the evening in a period

corresponding roughly to prime time my wife and i had spent more time supplying market data to the proprietors of preview house than

we had spent watching the free entertainment which had brought us

there i began to suspect that we had been exploited as the gifts were

distributed i became certain of it there were four of them all prod-

ucts from the test commercials a six box case of soap powder an

assortment of cheese snacks a box of felt tipped pens and a months

supply of dry spray deodorant

WORD-FORM CHART

Use your dictionary to complete the following table. Follow
the example shown with item 1, *misconception*. If there is no
commonly used form for a particular part of speech, write
the symbol XXX.

Noun	Verb	Adjective	Adverb
1. misconception	misconceive	misconceived	XXX
2.	advertise		
3.			potentially
4.		demographic	
5. ubiquity			
6.	synthesize		
7. relative			
8.	record		
9. datum			
10.		bare	

WORD-FORM EXERCISE

Using your completed Word-Form Chart, select the correct form to fit into each sentence. Use the appropriate tense of the verb, the singular or plural form of the noun, and the passive voice where necessary.
Follow the sequence of numbers from the Word-Form Chart to select the correct form.

1. We _____ the idea that television is free.

2. The costs of television advertising are passed along to con-

    sumers in the price of the _____ goods.

3. In the fifties and sixties it was assumed that all viewers were

    _____ consumers.

4. The television industry takes advantage of _____

    research to determine the age, race, and class of their viewers.

5. Television became a _____ medium, reaching 98

    per cent of American homes.

6. The task of American commercial television is to create an

    electronically _____ marketplace.

7. All of the people in that particular audience were white, well-

    dressed, and _____ youthful.

8. A computer in the rear of the auditorium _____

    and tabulated the responses.

9. The viewers in the test audience spent more time supplying

    marketing _____ than they had spent watching the

    "free entertainment."

10. The viewers _____ noticed the shabbiness of their

experience in the test group.

QUESTIONS FOR DISCUSSION

1. How does demography affect a person's choice of television programs?

2. Discuss the way that you feel about television taking away time that you might otherwise spend on reading, studying, talking with family and friends, or doing household tasks.

3. Cook says that because only the very largest corporations can afford to purchase network advertising, the 400,000 incorporated American businesses that can't afford network time have little voice in contemporary American television. In what ways might television programming differ if small corporations could sponsor programs?

TOPICS FOR WRITING

1. A common argument against television is that it shows too much violence and sex and does not challenge the intelligence of the viewer. Compare that argument with Cook's and decide whether either is valid as a reason for restricting your television habits. Once you have formulated your point of view in a thesis sentence*, write an argument presenting your evidence either inductively or deductively.

2. Write an argument from the point of view of a parent of young children (five to ten years of age) either supporting television watching or condemning it. Include your attitudes toward viewing hours, programming, and commercials directed toward children.

3. Argue for or against government ownership and operation of television broadcasting. Discuss programming, commercials, and propaganda.

CAREER EDUCATION AT THE COLLEGE LEVEL
Clifton R. Wharton, Jr.

[1] The amazing growth of career education in the past several years has been one of the significant developments of American education in the 1970's.

[2] In 1971, the then U.S. Commissioner of Education, Sidney Marland, gave career education a new impetus. Since then, federal funds for career training and counseling have increased 750 percent, from $9 million in 1971 to nearly $70 million in 1977. Moreover, state and local funds have been generated by this federal investment.

[3] Foundations and corporations also have supported career education. So have a wide range of national organizations, from the Chamber of Commerce and the AFL-CIO to the National Council of Churches and the Girl Scouts.

[4] High schools and colleges throughout the land have added more "practical" courses to their curriculums. Some small colleges have switched almost entirely from liberal education to career programs. Students, astonishingly alert to new educational fashions and new sources of financial support, are flocking to vocational, career, and professional courses.

[5] The pressure is so strong that more professors each year are relabeling their courses so that they seem directly related to paid employment.

[6] At this point, I want to urge that we keep career education in perspective. At present, the growth of career education is so explosive that liberal arts education in America is dying—or is at least seriously weakened. In 1970, according to A. W. Astin's studies of college freshmen, 12.7 percent of all freshmen were arts and humanities majors. By 1975, only 8.3 percent were. The number of English majors has dropped from 3 percent in 1970 to less than 1 percent today.

[7] There are many reasons for the recent spread of career education. Some are real, some merely perceived.

- More and more, people consider the content of college courses to be removed from and irrelevant to the world of work.
- People think that what career education there is, is misdirected —that colleges train too many teachers, say, and too few electronic technicians.
- Unemployment of young people has risen, partly because, the arguments run, young people are not trained for existing jobs.
- Too many professors appear disdainful, if not hostile, toward business and industry.

- A few scholars publicize the idea that students are being over-educated—prepared through humane learning and science to be leaders rather than technicians and service workers.
- Hard times—slower economic growth, inflation, and high taxes—are ahead for the United States. People have to get back to basics, to do-it-yourself, to the ethic of hard work.

[8] The swift rise of career education has other reasons, too. It started near the end of the Vietnam War, when some thought that college students had simplistically rejected reality, work, and achievement and were filled with fancy ideas fertilized by too much leisure, too much money, and too much permissiveness.

[9] Further, the costs of higher education are rising, and the share borne by students and their families is increasing. So the demand increases for courses that are helpful in getting jobs. Students and their parents ask, Why should we use our hard-earned dollars to pay

for general education "frills"? Every course taken and paid for, it seems, should pay off directly by helping the student get a job.

[10] The most fundamental reason of all, however, may be the movement of masses of formerly excluded young people—children of blue-collar workers, minorities, women, and the less academically gifted—into our colleges. Proponents of career education argue, "Surely most of them can't be trained for traditional careers in law, medicine, theology, university teaching, engineering, business, and the government bureaucracy. Surely, they need to be trained for new kinds of careers." The emphasis on vocational and career education almost implies a two-track college approach.

[11] So the arguments run.

[12] Two things are very clear. One is that we are being swept away by a tidal wave of new enthusiasm, in both public and private institutions, for vocational and career higher education. The other is that colleges and universities have superficially attractive and plausible reasons to move in this direction in the 1970's. I am acutely aware of these developments, and I support the trend—to a limited extent.

[13] But I also have some grave doubts. At times career education seems to be to the 1970's what free electives and so-called "relevant" courses and "nontraditional" teaching were to the 1960's. Let me give some reasons for my reluctance to jump on the bandwagon.

[14] First, career education, which seems so new to some educators, is really as old as education itself. The earliest universities in Western civilization—Bologna, Paris, Salamanca, Oxford—all had the express purpose of training people for careers: in the churches, the courts, medicine, teaching, and royal administration.

[15] Sir Walter Scott has reminded us that chivalric education for the elite in the Middle Ages was education for performance. One manual of the time stated, "The squire must be able to spring upon a horse while fully armed; to exercise himself in running; to strike for a length of time with the axe or club; to dance and do somersaults entirely armed except for his helmet . . ." and so forth. Being a squire in the twelfth century was a career that needed special training.

[16] To go even further back, Plato's *The Republic* was basically an examination of what kind of education Greece should provide in order to get real philosopher-kings as rulers and the best people into other careers of leadership.

[17] In 1636, Harvard was established mainly to train men for careers in the church and in teaching. Two centuries later, the Land-Grant Act, which gave birth to some of our leading state universities, was specifically designed to set up new kinds of colleges for what were called "the laboring classes"—in agriculture, the military arts, and mechanics (which we today would call engineering and technology).

[18] So American higher education, and indeed most higher education since its origins, has been in great part devoted to training for careers. To some extent the "discovery" in 1971 of career education is akin to the discovery by Monsieur Jourdain in Moliere's play *The Bourgeois Gentleman* that he had been speaking prose all his life.

[19] A second cause of doubt is that as hard as I have tried, I have been unable to pin down exactly what is meant by "career education."

[20] Many of the strongest advocates stress that career education is not vocational education, that it has more to do with counseling and with work generally than with specific jobs. Yet there is little doubt that career education has its roots in the Vocational Educational Amendments of 1968 and that former Commissioner of Education Terrel Bell in speaking of it said, "It is our duty to provide students with salable skills."

[21] Kenneth Hoyt, the director of the U.S. Office of Career Education, has said, "Career education is the totality of experiences through which one learns about, and prepares to engage in, work as part of his or her way of living." That is a very broad definition. It can include such things as preschool toys, talks with a grandfather about his preretirement days, and postdoctoral training. Others have written of "finding meaningful work," "deciding upon a satisfying career," and "improving the relations between schools and society."

[22] The American Association of State Colleges and Universities' statement on career education is one of the best. It speaks of career education as "a composition of activities, experiences, and results that prepare people for a successful transition to work, along with a rewarding personal life-style." It also says career education is a life-long process that begins in the primary years and that increases occupational training but keeps what the Association calls "a liberal arts base."

[23] Even the National Advisory Council on Career Education found in its 1976 Interim Report that what constitutes career education is still "untidy." I myself think that career education is at bottom a spirit, a mood, a vague sense that all education ought to be more related than it has been to manpower needs and the demands of the economy.

[24] Third, career education may be based on a misreading of what the leaders of American business really want.

[25] It is true that some employers, particularly small business people, have applauded the increase in vocationalism on our campuses. But a major study in 1976 by The Conference Board, which does studies for U.S. industry, found several interesting things. In 1975—a recession year—the nation's 7,500 largest employers spent more than $2 billion to train employees and executives. (This sum equals the total amount given to all American colleges and universities by all sources in that year.)

[26] Most business leaders said they did not consider this kind of training "the responsibility of the schools to provide." Most said that what they most desire from the schools and colleges is not more vocational education but elimination of the serious deficiencies among younger employees in basic skills such as writing, speech, mathematics, computer use, and knowledge of how our government and economy really work.

[27] The message is this. Most business people, especially corporate leaders, prefer to train employees in their own way of doing things. But they would like to have the schools graduate young persons who are articulate, literate, good at using numbers, informed about democracy and capitalism—and above all, persons who can think. They want soundly educated persons, not vocationally trained employees.

[28] Fourth, the career education movement may contain an unintended class and racial bias. Large numbers of students from blue-collar backgrounds, minorities, women, and those not in the top third of their classes by traditional measurements are now entering our colleges. It is interesting that we seem to think of them mostly as material for the middle-level and upper-lower-level positions in society.

[29] Some colleges have refused to slot these students for low-level careers. The City College of New York, for example, has for a century given a solid, liberal education to the children of immigrants, workers, and minorities. Its graduates have become poets and professors, financiers and surgeons.

[30] We must be careful not to identify what K. Patricia Cross calls the "new students" as fit only for technical and vocational positions. If their primary and secondary school preparation is sound, these students can handle the more rigorous liberal arts and sciences programs in college as well as anyone else, and become as competent leaders as anyone else. If their preparation is deficient, it will be harder for many of them, and we may have to provide extra help, guidance, and direction at the college level.

[31] In any case, those responsible for career education must guard against unintentional class or racial insult and stereotyping.

[32] Fifth, insofar as career education is preparation mainly for one kind of work, it puts individuals in jeopardy because our economy is changing.

[33] Perhaps because I am an economist, I have been particularly sensitive to the fact that people today change jobs with greater frequency than before. More and more persons even change careers two or three times.

[34] Therefore, if we spend much time in those precious college years educating people not for the dynamics and uncertainties of life but for one job or career, we may be doing them—and society—a disservice. We may produce a highly specialized graduate whose training is so narrow that his or her career is limited to one job. Any

major change in that field could suddenly result in unemployment, and the graduate would have neither the skills nor the intellectual flexibility for an alternative career.

[35] Career education, I fear, is education with a low ceiling. It may help get that first job or position but actually retard growth and work opportunities as time passes.

[36] Sixth, one of the few recent developments in higher education that has seen growth as dramatic as that of career education is life-long education. The explosion of information and the escalating obsolescence of information is forcing upon higher education a new set of demands: for updating, retooling, and recertification. The university is losing its traditional character as a community of youth.

[37] There are now more adults over 25 than college-age students enrolled in classes in the United States. In a world of rapid demands for new and better knowledge, lifelong learning has become the new pattern of education in our land. Career education, however, usually ends at what is so wisely called commencement.

[38] Higher education must respond to the new pattern of con-tinuing education. One of the ways it can respond best is to provide those vital skills of learning, those habits of thought, those sensi-bilities, and those core subjects that best allow people to go on learn-ing, stretching their minds and their dreams throughout their lives.

[39] The really critical question for higher education today is not how to provide more career education. It is how to revise the struc-ture and content of undergraduate education so that it will prepare students for a lifetime of continuous learning and a changing array of jobs, positions, and careers.

[40] Career education, by concentrating so heavily on the short-term economic ends of university training, is in danger of neglecting the political and personal ends. It is important that our graduates be intelligent, discerning, tolerant, humane citizens. Our democratic way of life demands it.

[41] It is important, too, that our graduates engage in humanistic thinking and exploring because people not only need jobs, they also need fulfillment both in their work and in their leisure. The decline in the length of the work week means that today many have almost as much time for leisure as for work. Self-fulfillment in work must be matched by self-fulfillment in leisure. Such fulfillment will come primarily from a clear understanding of oneself and society, from knowing what is valuable, from possessing an educated heart.

[42] I have a deeper concern about higher education and the current national mood. It seems to me that our nation is going through a gigantic loss of nerve, a massive decline in faith in our-selves. We seem to be suffering from creeping shrinkage of vision.

[43] Yet what we need at this pivotal point in our history is fresh thinking, fresh courage, and fresh values. That is, we need more

people who are creative, ingenious, vigorous, bold, and humane. We need more and better education, not less. And we certainly need more rigorous general education—for all our citizens—that will provide the tools and daring to build anew in disturbing new conditions.

[44] If higher education is a preparation for a better life, work is still the most time-consuming, consequential, even passionate component of our waking lives. I agree with the philosopher Alfred North Whitehead that "education should turn out a student with something he knows well and something he can do well. The intellect does not work in a vacuum." Our universities must continue to train people for both good lives and good work.

[45] I hope, however, that our vision as educators will not be short-sighted. Our present students will be at their greatest powers some 40 years from now. Surely we should prepare them for life in the year 2020 as much as for their first jobs in the next year or two.

[46] Every college and university worth its name has an obligation to be responsive. But it has a greater obligation to be responsible. To yield to the present cries for more careerism is to be responsive. Our responsibility, however, is to lead as well as follow, to prepare young men and women to shape our civilization during the next half century. No other institution in our society can exercise such leadership.

[47] We should never forget that the main purpose of higher education—the purpose that makes all the efforts and anguish worthwhile—is to help build a better society by graduating better people with better ideas. As a by-product of carrying out that large and critical task, we can help men and women get better jobs.

[48] I hope we never confuse the byproduct with our central purpose.

VOCABULARY

Look up the following words in your dictionary. Use the system developed in the dictionary section in the back of the text. Be sure to write the part of speech, the pronunciation, and the meaning(s) of each word.

im·pe·tus (ĭm′pə-təs) *n.*, *pl.* -tuses. 1. a. An impelling force; impulse. b. Something that incites; a stimulus. 2. Loosely, the force or energy associated with a moving body. [Latin, attack, from *impetere*, to assail, attack : *in-*, against + *petere*, to go toward, seek, attack (see pet-¹ in Appendix*).]

Definition ©1981 Houghton Mifflin Company. Reprinted by permission from *The American Heritage Dictionary of the English Language, New College Edition.*

generated

perspective

irrelevant

ethic

superficially

plausible

acutely

chivalric

elite

akin

salable

jeopardy

escalating

obsolescence

array

ingenious

consequential

component

STUDY QUESTIONS

Finding the Matter

1. How has the rising cost of higher education contributed to the increased interest in career programs?

2. For what careers did the earliest western universities (Oxford, Paris) train their students?

3. According to a 1976 survey, what qualities do most business leaders want in their college-educated employees?

4. Why does the author say that the "career education movement may contain an unintended class and racial bias"?

5. What is the danger of preparing for a single career in a changing economy?

Exploring the Manner

1. What is the author's position on the subject of career education?

2. Why does he begin his essay by listing several reasons for the spread of career education? Which ones do you think are "real" reasons and which ones "perceived" reasons?

3. Outline Wharton's reasons for hesitating to support career education fully. Which of these reasons do you agree with and which ones seem unconvincing? Support your opinions.

4. Does Wharton use deduction* or induction* to develop his argument? Support your answer.

SYNONYMS

From the column at the right, select the best synonym for the italicized word in each sentence. Rewrite each sentence using the appropriate synonym.

1. In 1971, the U.S. Commissioner of Education gave career education a new *stimulus*.

2. State and local funds were *produced* because of federal investments.

3. The discovery of career education is *related* to the discovery by Jourdain in Moliere's play *The Bourgeois Gentleman* that he had been speaking prose all his life.

4. The public must be *keenly* aware of the necessity of

A. akin

B. salable

C. generated

D. escalation

E. impetus

F. acutely

G. ingenious

H. obsolete

establishing career education
courses.

5. These courses provide students with *marketable* skills.

6. Career education was a
brilliant plan to provide new
jobs for the "blue collar"
class.

7. There is a rapid *increase* in
the number of colleges offering career education courses.

8. As new sets of demands are
put upon higher education,
it becomes necessary to up-
date information that
already shows signs of
being *outdated*.

PARAPHRASE

Read these paragraphs twice; then close your book. Using
your own words, rewrite the paragraphs as clearly and completely as you can.

There are many reasons for the recent spread of career
education. Some are real, some merely perceived.

- More and more, people consider the content of college
  courses to be removed from and irrelevant to the world
  of work.
- People think that what career education there is is misdirected—that colleges train too many teachers, say, and
  too few electronic technicians.
- Unemployment of young people has risen, partly because, the arguments run, young people are not trained
  for existing jobs.
- Too many professors appear disdainful, if not hostile,
  toward business and industry.
- A few scholars publicize the idea that students are being
  overeducated—prepared through humane learning and
  science to be leaders rather than technicians and service
  workers.
- Hard times—slower economic growth, inflation, and high
  taxes—are ahead for the United States. People have to
  get back to basics, to do-it-yourself, to the ethic of hard
  work.

VERB FILL-IN

Fill in each blank with the verb form that is appropriate for each sentence.

Two things _____ very clear. One is that we
           be

_____ away by a tidal wave of new enthusiasm, in both
   sweep

public and private institutions, for vocational and career higher

education. The other _____ that colleges and universities
                     be

_____ superficially attractive and plausible reasons to
   have

move in this direction in the 1970s. I _____ acutely
                                        be

aware of these developments, and I _____ the trend—
                                   support

to a limited extent.

But I also _____ some grave doubts. At times, career
           have

education _____ to be to the 1970s what free electives
          seem

and so-called "relevant" courses and "nontraditional" teaching were

to the 1960s. Let me _____ some reasons for my reluctance
                     give

to jump on the bandwagon.

SENTENCE COMPLETION

From the column at the right, select the correct line to complete each of the numbered lines at the left. Write each sentence in its correct form.

1. High schools and colleges throughout the land

2. The costs of higher education are rising,

3. The emphasis on vocational and career education almost implies

4. Harvard was established mainly to train men

5. The Land Grant Act gave birth to some of our leading state universities

6. Many of the strongest advocates stress that career education

7. Commissioner of Education Terrel Bell said, "It is our duty to provide students

8. Career education should be a composition of activities, experiences, and results

9. The City College of New York has for a century

10. If higher education is a preparation for a better life,

A. for careers in the church and in teaching.

B. and was specifically designed to set up new kinds of colleges for what were called "the laboring classes."

C. is not vocational education.

D. and the share borne by students and their families is increasing.

E. work is still the most time-consuming, consequential, even passionate component of our waking lives.

F. a two-track college approach.

G. given a solid, liberal education to the children of immigrants, workers, and minorities.

H. that prepare people for a successful transition to work, along with a rewarding personal life-style.

I. have added more "practical" courses to their curriculums.

J. with salable skills."

CLOZE EXERCISE

Fill in each blank with the best word to complete the meaning of the sentence.

Career education, by concentrating so heavily _____ the short-term economic ends of university _____, is in danger of neglecting the _____ and personal ends. It is important _____ our graduates be intelligent, discerning, tolerant, _____ citizens. Our democratic way of life _____ it.

It is important, too, that _____ graduates engage in humanistic thinking and _____ because people not only need jobs, _____ also need fulfillment both in their _____ and in their leisure. The decline _____ the length of the work week _____ that today many have almost as _____ time for leisure as for work. _____ in work must be matched by _____ in leisure. Such fulfillment will come _____ from a clear understanding of oneself _____ society, from knowing what is valuable, _____ possessing an educated heart.

SENTENCE COMBINING

Combine each pair of sentences into a single grammatical sentence.

1. Foundations and corporations have supported career education. National organizations from the Chamber of Commerce to the Girl Scouts have supported career education.

2. The growth of career education is so explosive that liberal arts education in America is dying.
   Liberal arts education in America is seriously weakened, if not dying.

3. Too many professors seem disdainful toward business and industry.
   Too many professors seem hostile toward business and industry.

4. Career education is really as old as education itself.
   Career education seems so new to some educators.

5. The strongest advocates stress that career education is not vocational education.
   They say it has more to do with counseling and with work generally than with specific jobs.

6. Some employers like the new vocationalism.
   Small business people applaud the increase of vocationalism on our campuses.

PUNCTUATION

Read the following paragraph. Write in the capital letters and place commas, periods, colons, semicolons, dashes, and quotation marks where needed.

kenneth hoyt the director of the u s office of career education has said career education is the totality of experiences through which one learns about and prepares to engage in work as part of his or her way of living that is a very broad definition it can include such things as preschool toys talks with a grandfather about his preretirement days and postdoctoral training others have written of finding meaningful work deciding upon a satisfying career and improving the relations between schools and society

WORD-FORM CHART

Use your dictionary to complete the following table. Follow the example shown with item 1, *liberalize*. If there is no commonly used form for a particular part of speech, write the symbol XXX.

Noun	Verb	Adjective	Adverb
1. XXX	liberalize	liberal	liberally
2.			humanely
3. tide			
4.		total	
5.		responsible	
6.	finance		
7. competence			
8.		frequent	
9.			continuously
10.	graduate		

WORD-FORM EXERCISE

Using your completed Word-Form Chart, select the correct form to fit into each sentence. Use the appropriate tense of the verb, the singular or plural form of the noun, and the passive voice where necessary.

Follow the sequence of numbers from the Word-Form Chart to select the correct form.

1. Some small colleges have switched almost entirely from

    _____ education to career programs.

2. A few scholars publicize the idea that students are being over-

educated—prepared through _____ learning and science

to be leaders rather than technicians and service workers.

3. We are being swept away by a _____ wave of enthu-

siam for this new education.

4. Hoyt said that career education is the _____ of expe-

riences through which one learns about work as part of a way of

living.

5. Many business leaders did not consider this kind of training to

be the _____ of the school.

6. Graduates of the City College of New York have become famous

in the fields of the arts, _____ , and medicine.

7. If the primary and secondary education of these new students is

sound, they will be able to become as _____ leaders

as anyone else.

8. People today change jobs with greater _____ than

before.

9. The critical question today is how to revise the structure and

content of undergraduate education so that it will prepare stu-

dents for a lifetime of _____ learning.

10. We should never forget that the main purpose of higher educa-

tion is to help build a better society by _____ better

people with better ideas.

QUESTIONS FOR DISCUSSION

1. What are the requirements for college or university admission in your native country? Explain how they differ from the requirements at the college you are now attending.

2. Are there career programs in the colleges in your native country, or are there separate schools devoted to career training? Give details.

3. What college courses are required for your curriculum? What electives do you plan to take? Explain your reasons for selecting these electives.

4. What courses do you think that every college student should take, no matter what his or her intended major? Give supporting reasons for your choices.

TOPICS FOR WRITING

1. Complete the following statement and then argue for or against it: A college education should train a person not only for a job but also for _____.

2. Write an argument in favor of or against the policy of requiring students to take college courses outside their major areas of study.

3. Pretend that you are the president of a successful business. Write a letter to the personnel director at the college from which you were graduated. Tell the director what kind of education and training you would like your future executives to receive in college. Give specific reasons for the qualifications that you require.

PRIVACY AND THE PRESS: IS NOTHING SACRED?

Nat Hentoff

[1] For several years, I have taught a course on investigative reporting at New York's New School for Social Research. Many of the students and nearly all the guest experts are journalists. I ask each guest if there is anything he or she would *not* do to get a story. Most react as if they had never even thought of the question before. They have simply taken it for granted that a diligent journalist may—and indeed, must—get the news by whatever means are necessary.

[2] I ask these reporters if they would bug and wiretap an uncooperative subject. Would they disguise their identities and infiltrate the subject's business or even family? The answer usually is affirmative, proudly so. After all, in order to satisfy "the people's right to know" —the basic credo of our calling—a reporter has to be uncommonly resourceful, daringly inventive.

[3] Outside of class, other journalists tell me of secret grand jury minutes that they have somehow obtained and printed. This, mind you, before the person being investigated by the grand jury has been indicted. What about the presumption of his innocence? Because he has been brought before the grand jury, I am told, he is news and that's all that ultimately counts.

[4] My own maverick view is that journalists are second only to the state in their imperiling of individual privacy. They often act like undercover cops and sometimes like righteously aggressive prosecutors. It is a citizen's right, for example, not to speak to the press; but a "no comment" almost invariably leads the reporter to assume guilt. That assumption having been made, the reporter feels free to "get" the silent citizen. If I were recruiting for the FBI these days, I would surely canvass the press for prospects.

[5] What most disturbs me is that exceedingly few journalists see anything wrong with this way of doing their job. They apparently forget, for one thing, that the First Amendment is a shield, increasingly battered, against state interference with the press's functions. It was not intended to be a blunt instrument against individual citizens who would be strewn about in the wake of journalists gathering news. But most reporters think only of getting the story. The notion that they should be sensitive to individuals' privacy rights strikes them as a dangerous form of outside meddling with their special status. (Again, they react like cops.)

[6] This is not to say that privacy should always be inviolate. Then we'd have nothing to read but press releases and shopping news. The privacy of Richard Nixon's White House was legitimately invaded because crimes were being committed there. Similarly, I have printed

information about private meetings in and outside of municipal agencies because public lies were being concocted there.

[7] On the other hand, years ago I did not print a tip from a cop that a legislator had been swept up in a dragnet raid of a homosexual bar. I knew his public record, and I saw no relevant relationship between that apparent aspect of his private life and what he did as a lawmaker. Conversely, I do think the Washington press has been remiss through the years in not naming those members of Congress who are manifestly drunk during the course of legislative business. That is news their constituents should surely have. But what about extramarital affairs? It depends on whether the liaison affects the public figure's public life. If the inamorata is on the payroll of, let's say, the Chilean government, and her friend is on the Foreign Relations Committee, that's legitimate news. And if a President is an active satyr, the electorate ought to be told, if only on grounds of national security.

[8] No clear line of judgment can be drawn in these matters, but reporters must at least be continually aware of a conflict between the colliding interests of privacy and the free flow of information. Instead the trend has been toward publishing just about anything that can be obtained, by whatever means. I am not, however, particularly concerned with the steamy proliferation of gossip in the nation's press, since no one gets into those columns unless they're renowned or notorious and indeed have worked at achieving such visibility. Accordingly, they have voluntarily given up much of their privacy.

[9] What does greatly concern me are those private citizens who can be severely injured by needless press attention. Consider the printing of arrest records. News organizations have been fighting for years to get at that information. Their opponents, including the American Civil Liberties Union, maintain that there is no public need to know if someone has been arrested if the arrest has not resulted in a conviction. The vast majority of arrests do not. Why, then, if someone has been found innocent, subject him to public obloquy by publishing the fact that he was arrested? Yet in many states the press has won this dubious right.

[10] In New York State, for instance, the law says that no employer, public or private, and no agency, can ask anyone if he's ever been arrested. Furthermore, anyone exonerated of a criminal charge can have his fingerprints expunged from all official records. The privacy of such individuals is thus safeguarded—except from the press, which can search out the arrest records and print them.

[11] As an illustration of the press's zeal in these matters, there was a triumphant tour of Maine last October by a task force of 100 reporters testing the state's "right-to-know" law. Marching into local police stations, they demanded to see the complete records of the most recent arrests. (Not convictions, arrests.) Out of 111 police stations, 99 complied entirely. One of the tiny minority of officers defending privacy rights was the sole cop in the town of New Gloucester. He told the posse that he hadn't arrested anybody during the past four years, but if he had, those records would be out-of-bounds to reporters. As they should be.

[12] Similarly, there have been moves in some states to seal juvenile records and accounts of certain misdemeanors committed by adults. If the once and former defendants don't get into any more trouble, the slate is wiped clean. This too offends the press, which insists that every record should be open and publishable. Otherwise, how can vigilant reporters keep a check on the criminal justice system?

[13] Arthur Miller, an expert on privacy and a professor at Harvard Law School, states:

> Vigorous and diligent reporters can effectively monitor the criminal justice system without examining the records of those who have paid their debt to society, who have met the stringent conditions of the

statutes, and who deserve a second chance. If we believe in rehabilitation . . . then we must tolerate some risks. We should permit some people to reenter the mainstream of society by eliminating the social and vocational ostracism associated with an ancient record that does not reflect their present worth. How can you quarrel with the principle of sealing the record of a youthful peccadillo which has never been repeated?

[14] Much of the press eagerly does quarrel with that principle, as with the principle that the names of people on welfare should not be published. But what is the point of doing that, except to embarrass those on the rolls? The public is entitled to know the cost of welfare and the percentage of the population being aided. But not the individual names.

[15] The press's mania for going after just about everything is not unlike the sleuthing habits of the FBI, other government agencies, and insurance companies—all of whom are criticized by much of the press for invading privacy. Now, however, as *the press* is being recognized as one of the more fearsome enemies of privacy, there is some movement toward trying to legislate journalists into becoming "responsible." Professor Arthur Miller, for instance, speaks darkly, if unspecifically, of "a reexamination of the favored position currently enjoyed by the press."

[16] Wherever that "corrective" route might lead would be worse than the disease, for it would necessarily involve weakening the First Amendment even further than has the present Supreme Court. Although Justice William O. Douglas said in the tradition of Louis Brandeis that "the right to be let alone is indeed the beginning of all freedom," he also persistently maintained that the First Amendment cannot be balanced. I am also largely of that view. Even if I were not, I cannot conceive of any "privacy" strictures on what the press can print—or additions to present punishments for what is published— that would not be subject to crippling abuse by the state. To make the press "responsible" in this way is to paralyze it.

[17] In terms, however, of *how* privacy is sometimes invaded by journalists, there are already laws that can be applied without violating the First Amendment. If, without color of law, a journalist breaks into an apartment to snatch diaries or other such material, he can and ought to be charged, just like an errant FBI agent, with breaking and entering. If he unlawfully wiretaps, he should be punished for breaking the relevant law.

[18] But what of those invasions of privacy that occur without crimes being committed? Visiting notoriety, for instance, upon a public official's son for living with another man. Is all privacy to be lost to the families of newsworthy figures? And what of the continuing, quasi-religious crusade of the press to be allowed to poke

into all kinds of dossiers, from everyone's arrest records to reckless driving charges (later dismissed) against a public official?

[19] I have no confident answer. The press as a whole is no more likely to become more humane on its own, than bill-collecting agencies. When I most despair of the majority of journalists ever growing less reckless about the privacy of everyone else, I think that it might be grandly therapeutic—though contrary to the spirit of this article —if one paper in a city would subject reporters and editors at another paper to exactly this kind of privacy-shredding. That is, headlining the extramarital affairs and ancient arrest records of some of these journalists. The experience could greatly concentrate the victims' minds on privacy when next they went on assignment.

VOCABULARY

Look up the following words in your dictionary. Use the system developed in the dictionary section in the back of the text. Be sure to write the part of speech, the pronunciation, and the meaning(s) of each word.

> **pri·va·cy** (prī'və-sē) *n., pl.* -cies. **1.** The condition of being secluded or isolated from the view of, or from contact with, others. **2.** Concealment; secrecy.
> Definition ©1981 Houghton Mifflin Company. Reprinted by permission from *The American Heritage Dictionary of the English Language, New College Edition.*

investigate

diligent

bug

wiretap

infiltrate

credo

indicted

presumption

aggressive

prosecutors

posse

misdemeanors

vigilant

stringent

ostracism

peccadillo

assume

canvass

shield

battered

blunt

strewn

meddling

inviolate

concocted

sleuthing

strictures

snatch

errant

dossiers

relevant

remiss

constituents

extramarital

liaison

inamorata

satyr

proliferation

notorious

obloquy

dubious

exonerate

expunge

zeal

sole

humane

therapeutic

STUDY QUESTIONS

Finding the Matter

1. How do most reporters justify using questionable methods to obtain a story?

2. Hentoff says that journalists are the second worst violators of individual privacy. Who is the worst violator?

3. In what ways do some journalists act like undercover policemen and prosecutors?

4. Why does Hentoff say that a reporter might be an effective FBI agent?

5. How does Hentoff distinguish between "private" and "public" news? What examples does he offer of each?

6. What does Hentoff say about public figures who may be attacked in gossip columns?

7. What is the danger in a newspaper's printing the arrest records of a private citizen who is not convicted?

8. What is the First Amendment of the United States Constitution? How might this amendment be weakened if laws were passed to try to make reporters more responsible?

Exploring the Manner

1. How does Hentoff's opening anecdote about his course on investigative reporting suggest his attitude toward privacy and the press?

2. Although he uses sophisticated vocabulary in this essay, Hentoff refers twice to policemen as "cops." What does this informal usage suggest about the nature of his professional relationship with members of the police force?

3. Hentoff's choice of words reveals his attitude* toward privacy and the press. Why, for example, does he call the 100 reporters testing Maine's right-to-know law "the posse"? What ideas are suggested by the phrases "quasi-religious crusade of the press" and "the mania of the press"?

4. Does Hentoff use both induction* and deduction* to develop his argument? What kind of evidence does he use?

5. Hentoff admits that he has no certain answer to the problem of the press's invasion of citizens' privacy. Does this admission weaken his argument?

SYNONYMS

From the column at the right, select the best synonym for the italicized word in each sentence. Rewrite each sentence using the appropriate synonym.

1. Reporters should be sensitive to the rights of privacy of individuals and should not *interfere* with such rights.

2. People who have met the *strict* conditions of the law should not be prosecuted.

3. When the press reports on a person's arrest, it is *doubtful* that this informa-

A. sole

B. stringent

C. snatch

D. diligent

E. remiss

F. dubious

G. meddle

tion is important unless the person is convicted.

H. mania

I. expunged

J. vigilant

4. One officer, defending privacy rights, was the *only* cop in the town of New Gloucester.

5. Reporters must be *watchful* in keeping a check on the criminal justice system.

6. The Washington Press has been *careless* in not naming Congressmen who are drunk during the course of legislative business.

7. The *madness* of the press for going after just about everything is not unlike the sleuthing habits of the FBI.

8. Anyone exonerated of a criminal charge can have his fingerprints *erased* from all official records.

9. If a journalist breaks into an apartment to *grab* diaries or like materials, he ought to be arrested.

10. People take it for granted that an *industrious* journalist must get the news by whatever means are necessary.

PARAPHRASE

Read these paragraphs twice; then close your book. Using your own words, rewrite the paragraphs as clearly and completely as you can.

My own maverick view is that journalists are second only to the state in their imperiling of individual privacy. They often act like undercover cops and sometimes like righteously aggressive prosecutors. It is a citizen's right, for example, not to speak to the press; but a "no comment" almost invariably leads the reporter to assume guilt. That assumption having been made, the reporter feels free to "get" the silent citizen. If I were recruiting for the FBI these days, I would surely canvass the press for prospects.

What most disturbs me is that exceedingly few journalists see anything wrong with this way of doing their job. They apparently forget, for one thing, that the First Amendment is a shield, increasingly battered, against state interference with the press's functions. It was not intended to be a blunt instrument against individual citizens who would be strewn about in the wake of journalists gathering news. But most reporters think only of getting the story. The notion that they should be sensitive to individuals' privacy rights strikes them as a dangerous form of outside meddling with their special status. (Again, they react like cops.)

VERB FILL-IN

Fill in each blank with the verb form that is appropriate for each sentence.

1. The First Amendment acts as a shield for the individual; it was

   not _____ to be an instrument against him.
          intend

2. No clear line of judgment can be _____ on what is
               draw

   important in regard to national security.

3. News organizations _____ for years to get permis-
         fight

   sion to print arrest records.

4. If someone _____ innocent, why should he be sub-
        find

   jected to undue publicity?

5. The policeman told the reporters that he _____ no one

                                                arrest

during the past four years.

6. Professor Miller _____ darkly of a "reexamination of

                              speak

the favored position currently enjoyed by the press."

7. If a journalist unlawfully wiretaps, he _____ for break-

                                           punish

ing the law.

8. Is all privacy to be _____ to the families of noteworthy

                                  lose

people?

9. The press _____ no more likely to become more

                            be

humane on its own than are bill-collecting agencies.

10. The press usually _____ with great zeal, diligence, and

                                perform

inventiveness.

SENTENCE COMPLETION

From the column at the right, select the correct line to complete each of the numbered lines at the left. Write each sentence in its correct form.

1. Students have simply taken it for granted that journalists

2. It is a citizen's right not to speak to the press,

A. by needless press attention.

B. must get the news by whatever means they think necessary.

3. Most reporters think only

4. The privacy of Richard Nixon's White House was legitimately invaded

5. What should concern us is that private citizens can be severely injured

6. In New York State the law says that no employer, public or private, and no agency

7. As the press is being recognized as one of the more fearsome enemies of privacy,

8. Is all privacy to be lost

9. A newspaper should headline the extramarital affairs and ancient arrest records

10. These "exposed" reporters could then concentrate on the rights of privacy

C. there is some movement toward trying to legislate them into becoming more "responsible."

D. of getting the story.

E. of some of the journalists who do not use good judgment in dealing with the public.

F. to the families of newsworthy figures?

G. but a "no comment" invariably leads the reporter to assume guilt.

H. can ask anyone if he's been arrested.

I. when they went out on their next assignment.

J. because crimes were being committed there.

CLOZE EXERCISE

Fill in each blank with the best word to complete the meaning of the sentence.

Vigorous and diligent reporters can _____ monitor the criminal justice system _____ examining the records of those _____ have paid their debt to _____, who have met the stringent _____ of the statutes, and who _____ a second chance. If we _____ in rehabilitation, then we must _____ some risks. We should permit _____ people to reenter the mainstream _____ society by eliminating the social ＿＿＿＿＿＿ vocational ostracism

associated with an ＿＿＿＿＿＿ record that does not reflect

＿＿＿＿＿＿ present worth. How can you ＿＿＿＿＿＿ with the

principle of sealing ＿＿＿＿＿＿ records of a youthful peccadillo

＿＿＿＿＿＿ has never been repeated?

SENTENCE COMBINING

Combine each pair of sentences into a single grammatical
sentence.

1. Journalists forget one thing.
   Journalists forget that the First Amendment is a shield.

2. The First Amendment was not intended to be a blunt instrument
   against individual citizens.
   These citizens would be strewn about in the wake of journalists
   gathering news.

3. The privacy of individuals is safeguarded except from the press.
   The press can search out arrest records and print them.

4. The public is entitled to know the cost of welfare.
   The public is entitled to know the percentage of the population
   being aided.

5. Sometimes a journalist unlawfully wiretaps.
   The journalist should be punished for breaking the law.

6. The press established a quasi-religious crusade to be permitted
   to examine all kinds of dossiers.
   These dossiers show everything from arrest records to reckless-
   driving charges.

PUNCTUATION

Read the following paragraph. Write in the capital letters
and place commas, periods, colons, semicolons, dashes, and
quotation marks where needed.

as an illustration of the presss zeal in these matters there was a

triumphant tour of maine last october by a task force of 100 reporters testing the states right to know law marching into local

police stations they demanded to see the complete records of the

most recent arrests not convictions arrests out of 111 police stations

99 complied entirely one of the tiny minority of officers defending

privacy rights was the sole cop in the town of new gloucester he told

the posse that he hadnt arrested anybody during the past four years

but if he had those records would be out of bounds to reporters

as they should be

WORD-FORM CHART

Use your dictionary to complete the following table. Follow the example shown with item 1, *investigation*. If there is no commonly used form for a particular part of speech, write the symbol XXX.

Noun	Verb	Adjective	Adverb
1. investigation	investigate	investigative	investigatively
2.			diligently
3. aggression			
4.		invariable	
5.		legitimate	
6.	proliferate		
7.			dubiously
8. maintenance			
9.			maniacally
10. humanism			

WORD-FORM EXERCISE

Using your completed Word-Form Chart, select the correct
form to fit into each sentence. Use the appropriate tense of
the verb, the singular or plural form of the noun, and the
passive voice where necessary.
Follow the sequence of numbers from the Word-Form Chart
to select the correct form.

1. Mr. Hentoff taught a course on ⎯⎯⎯⎯⎯⎯ reporting.

2. Students thought that a ⎯⎯⎯⎯⎯⎯ journalist must get

   the news by whatever means necessary.

3. Reporters often act like undercover cops and exhibit

   ⎯⎯⎯⎯⎯⎯ behavior.

4. When a person being interviewed says "no comment," it

   ⎯⎯⎯⎯⎯⎯ leads a reporter to assume that person is guilty.

5. The privacy of Mr. Nixon's White House was ⎯⎯⎯⎯⎯⎯

   invaded because crimes were being committed there.

6. There is a great ⎯⎯⎯⎯⎯⎯ of gossip in the nation's press.

7. Reporters feel no compunction about printing intimate informa-

   tion that is of ⎯⎯⎯⎯⎯⎯ value.

8. The American Civil Liberties Union is one group that

   ⎯⎯⎯⎯⎯⎯ that there is no public need to know if someone

   has been arrested if the arrest has not resulted in a conviction.

9. The press's ⎯⎯⎯⎯⎯⎯ for going after just about every-

   thing is not unlike the sleuthing habits of the FBI.

10. The press is not likely to become more ⎯⎯⎯⎯⎯⎯ on its

    own; laws have to be enacted to temper the press in this regard.

QUESTIONS FOR DISCUSSION

1. Make your own list of justifiable and unjustifiable invasions of privacy by the press. Compare this list with Hentoff's examples and with the lists of other classmates. Do they differ? How?

2. Why can't laws be passed in order to make the press more responsible?

3. Is the invasion of a person's privacy an American problem? Where else does it occur, and how does it differ from one country to another?

TOPICS FOR WRITING

1. From the list you have compiled, choose an example of an invasion of privacy and write an argument showing either that it *is* or *is not* justifiable. Give specific reasons to support your point of view.

2. Imagine that a famous celebrity has just been killed. Argue in favor of or against the right of reporters to film and interview members of the immediate family, friends, and grieving fans.

3. Discuss how freedom of speech and of the press is interpreted in your native country. Argue in favor of or against this interpretation.

Appendix

Using the Dictionary

It is essential for you as an advanced ESL student to make greater use of the American English dictionary in order to overcome your reliance on your bilingual dictionary. You should familiarize yourself completely with all aspects of information that the dictionary provides. Dictionary study must become an integral part of your growth in language usage, since improving your vocabulary will improve your fluency.

As an ESL student, you have been using a dictionary since the beginning of your second-language learning; however, you may not know the various kinds of information dictionaries contain. Moreover, you may be unable to benefit from the most common uses of the dictionary: finding the pronunciations and the definitions of words. This inability occurs largely because you do not familiarize yourself with the methods and symbols by which the material is conveyed. If you pay attention to the following information, you will be assured of progress.

The first step is to examine the way in which the dictionary presents information. Let us look at one entry:

tri·umph (trī'əmf) *intr.v.* **-umphed, -umphing, -umphs. 1.** To be victorious or successful; to win; prevail. **2.** To rejoice over a success or victory; exult. **3.** In ancient Rome, to receive honors upon return from a victory. *—n.* **1.** The instance or fact of being victorious; success. **2.** Exultation or merriment derived from victory. **3.** A public celebration in ancient Rome to welcome a returning victorious commander and his army. **4.** *Obsolete.* Any public celebration or spectacular pageant. *—See* Synonyms at **victory.** [Latin *triumphāre,* from *triumphus,* a triumph, variant of Old Latin *triumpus,* akin to or possibly from Greek *thriambos,* hymn to Bacchus, of Aegean origin.] *—tri'umph·er n.*

Definition ©1981 Houghton Mifflin Company. Reprinted by permission from *The American Heritage Dictionary of the English Language, New College Edition.*

If you examine this entry, you can see that the dictionary gives the following information: (1) spelling of the word and the way it is divided into syllables; (2) pronunciation, including syllable stress; (3) grammatical function or functions of the word; (4) definition or definitions; (5) etymology or history of the word; (6) synonyms or antonyms when available.

Information is also given about principal parts of irregular verbs, irregular plurals of nouns, case forms of pronouns, capitalization of proper nouns and adjectives derived from proper nouns. Dictionaries also include idiomatic expressions and idiomatic use of particular words.

You should take the time to read the front and back sections of the dictionary in order to use this special information for easy reference. You should be aware of all abbreviations because they indicate the grammatical function of the word; for example, *intr. v.* (intransitive verb) or *n.* (noun). Some abbreviations indicate etymology; for example, *GK* (Greek), *L* (Latin), and others indicate status or style, such as *obs.* (obsolete); *dial.* (dialect).

Mastering the use of your dictionary will help you to cope with the ways in which English words change from one occurrence to the next. For example, many words have a set of related though clearly different meanings. Since these different meanings are not accompanied by variations in the spelling of a word, they will all be found within a single citation. The citation for *triumph,* above, is an example of a word with multiple meanings. Several meanings of a word are often related to each other, and the differences among these meanings are often not clear to the nonnative speaker. Therefore it is important for you to use the entire citation of a word as the basis for the entry in the vocabulary section of your notebook.

Another way in which words may vary is in their spelling, or form. For example, many words with the same *basic* meaning may appear as different parts of speech. When they do, the different grammatical classes of the word are often indicated by differences in spelling, usually by the addition of a word ending (suffix) such as *-ly*, which signals most adverbs. Changes in spelling, however, may also modify the meaning of a word as well as its grammatical category. For this reason, the careful dictionary user will look at the citations both above and below the one of primary interest. Consider, for example, the citation for *statistician*:

> **stat·is·ti·cian** (stăt-ə-stĭsh′ən) *n.* **1.** A mathematician specializing in statistics. **2.** A compiler of statistical data.
>
> Definitions © 1981 Houghton Mifflin Company. Reprinted by permission from *The American Heritage Dictionary of the English Language, New College Edition.*

Note how the meaning changes in the citation for *statistics*:

> **sta·tis·tics** (stə-tĭs′tĭks) *n. Abbr.* **stat.** **1.** The mathematics of the collection, organization, and interpretation of numerical data; especially, the analysis of population characteristics by inference from sampling. Used with a singular verb. **2.** A collection of numerical data. Used with a plural verb. [German *Statistik,* originally "political science dealing with state affairs," from New Latin *statisticus,* of state affairs, from Latin *status,* manner of standing, position, state. See **stā-** in Appendix.*]

And in the citation for *statistic*:

> **sta·tis·tic** (stə-tĭs′tĭk) *n.* **1.** Any numerical datum. **2.** An estimate of a parameter, as of the population mean or variance, obtained from a sample. [Back-formation from ṢTATISTICS.] —**sta·tis′ti·cal** (-tĭ-kəl) *adj.* —**sta·tis′ti·cal·ly** *adv.*

In summary, taking the time to use the dictionary properly will help you not only to increase your vocabulary but also to become aware of the different forms that words can take in English. You should rely on the dictionary to look up words before you read an essay and to check your own spelling as you write compositions. Of all reference books, the dictionary is the most essential for the student learning English.

Glossary

Analysis Analysis is the form of expository writing in which the subject is broken down into its parts. The three most common forms of analysis are *division, classification,* and *process analysis.* For a thorough discussion of analysis, see Chapter 6. Also see *division, classification,* and *process analysis.*

Argumentation Argumentation is one of the four traditional divisions of prose (The others are *narration, description,* and *exposition.*) It is the method by which a writer attempts to persuade his or her audience to accept a particular belief or to take specific actions consistent with that belief. For a thorough discussion of argumentation, see Chapter 8. Also see *deduction, induction,* and *syllogism.*

Attitude The writer's attitude toward his or her subject consists of the feelings communicated to the reader. The choice of words and selection of detail tell the reader if the writer is friendly, hostile, disinterested, or doubtful. This sentence, for example, illustrates the hostile attitude of a television critic: "This evening's television viewing consisted of the usual mindless situation comedies, dull dramatic series, and inane quiz shows." See *tone.*

Audience The audience for a writer consists of the readers who are expected to read his or her work. For example, the audience for an article in *Sports Illustrated* magazine is composed of well-informed sports fans.

Cause and effect Cause and effect is the form of expository writing that is concerned with the reasons for an action or event and the results of one. For a thorough discussion of cause and effect, see Chapter 7.

Central image A central image is a single word-picture used to unify descriptive writing when spatial organization is not appropriate. For example, in his essay "The Rainbow City," Pete Hamill uses the word *rainbow* to emphasize the spectrum of colors and races in New York City.

Chronological order Chronological order is the presentation of events as they occur in time. Example: "After gulping down his milk, he seized his books and then rushed to catch the school bus."

Classification Classification is the form of expository writing in which people, places, objects, or ideas are grouped into categories. Items within a category share similar characteristics that distinguish them from items in other categories. For a thorough discussion of classification, see Chapter 6.

Coherence Coherence is literally a sticking together. To achieve coherence, the writer must logically connect one idea to the next, leading his or her reader from sentence to sentence and from paragraph to paragraph by means of connectives called transitions. See *transitions.*

Colloquial Colloquial words are characteristic of and appropriate to informal spoken language rather than to formal written language. For example, "I *failed* the test" is formal style. "I *flunked* the test" is colloquial style.

Comparison and contrast Comparison and contrast is the form of expository writing that discusses similarities and differences between two persons, places, things, or ideas. Usually, the items belong to the same class, such as two baseball stars or two diets. For a thorough discussion of comparison and contrast see Chapter 4.

Conclusion The conclusion is the final, closing part of an essay. It ties together the different parts by reinforcing the thesis, or main idea. A conclusion may also raise a pertinent question, present a challenge, or suggest a solution. See "How to Read an Essay."

Connotation The connotation of a word is its literal meaning plus the associations, attitudes, and emotions surrounding it. For example, both *cheap* and *inexpensive* mean relatively low in cost. *Cheap*, however, implies inferior quality while *inexpensive* suggests value at low cost. See "How to Read an Essay."

Deduction Deduction is a method of arguing or reasoning from general principles to specific conclusions. One of the most commonly used forms of the deductive argument is the syllogism. For a thorough discussion of deduction, see Chapter 8. Also see *syllogism*.

Definition Definition is the form of expository writing in which the author identifies all the characteristics that are unique to an object or concept and which, therefore, differentiate it from all other objects or concepts. For a thorough discussion of definition, see Chapter 5.

Denotation The denotation of a word is its dictionary definition. It is the literal, most limited meaning of a word. For example, *cheap* means relatively low in cost, inexpensive. See "How to Read an Essay."

Description Description is one of the four traditional divisions of prose (The others are *narration, exposition,* and *argumentation.*) It is a form of writing in which the writer uses the five senses to convey his or her impressions to the reader. For a thorough discussion of description, see Chapter 2.

Dialogue Dialogue is a conversation between two or more people. The spoken speech is enclosed within quotation marks. The change from one speaker to the next is indicated by a new paragraph.
Example: He said, "I must hurry to catch the bus."
　　　　　　 She replied, "Don't worry, I won't keep you."

Division Division is the form of expository writing in which a subject is broken down into categories. For a thorough discussion of division, see Chapter 6.

Dominant impression In description, the dominant impression is the writer's major response to his or her subject, usually expressed in sensory language. For example, a writer might describe an attic in terms of the nostalgic mood that it suggests. See Chapter 2, page 52.

Effect See *cause and effect*.

Example See *illustration*.

Exposition Exposition is one of the four traditional divisions of prose. (The others are *narration, description,* and *argumentation.*) It attempts to explain something or give information about it. Exposition is the most common form of college writing and is used in compositions, essay examinations, and laboratory reports. The examples of exposition in this text are to be found in the following chapters: "Illustration," "Comparison and Contrast," "Definition," "Analysis," and "Cause and Effect."

Extended definition An extended definition is the expansion of a definition beyond its dictionary meaning. The extended definition uses various methods of organization, including illustration, comparison and contrast, and analysis. For a thorough discussion of definition, see Chapter 5.

Figurative language Figurative language is a form of writing using comparison to go beyond the literal meanings of words. The two most common types are *simile* and *metaphor.* The *simile* uses the word *as* or *like* to indicate the comparison; for example, "She was as tired as a runner after a marathon." The *metaphor* equates the objects being compared and does not use a connecting word, as in "He was a lion in battle."

Illustration Illustration is the form of expository writing in which examples are used to clarify ideas. Examples show ideas in action instead of simply telling about them. For a thorough discussion of illustration, see Chapter 3.

Image, imagery See *figurative language.*

Induction Induction is a method of arguing or reasoning from specific evidence to general conclusions. The inductive method is used by scientists and detectives, both real and fictional. For a thorough discussion of induction, see Chapter 8.

Introduction The introduction is the beginning of an essay. It presents the subject (and its limited scope), the writer's attitude toward the subject, and the thesis. An effective introduction should gain the reader's interest. See "How to Read an Essay."

Lexical definition See *literal meaning.*

Literal meaning The literal meaning is the most limited meaning of a word, as it is found in the dictionary. It is what a word actually refers to exclusive of feelings or attitudes. Example: "*House* refers to a residence or dwelling." See *denotation.*

Metaphor See *figurative language.*

Method of organization A method of organization is any one of the ways of ordering ideas in an essay. See the chapter headings in the table of contents.

Narration Narration is one of the four traditional divisions of prose. (The others are *description, exposition,* and *argumentation.*) Narration is telling a story. Used primarily in fiction, it is also valuable in nonfiction whenever there is a need to relate an incident. For a thorough discussion of narration, see Chapter 1.

Objective/subjective Objective and subjective are two kinds of description. Objective description is impartial description, such as might be found in a nurse's report on a patient's progress: "The vital signs returned to normal: blood pressure, body temperature, respiration, and pulse rate." Subjective description is biased reporting and might describe the same patient's condition from the point of view of a family member: "Henry looks terrible. He is pale, has lost weight, and seems weak." For a thorough discussion of description, see Chapter 2.

Person *Person* is a grammatical term referring to the voice that speaks to the reader. The first person (*I*) reveals information about the speaker: "*I* had a terrible dream last night." The second person (*you*) emphasizes the reader as well as the speaker: "*You* learn how to ride a bicycle through repeated effort." The third person (*he, she, it, they*) concentrates on the subject being discussed: "He spoke softly to his sister and they both began to cry." The choice of person determines the nature of the relationship between the writer and the reader. See *point of view*.

Point of view The point of view is the way in which a writer decides to relate his or her story or essay. This is determined by the choice of grammatical person. In this text Randi Kreiss uses the first person (*I*) in her narrative essay because it is personal history. Roger Cox uses the second person (*you*) because he is giving instructions to the reader. And Anthony Lewis uses the third person (*it*) because he wants to concentrate solely on his subject: school desegregation. See *person*.

Process analysis Process analysis is the form of expository writing in which the writer demonstrates a process to the reader ("How to Frame a Picture") or describes a process ("How the Caterpillar Becomes a Butterfly"). In either case, a step-by-step analysis of the procedure is necessary. For a thorough discussion of process analysis, see Chapter 6.

Rhetoric Rhetoric is the art of effective verbal communication, both written and spoken. Examples of effective communication such as the essays in this collection enable students to strengthen their reading and writing skills.

Simile See *figurative language*.

Slang Slang words or expressions are recent additions to the language which extend the meaning of an existing word in its present form or in an altered form (for example, the use of *bread* to mean money or *junkie* to mean a person using drugs.) Slang is usually considered inappropriate for formal or, occasionally, for polite use.

Spatial organization Spatial organization is the most common way of arranging details in a description. The writer using a spatial plan of organization first selects a point at which to begin his or her description of a person, object, or place and then selects the direction the description will follow (for example, left to right, top to bottom, inside to outside). See Chapter 2.

Stipulative definition A stipulative definition is one which either extends or limits the meaning of a word so that it includes a particular concept with which the writer is concerned. For example, the author might stipulate that he or she is using the word *sports* to include *any* competitive activity, so that chess or bridge might be included in the essay. On the other hand, the author might stipulate that he or she is limiting the definition of *sports* to competitive activities that involve strenuous physical activity, so that activities such as chess or bridge might be excluded from the essay. See Chapter 5.

Subjective See *objective/subjective.*

Syllogism A syllogism is a three-part deductive proof consisting of a general or major premise, a specific or minor premise, and a conclusion.

> Example: All state senators are elected officials.
>   Mr. Jones is a state senator.
>   Mr. Jones is an elected official.

For a thorough discussion of the syllogism see Chapter 8.

Thesis The thesis is the central idea of an essay. It may be stated directly or implied. See "How to Read an Essay."

Tone Tone is the stylistic manner by which the writer conveys his or her attitude toward subject and audience. Unlike tone of voice in speech, written tone depends more heavily on word choice and sentence structure. Like tone of voice, written tone can be critical, angry, approving, humorous, or sympathetic. See "How to Read an Essay." Also see *attitude.*

Topic sentence The topic sentence is the sentence that states the central idea of the paragraph. It may appear anywhere in the paragraph, although the beginning is the most popular location. In a well-organized paragraph, all the sentences relate to and support the topic sentence. See "How to Read an Essay." Also see *unity.*

Transitions Transitions are the connecting devices that link sentence to sentence, paragraph to paragraph, and one section of an essay to the next. The connection is achieved by the use of a logical sequence of ideas (chronological order, for example), transitional words (such as *in addition, next, therefore*), the repetition of key words or phrases, and pronouns referring to the previous sentence. A sentence or even a paragraph can function as a transition. See *coherence.*

Unity Unity exists when all the elements of an essay work together to support the thesis. The sentences in a unified paragraph relate to the topic sentence, and the paragraphs relate to the thesis. See *topic sentence.*